THE FIRST CLASS LESSONS AND MANTRAS

Rudolf Steiner, 1907

Rudolf Steiner's Esoteric Legacy of 1924

THE FIRST CLASS
LESSONS AND MANTRAS

The Michael School Meditative Path in Nineteen Steps

RUDOLF STEINER

T. H. MEYER, editor

SteinerBooks – Perseus Basel

2017
SteinerBooks
An imprint of Anthroposophic Press, Inc.
610 Main Street, Great Barrington, MA 01230
www.steinerbooks.org

Copyright © 2017 by SteinerBooks/Perseus Basel.
All rights reserved. No part of this book may be reproduced, stored in a retrieval system, or transmitted in any form or by any means, electronic, mechanical, photocopying, recording, or otherwise, without the written permission of SteinerBooks. This book was originally published by Perseus Verlag in Basel, Switzerland, with the title *Der Meditationsweg der Michaelschule in neunzehn Stufen*.

The nineteen class lessons were translated by
Jannebeth Röell, Paul V. O'Leary, and James Lee;
all other text was translated by
Jannebeth Röell and James Lee.

Cover and book design by Jens Jensen

LIBRARY OF CONGRESS CONTROL NUMBER: 2016944224

ISBN: 978-1-62148-173-7 (hardcover)
ISBN: 978-1-62148-174-4 (eBook)

Printed in the United States of America

Contents

Preface to the First English Edition *by T. H. Meyer* — vii

Introduction to the Third German Edition *by T. H. Meyer* — ix

The Nineteen Lessons of the Michael School — 1

    First Lesson — 3

    Second Lesson — 17

    Third Lesson — 33

    Fourth Lesson — 52

    Fifth Lesson — 69

    Sixth Lesson — 87

    Seventh Lesson — 108

    Eighth Lesson — 120

    Ninth Lesson — 132

    Tenth Lesson — 145

    Eleventh Lesson — 160

    Twelfth Lesson — 174

    Thirteenth Lesson — 190

    Fourteenth Lesson — 206

    Fifteenth Lesson — 221

    Sixteenth Lesson — 236

    Seventeenth Lesson — 250

    Eighteenth Lesson — 263

    Nineteenth Lesson — 277

PASSAGES OMITTED FROM THE TEXT	291
MANTRAS OF THE MICHAEL SCHOOL IN ENGLISH AND GERMAN	313
APPENDIX: THE MEDITATIVE PATH OF THE MICHAEL SCHOOL TODAY by T. H. Meyer	357
Rudolf Steiner and the Time Spirit Michael	359
The Suprasensory Michael School	364
The Earthly Michael School and the Role of Ita Wegman	369
The Role of Ludwig Polzer-Hoditz	373
Who is the Guardian of the Threshold?	386
The Structure and Levels of the Nineteen Lessons	391
The Form Language of the Michael Sign	395
NOTES	403
ABOUT THE FRONTISPIECE	409
RUDOLF STEINER'S BLACKBOARD DRAWINGS	411

Preface to the First English Edition

T. H. Meyer

It is with great satisfaction that I welcome this first public English edition of *The Michael School Meditative Path*.

Since the initial publication of the German version in 2011—which coincided with the 150th anniversary of Rudolf Steiner's birth—many positive reactions have been received, including those from class members and class readers all over Europe. The taboo has now been broken with regard to these esoteric texts by Rudolf Steiner as something to be spread exclusively within the circle of the Anthroposophical Society. There is good reason for this. According to Anna Samweber, a close associate of Rudolf Steiner in Berlin, Marie Steiner made a significant remark to her; "In 1926, Marie Steiner told us the following during a conversation about the class lessons in Dornach: 'Doctor Steiner told me that, when the class lessons lead to sectarian behavior and pretensions of power, they will have to be published like all of my other lectures.'"[1]

Since the German edition was published a significant discovery was made. In the Kolisko Archive in England, a stenographer's notebook was discovered that contains the stenographic notes of two recapitulation lessons by Rudolf Steiner that have never before been published. These notes were taken by Lily Kolisko and written down in the Gabelsberger stenographic writing system. After an extensive search, someone was found who is familiar with this stenographic system, which enabled a transcription of the material. These previously unknown recapitulation lessons

---

1 See volume 2, *Der Meditationsweg der Michaelschule* (Perseus Verlag, Basel, 2011), p. 250. This volume is scheduled to be published in English in 2017.

were given in Breslau on June 11 and 13, 1924. They will be incorporated into the second volume of *The Michael School Meditative Path*, scheduled for publication in 2017.

A word about the English-language version of the mantras: It should be evident that there is difficulty in translating these mantras into English from the original German. Today, there are several English versions circulating in publications for private and limited distribution. The spiritual content of the mantras was brought by Rudolf Steiner from the spiritual world into the German language. That language has a special kinship to spiritual facts and beings as probably no other language in use at present. Ita Wegman wrote to the Swedish class holder Anna Gunnarsson Wager that, although the mantras could be given in translations, "one should nevertheless try to meditate them in German, because the rhythm of it has a great effect. If one has no access to the German language at all, then one can meditate in the translation" (16.10.1924, Ita Wegman Archive Arlesheim).

David Clement, a leading personality within the British biodynamic movement and who knew Ita Wegman and D. N. Dunlop, once told me that he meditated the mantras in German. He did not speak this language but found it helpful to look at the German version after having worked with the English. Those who are moving seriously onward on the meditative path of the Michael School may find it equally useful to have access to the German version of the mantras, which are included in this edition.

I am indebted in gratitude to Jannebeth Röell, James Lee, and Paul V. O'Leary for translating and editing the text, to Paul V. O'Leary for translating the mantras, and to Gene Gollogly for his courage in publishing this book.

I hope this publication will be met with the same unbiased interest and attention in the English-speaking world as was the case with the German edition.

T. H. Meyer
June 25, 2016

Introduction to the Third German Edition

They can rely on the words
I previously spoke in earth existence.
They don't see how those words can only be given life
if in the proper sense they are enlivened and renewed.
— Rudolf Steiner
(Benedictus, *The Trials of the Soul*, scene 7)

This newly revised, third edition of Rudolf Steiner's esoteric legacy from the year 1924 is intended for all people who possess an earnest need for a contemporary meditative path of training.

Today, meditation is often spoken about, both inside and outside of the anthroposophic movement. The path of meditation that Rudolf Steiner made available to humanity at the end of his life is the quintessence of all his prior presentations and yet, it has received little consideration. This can be regretted all the more because he touched upon and listened to the intentions of the true spirit of our time, which in Spiritual Science bears the name of Michael. This is a path of self-knowledge from which world knowledge can be gained.

The prerequisites for taking this path are a will fired by a healthy common sense and a healthy trust in the human capacity to develop and enter into the field of spiritual knowledge.

The path described here stretches over nineteen lessons or levels that will, perhaps, be challenging for many spiritual seekers. It is, however, a secure path. Those who enter upon this path strengthen themselves to meet the dangers of self-illusion, such as grandiosity and vanity. At present, the human being taking what may seem to be an easier path providing less security than the one set forth here, immediately meets these dangers when taking their first steps into the suprasensory world.

A very important reason for this publication is the fact that certain of its mantric elements prepare the spiritual seeker for corresponding stations in the life after death. These stations, which every human soul experiences, involve meetings with certain beings and processes that must remain painfully unintelligible *without* such preparation on earth. One can think about the many people who cross the threshold of death today, either naturally or violently, without ever having heard of such a preparation. One can see the objective necessity for humanity in distributing the content of this book in a gracious manner and without reservation.

The fact that these meditative provisions have remained inaccessible to many souls was, in part, caused by the history of their origin in the twentieth century, and the ensuing destiny of the content of this meditative path. The content originally formed the substance of the nineteen lessons of the "First Class" of the School of Spiritual Science, which itself was founded by Rudolf Steiner after forming the newly-constituted General Anthroposophical Society at the "Christmas Conference" during Christmastime 1923. The lessons are, accordingly, called "Class Lessons" and were given in Dornach, Switzerland between February 15 and August 2, 1924. They were accessible only to members of the General Anthroposophical Society and the School of Spiritual Science. This last membership results from a declaration of will by its members not only to take up Anthroposophy for oneself, but to also be responsible for Anthroposophy in the world.[1]

Steiner demanded observance of the strictest rules for the handling of the "Class Lessons." From respect for an esoteric law, he forewarned that the "mantras" would become ineffective if they were to fall into the wrong hands. He hoped by such means to effectively safeguard the lessons as long as possible.

Rudolf Steiner often preceded the Class lessons with explanations about their spiritual place of origin in Dornach, the "Christmas Conference,"

Introduction to the Third German Edition

and the "School of Spiritual Science." These separate talks can clearly be distinguished from the actual *Class content*.

In light of the further development of the General Anthroposophical Society after Rudolf Steiner's death, these references to the "Christmas Conference" and the "School of Spiritual Science" seem to the editor to be no longer relevant *today*. Even more so, they can give the current reader the impression that the legacy of Rudolf Steiner's esoteric indications continue to be exclusively for a special group of people. This would signify a denial of its relevance for *humanity* that was previously discussed.

In 1948, Marie Steiner ascertained that the text of the Class lessons "had been confiscated by the Cheka and Gestapo. This means they are desecrated and only through individual work can they become productive again."[2] Furthermore, the text and mantras can be found today in bookstores and on the Internet. It only leads to illusion when a person closes their eyes to the ramifications of these facts.

On these grounds, the editor felt compelled to create a new title and to make one other change to the two prior German language editions of *The Michael School Meditative Path*: the previously mentioned "separate talks" have been excised from the text of the lessons and, where this occurs, an ellipsis is used to mark the spot and the removed text is reproduced in a separate part of this book.[3]

The editor is of the opinion that this editorial decision is in harmony with the current intentions of the continuously working individuality of Rudolf Steiner. It is also in accordance with the words of Benedictus, who, from the spiritual world, inspires a faithful student to pay attention to necessary modifications of the words he spoke on earth and not to hold too tightly to the printed letter of the *past*.

Historically, this edition connects with the fact that one of Rudolf Steiner's most esteemed students, who in November 1924 was authorized by Steiner to read and hold *Class lessons*, did that work for twelve years *within* the framework of the General Anthroposophical Society and the School of Spiritual Science. He continued to do this work *outside* of the framework of these same institutions for nine years after the catastrophic events of 1935. The student in question is Ludwig Polzer-Hoditz (1869–1945).

In the figure of Ludwig Polzer-Hoditz, a serious and worthy carrying of these contents was severed from the concerned institutions.[4] This does not mean that no earnest and dignified work was or can be done within these institutions. But it does mean that the connection of the institutions with the handling of the esoteric legacy of Rudolf Steiner is today no longer *the only right one*. Whoever is convinced of the opposite opinion can work with the 1992 edition of the four books of the School of Spiritual Science, including a book of drawings, or with the 1997 edition (sold out) published within the framework the anthroposophic institutions.[5]

In addition, this third edition differs from prior editions through a series of contemplations that are found in the back of the book. They concern the question of the centuries-long working of the suprasensory Michael School and the meaning of Rudolf Steiner's deed in bringing this school down to the physical plane in the short period between February and September 1924. Then there is the question of the being of the Guardian of the Threshold, who plays a central role on the meditative path of the Michael School, contrary to most other current esoteric trainings. One special contemplation concerns the Michael sign pictured on the cover of this book. The fact that Ludwig Polzer-Hoditz's relationship to the "Class" had to be studied in depth should be obvious after what was previously said.[6]

It is hardly necessary to mention that a proper treatment of these published mantras and text by Rudolf Steiner is connected with a certain familiarity with the basics of the anthroposophic path of training as indicated in *How to Know Higher Worlds* (CW 10), *An Outline of Esoteric Science* (CW 13), and other works.

It is a happy coincidence that the original publication of this work in the German language coincides with Rudolf Steiner's 150th birthday and the period of two-times-thirty-three years after the death of Ludwig Polzer-Hoditz.[7]

Introduction to the Third German Edition

May the contents of this book, which literally can be found on the streets today, be taken up seriously and worked with fruitfully. They enable a contemporary grasp of the current world mission and can give a future-oriented spiritual foundation to all people who want to represent the anthroposophic world impulse in a concrete way.

Thomas Meyer
January 8, 2011

The Nineteen Lessons of the Michael School

Rudolf Steiner

Notes

(…) Ellipsis in parentheses indicates omitted text; see passages omitted from the text starting on page 291.

[ ] Text in square brackets indicates changes made by the current editor; see page....for notes and indications.

{ } Text in curly brackets (or braces) represent indications by the stenographer.

Text in italics: words written on a blackboard.

Bold print: words spoken with strong emphasis according to the stenographer.

Pictures of the blackboard drawings are included at the end of the book.

First Lesson

Dornach, February 15, 1924

M y dear friends! (...) Before all else, I would like to present to your hearts and souls what should stand as a first-engraved tablet over our School. It is important that we completely identify with what comes to us in this School from the life of the spirit to our soul's ear and our soul's understanding.

So we begin with the words:

> Where on Earth foundations, color upon color,
> Life, creative life, manifests itself;
> Where from earthly substance, form on form,
> The lifeless world is fashioned;
> Where sentient beings, powerful in will,
> Warm themselves with joy in their existence;
> Where you, yourself, O Man, acquire
> Your body from earth, air and light:
>
> There you enter with your own true being
> Deep into night-enveloped cold and darkness;
> From the dumb expanse you ask in vain
> Who you are and were and will become.
> For your own being the light of day fades into
> Soul's night and spirit-darkness;
> With anxious seeking you turn your soul
> To that light that takes its strength from darkness.

I will repeat it:

> Where on Earth foundations, color upon color,
> Life, creative life, manifests itself;
> Where from earthly substance, form on form,
> The lifeless world is fashioned;
> Where sentient beings, powerful in will,
> Warm themselves with joy in their existence;
> Where you, yourself, O Man, acquire
> Your body from earth, air and light:
>
> There you enter with your own true being
> Deep into night-enveloped cold and darkness;
> From the dumb expanse you ask in vain
> Who you are and were and will become.
> For your own being the light of day fades into
> Soul's night and spirit-darkness;
> With anxious seeking you turn your soul
> To that light that takes its strength from darkness.

These words should tell us that the world is indeed beautiful, great, and majestic. Endless is the light of revelation that flows to us from all that lives in leaf and blossom and meets our eye in colors from the entire visible universe. We should remember that the Divine is revealed to us through manifestations of lifeless Earth substances, the many crystalline and non-crystalline forms under our feet, in water, air, clouds and stars. It should be clear to us that all the animal life in the wide world around us—delighting in its own existence and in its own warmth—is divine spiritual revelation. And it should remind us that we derive our own bodies from this world of forms, from all that is greening and growing, color upon color. It should also be brought to our awareness that all that is beautiful, glorious, grand and divine in the world of our senses cannot tell us who we are as human beings.

Nature, however great and powerful in tone, strength and warmth, meets our senses. But nature can never provide us with information about ourselves, although it does give us a vast amount of information about many divine aspects of the world. So we must always repeat to ourselves:

First Lesson

what we feel as our innermost Self is not woven from what we perceive from the outside as the beauty, grandeur, greatness and power of nature. The question arises in our soul: why does the reality of being all around us, of which we are also a part, remain dark and silent?

We must experience as a blessing what we may feel to be a kind of deprivation, so that we can say to ourselves in all seriousness and sternness: we must first make ourselves truly human, warm in soul and strong of spirit, so that we, as spirit in humanity, may find the spirit in the world.

It is necessary that we do not take this lightly, that we prepare ourselves to come to the boundary of the sense world where the spirit's revelation can arise in us. We must say to ourselves: if we arrive unprepared at this boundary and the full light of the spirit comes upon us all at once, because we have not yet developed the strength of spirit and the warmth of soul necessary for receiving the spirit, this would shatter us and cast us back into our nothingness.

That is why a messenger of the gods stands between the boundary of the sense world and the spirit world, that spirit messenger about whom we will hear more and more in the coming lessons, whom we will come to know more intimately. The spirit messenger stands there and speaks to us, cautioning how we must be and what we must discard so we can meet the revelations of the spiritual world in the right way.

And, my dear friends, when we have first understood that—in contrast to all the beauty, greatness and majesty in nature—at first there exists for human cognition a spiritual darkness from which a light must be born, a light that tells us who we are, who we were, and who we will become. We must first and foremost realize that from this darkness we have to perceive the spirit messenger who sends us the admonitions we need. Therefore, let us allow the words of the spirit messenger to resound in our soul and let the description of the spirit messenger rise up before our inner "I."

> And from the darkness there lights up
> To you—

(The human being is addressed.)

> Revealing your own likeness,
> Yet also shaping you into an image,
> Solemn spirit words powerfully working in the cosmic ether,
> Words that your heart can hear—
>
> The spirit messenger, who alone
> Can shed light upon your path.
> Before him lies the far spread world of the senses;
> Behind him yawn the depths of the abyss.
>
> And before his darkened realm of spirit,
> Close to the yawning chasm of existence,
> His creative word sounds with all primeval power:
> Behold, I am the only gate to knowledge.

We have to be completely clear and take in all that comes to our soul as admonitions from the spirit messenger before we seek to unveil what is not in the sense world on this side of the threshold, but is spread out on the other side of the gaping abyss. And, as has been said, we will come to know the spirit messenger more and more in the following lessons. At first, knowledge of what is on the other side is covered in a deep darkness from which only the earnest countenance of the spirit messenger lights forth. At first he appears like a human being but transformed into gigantic stature. At the same time, however, he is also like the human being in a shadow-like form. He warns that anyone lacking earnestness should not try to enter those realms that are on the other side of the gaping abyss.

This solemn spirit messenger implores us to be earnest. Then, when we have heard his voice with sufficient seriousness of soul, we should be conscious of how indications sound toward us from the spiritual world. At first they sound silently and almost abstractly from beyond the abyss that yawns before us, which the Spirit Messenger holds us back from, so that we don't take a careless step. These indications will give us guidance and orientation. Thus it sounds across the gaping chasm:

> From the far reaches of the beings of space,
> Who experience their being in light;
> From the beat of the course of time,
> Which finds its expression in creation;
> From the depths of the heart's experience,
> Where the world fathoms itself in your Self:
>
> There resounds in the speaking of the soul,
> There shines forth from the thoughts of the spirit,
> Working from divine, healing powers,
> Weaving in cosmic, formative forces,
> The Eternal Word of existence:
> O Man, Know Thy Self!

I will say it again,

> From the far reaches of the beings of space,
> Who experience their being in light;
> From the beat of the course of time,
> Which finds its expression in creation;
> From the depths of the heart's experience,
> Where the world fathoms itself in your Self:
>
> There resounds in the speaking of the soul,
> There shines forth from the thoughts of the spirit,
> Working from divine, healing powers,
> Weaving in cosmic, formative forces,
> The Eternal Word of existence:
> O Man, Know Thy Self!

With these words it can become clear to us how the secrets of existence must be comprehended from all that weaves, works and manifests in the wide expanses of space. Real knowledge must be discovered in what can be revealed in creative activity through the course of time. The world that can be revealed within the depths of a person's heart can be made manifest in the honest seeking of the soul. These things alone form the basis for what people need on the path of knowledge, for the foundation of self-knowledge—where the world has placed the sum total of its secrets. In this

Self, this human self-knowledge, the world has placed the sum total of its secrets so that all that is needed in days of health and illness can be found on the path between birth and death, as well as what has to be applied on the other path of existence between death and a new birth.

But all who feel themselves as members of this School should be very clear that what is not acquired in this spirit is not real knowledge but only a semblance of knowledge. All that is usually validated as knowledge, which has been received by a person before becoming aware of the admonitions about spiritual knowledge from the Guardian of the Threshold, all of this is only a semblance of knowledge, the illusion of knowledge. It doesn't need to remain a semblance of knowledge. We don't despise this outer semblance of knowledge, but we must be clear that semblance of knowledge is a stage that can only be transformed by people who seek to purify their own being. The next stage can only be achieved through the metamorphosis of a one's own being through understanding what the guarding spirit messenger cautions at the gaping abyss of knowledge. Cautioning, the guarding messenger of the spirit, shining from the darkness, calls to human beings. The Guardian is a messenger of the light of the spirit in the darkness and is commissioned by the best inhabitants of the spiritual world.

Anyone lacking consciousness of the gaping abyss, which is bounded by what exists in the sense world where we live our life on Earth between birth and death and what exists in the spirit world, cannot truly acquire real knowledge. A person can only enter into true, real knowledge with this consciousness. One does not need to be clairvoyant, although knowledge of the spirit is derived from clairvoyance. But a person must become conscious of the solemn warnings about space, time and the human heart that are always present at the abyss. The abyss is there when we go out into the expanses of space. The abyss is there when we enter into the cycles of time. When we descend into the depths of our own heart, the abyss is there.

These three abysses are not three separate abysses; they are but one abyss. When we go to the limits of the expanses of space where we find the spirit, when we wander through the cycles of time where we find the beginnings of the cycles, when we enter into the depths of the human heart as deeply as only we can fathom in ourselves, these three paths all lead to one single endpoint, not to three different places. All three lead to the same divine-spirit-life that is the origin of the world, where eternal fountains fertilize and nourish all existence, where human beings learn and are taught about the ground of all existence.

In all earnestness, we must imagine ourselves in thought at that place where the solemn spirit messenger speaks. We must listen precisely to what he considers to be the hindrances of our time, the special character of our time. We should listen precisely to what the solemn spirit messenger considers hindrances of the spirit, the special character of our time that we have to overcome in order to arrive at true spiritual knowledge. My dear friends, hindrances to spiritual knowledge have existed at all times. Human beings at all times had to discard one thing or another that was warned against by the Guardian of the Threshold of the spiritual world. But every age has its peculiar hindrances. What comes from earthly human civilization is for the most part not a help but a hindrance for entering the spiritual world. People have to discover what emerges from the ordinary earthly civilization of their time. They have to discover the specific hindrances implanted in nature by that very time and that must be discarded before crossing the gaping abyss. Let us hear the serious guarding spirit messenger speak to this.

> Yet, beware of the abyss!
> For its beasts would soon devour you
> If in heedless haste you passed me by.
> Your cosmic age has set them within you
> As the enemies of knowledge.
>
> Behold the foremost beast; its crooked back,
> Its bony head, its parched form,
> Dull blunt blue appears its skin.
> Your fear of creative spirit being
> Begat this monstrous foe within your will;
> Only courage on the path of knowledge will overcome it.

The First Class of the Michael School

    Behold the second beast; it bares its teeth
In its distorted countenance, and tells lies with scorn.
Yellow, streaked with gray, its loathsome shape.
Your hatred of the spirit's revelations
Begat this weakling in your feeling;
Your fire for knowledge must tame it.

    Behold the third beast with cloven snout;
Glassy is its eye, its posture slouching.
Dirty red its form appears.
Your doubt in the power of spirit light
Begat this spectral form within your thinking;
Your creative work in knowledge must make it yield.

    Only when you have overcome these three
Will your soul develop wings
To soar across the deep abyss
That severs you from the field of knowledge
Where the dearest longings of your heart,
Aspiring to wholeness, wish to consecrate themselves.

I will read it again.

    The Guardian speaks:

    Yet, beware of the abyss!
For its beasts would soon devour you
If in heedless haste you pass me by.
Your cosmic age has set them within you
As the enemies of knowledge.

    Behold the foremost beast; its crooked back,
Its bony head, its parched form,
Dull blunt blue appears its skin.
Your fear of creative spirit being
Begat this monstrous foe within your will;
Only courage on the path of knowledge will overcome it.

    Behold the second beast; it bares its teeth
In its distorted countenance, and tells lies with scorn.

> Yellow, streaked with gray, its loathsome shape.
> Your hatred of the spirit's revelations
> Begat this weakling in your feeling;
> Your fire for knowledge must tame it.
>
> Behold the third beast with cloven snout;
> Glassy is its eye, its posture slouching.
> Dirty red its form appears.
> Your doubt in the power of spirit light
> Begat the spectral form within your thinking;
> Your creative work in knowledge must make it yield.
>
> Only when you have overcome these three
> Will your soul develop wings
> To soar across the deep abyss
> That severs you from the field of knowledge
> Where the dearest longings of your heart,
> Aspiring to wholeness, wish to consecrate themselves.

These, my dear friends, are the three great enemies of knowledge in our time for the present day human being.

People fear the creative life of the spirit. This fear lies deep down in the soul and people like to deny that this fear exists. They clothe this fear in a selection of ostensible logic through which they refute the revelations of the spirit.

My dear friends, here or there you will hear objections against spiritual knowledge. These are occasionally clothed in clever, or foolish, forms of logical reasoning. Never, however, are these logical forms the real reason why some people reject spiritual knowledge. Truthfully, it is the spirit of fear that abides deep down in the human soul, which works and gains strength in order to surge into the head as haunting logical forms. It is fear.

But let us be clear. It is not enough to say, "I have no fear." Anyone can say that. We must first comprehend the real seat of fear and the true nature of this fear. We must realize that in our present time we are born and educated from the forces into which ahrimanic powers have put the spirits of fear. We ourselves are afflicted with the spirits of fear. Just because we deny them doesn't mean that we are really free of them. We must find the ways and means—the School will guide us—to find the courage of cognition to face these spirits of fear who lurk as monsters in our will. Today what a person says is driving her or him to knowledge cannot result in true knowledge. Only courage, inner bravery of the soul, seizes those forces and capacities needed to traverse the path leading to true, life-filled spiritual knowledge.

The second beast slips into the human soul from the spirit of our time to become an enemy of knowledge. People confront the second beast everywhere in most of the literary works of our time, and in galleries, sculptures and other works of art and music. It does mischief in schools and in society; the second beast is everywhere you go. The second beast feels inwardly stimulated to mock spiritual knowledge in order to avoid admitting fear of the spirit.

Such mocking is not always expressed because people are not conscious of what lives within them. I would like to say that a wall—as thin as a spider's web—separates our head consciousness from what wants to mock true spiritual knowledge in the hearts of human beings. When this derisive scorn comes to light, the conscious or semi-conscious disrespect people carry today for spiritual knowledge suppresses the fear. Indeed, there are strange forces in every human being inciting against the revelations of the spirit. This mocking attitude reveals itself through most peculiar means.

The third beast is laziness of thinking, the ease of thinking that would like to make the whole world into a movie. You don't need to think during a movie. Everything is reeled off before your eyes and your thoughts only need to follow. Today, even science would like to follow the outer existence of the world with passive thoughts. People are too easy going, too slack, to bring thinking into activity. This slack thinking of humanity is like a person who wants to lift something up from the floor, who stands there with their hands in their pockets and believes the object can be lifted just like that. It can't be done this way! Likewise, we cannot take hold of real existence with the type of thinking that is not connected with the will. Just as we have to move our arms and hands if we want to take hold of an object, so we must bring our thoughts into action if we want to ascertain what is spiritual.

The Guardian of the Threshold characterizes the lurking first beast as fear in our will. It is a beast with a curved back, a parched body and a bony, distorted face. This beast has a dull, blunt, blue shape and rises up for humanity today beside the Guardian of the Threshold at the abyss. The Guardian makes clear to people of today that this dull, blunt, blue beast with a curved back and a parched, bony, distorted face exists. This beast is actually within you. And this beast rises from the gaping abyss of your field of knowledge and mirrors what lives in you as one of the enemies of knowledge, the one that lurks in your will.

The Guardian today characterizes the second beast in a similar way; it is connected with the lust to mock the spiritual world. It rises next to the other monster and proves itself a weakling. Its bearing is saggy. With its saggy bearing and yellow-gray shape it bares its teeth in a distorted countenance. And baring its teeth, it wants to live but is lying in its laughter because its mocking is a lie. It grins at us as a mirror image of the beast that lives in our own feeling, hindering our knowledge—an enemy of knowledge.

The third beast does not want to come near the content of the spiritual world and is characterized by the Guardian as the third one rising from the abyss with a cloven snout and glassy eye. Its gaze is dull because its thinking does not want to be active. A weak posture and a dirty red shape, false doubt in spirit light, this then characterizes the third enemy of knowledge that lurks within us. They make us earth-bound and heavy.

If we approach spiritual knowledge disregarding the warnings of the Guardian of the Threshold the gaping abyss is there. One cannot cross the abyss when weighed down by the heaviness of Earth; we cannot cross it with fear, nor with mocking, nor with doubt. We can only cross the abyss: when with thinking we have understood the spirituality of being; when with feeling we have experienced the soul of being; and, when we have become strong in will with the creativity of being. Then will spirit, soul, and creativity of being become the wings that lift us from the heaviness of Earth. Then we will have the strength to cross the deep abyss.

Threefold is the prejudice that throws us into the abyss when we haven't acquired the courage of knowledge, the fire of knowledge and the creativity of knowledge. But if we take hold of creative knowledge in thinking, when we want to activate our thinking, if we don't passively approach the spirit but receive the spirit with inner fire of the heart; if we have the courage to take hold of the spirit as spirit and not as a material picture, then wings will begin to grow that will carry us across the abyss to a realm that all people today, who are honest with themselves, long for in their hearts. That, my dear friends, is what I want to bring before your souls in this introduction to the first lesson, the beginning of the School of Spiritual Science.

Let us now end by bringing again before our souls the beginning, middle, and end of the experiences with the Guardian of the Threshold:

> Where on Earth foundations, color on color,
> Life, creative life, manifests itself;
> Where from earthly substance, form on form,
> The lifeless world is fashioned;
> Where sentient beings, powerful in will,
> Warm themselves with joy in their existence;
> Where you, yourself, O Man, acquire
> Your body from earth, air and light:
>
> There you enter with your own true being
> Deep into night-enveloped cold and darkness;
> From the dumb expanse you ask in vain
> Who you are and were and will become.
> For your own being the light of day fades into
> Soul's night and spirit-darkness;
> With anxious seeking you turn your soul
> To the light that takes its strength from darkness.

First Lesson

And from the darkness there lights up
To you—
Revealing you in your own true likeness,
Yet also shaping you into an image,
Solemn spirit words powerfully working in the cosmic ether,
Words that your heart can hear—

The spirit messenger, who alone
Can shed light upon your path.
Before him lies the far spread world of the senses,
Behind him yawn the depths of the abyss.

And before his darkened realm of spirit,
Close to the yawning chasm of existence,
His creative word sounds with all primeval power:
Behold, I am the only gate to knowledge.

The Guardian Speaks:

From the far reaches of the beings of space,
Who experience their being in light;
From the beat of the course of time,
Which finds its expression in creation;
From the depths of the heart's experience,
Where the world fathoms itself in your Self:

There resounds in the speaking of the soul,
There shines forth from the thoughts of the spirit,
Working from divine, healing powers,
weaving in the cosmic, formative forces,
The Eternal Word of existence:
O Man, Know Thy Self!

The Guardian Speaks further:

Yet, beware of the abyss!
For its beasts would soon devour you
If in heedless haste you passed me by.
Your cosmic age has set them within you
As the enemies of knowledge.

Behold the foremost beast; its crooked back,
Its bony head, its parched form,
Dull blunt blue appears its skin.
Your fear of creative spirit being
Begat this monstrous foe within your will;
Only courage on the path of knowledge will overcome it.

Behold the second beast; it bares its teeth
In its distorted countenance, and tell lies with scorn.
Yellow, streaked with gray, its loathsome shape.
Your hatred of the spirit's revelations
Begat this weakling in your feeling;
Your fire for knowledge must tame it.

Behold the third beast with cloven snout;
Glassy is its eye, its posture slouching.
Dirty red its form appears.
Your doubt in the power of spirit light
Begat the spectral form within your thinking;
Your creative work in knowledge must make it yield.

Only when you have overcome these three
Will your soul develop wings
To soar across the deep abyss
That severs you from the field of knowledge
Where the dearest longings of your heart,
Aspiring to wholeness, wish to consecrate themselves.

What we shall discover when we go past the Guardian of the Threshold, and what is necessary to experience in thinking, feeling and willing when passing the light of the Guardian when entering the darkness from which that light will grow— where we recognize the light of our own Self and thus achieve "O Man, Know Thy Self"—what speaks to us from the darkness that will grow light in spirit as to all this, my dear friends, we shall hear more in the next lesson of the first Class.

Second Lesson

Dornach, February 22, 1924

My dear friends! We will begin today with what was said in the last lesson to maintain continuity and because new members will be with us. Today's lesson will begin with a short recapitulation of what we placed before our souls the last time.

We have moved ourselves in thought to that place where the human being is able to face and perceive the suprasensory whose essence is akin to our own being. In normal life, and for normal consciousness, the human being is surrounded by the sense-perceptible world that can be understood with the intellect. To begin with, we want to develop three moods before we approach the Mysteries of spiritual life, which we will do next time.

The first mood makes us conscious of how one is surrounded in the normal state of soul by the world of the senses. However, this external world does not provide insight into one's own being. Throughout the ages, when the words *"Know Thy Self"* resound in the human soul, they call forth your noblest activity. One cannot find any satisfaction or answer to these words when, under the impression of *"Know Thy Self,"* one only sees what spreads out before the senses, the content of the outer world. One is directed to something other than what is experienced in the sense world—a world that lies outside of the human being.

We can have this feeling while carrying the question about our own being, when looking out into the vast expanses of the world. We approach in thought with this feeling to the suprasensory world, a world that is akin to our own being. Then the corresponding mood is reflected in the words that stood before our souls last time:

Where on Earth foundations, color on color,
Life, creative life, manifests itself;
Where from earthly substance, form on form,
The lifeless world is fashioned;
Where sentient beings, powerful in will,
Warm themselves with joy in their existence;
Where you, yourself, O Man, acquire
Your body from earth, air and light:

There you enter with your own true being
Deep into night-enveloped cold and darkness;
From the dumb expanse you ask in vain
Who you are and were and will become.
For your own being the light of day fades into
To soul's night and spirit-darkness;
With anxious seeking you turn your soul
To the light that takes its strength from darkness.

We are now confronted in our soul with a feeling, a sense, that presents us with the grandeur, beauty and majesty of the outer world. How can we see all of this in the world, even though we will never able to find our own being there? It is necessary for someone who strives for the spirit to build up this mood repeatedly in their soul. We have a profound experience in this mood when we look out upon the world outside of us... and that world doesn't tell us who we are. Creating this mood in our soul again and again strengthens it so it can carry us into the spiritual world. Although we feel that these moods can carry us into the spiritual world, we must also realize how people in their normal life are unprepared to face the spiritual world, a world that is akin to their own essence.

This is why at the boundary between the sense world and the spiritual world there stands the Guardian who earnestly cautions us not to enter the spiritual world unprepared. And again, my friends, we must take it to heart that the Guardian stands there before the spiritual world for the benefit of an unprepared humanity. We will soon learn to know the Guardian better. From time to time we must let this mood arise in our soul, we must let the feeling of approaching this Guardian come to us so it will become clear that a certain disposition of soul is necessary to attain insight, to attain true knowledge.

The common type of insight that everyone has in today's materialistic time is, as we say, experienced on every street corner. It would be terrible for humanity if this common insight contained true spiritual knowledge because humanity would be unprepared to receive it. Human beings must receive insight while in the right mood, the preparatory mood for receiving real knowledge. That is why we have to imagine in an intimate way the second mood that will repeatedly speak to us about how we must approach the Guardian.

> And from the darkness there lights up
> To you—
> Revealing your own true likeness,
> Yet also shaping you into an image,
> Solemn spirit words powerfully working in the cosmic ether,
> Words that your heart can hear—
>
> The spirit messenger, who alone
> Can shed light upon your path.
> Before him lies the far spread world of the senses,
> Behind him yawn the depths of the abyss;
>
> And before his darkened realm of spirit,
> Close to the yawning chasm of existence,
> His creative word sounds with all primeval power:
> Behold, I am the only gate to knowledge.

While we are still on this side in the sense world, the Guardian points across to the realm where it looks to us like impenetrable darkness. He points to this darkness that must become bright and will lighten up for us through spiritual knowledge. At first only the Guardian grows brighter. Pointing to the seeming darkness, this Maya of darkness, he speaks:

> From the far reaches of the beings of space,
> Who experience their being in light;
> From the beat of the course of time,
> Which finds its expression in creation;
> From the depths of the heart's experience,
> Where the world fathoms itself in your Self:
>
> There resounds in the speaking of the soul,
> There shines forth from the thoughts of the spirit,
> Working from divine, healing powers,
> Weaving in the cosmic, formative forces,
> The Eternal Word of existence:
> O Man, Know Thy Self!

If one can feel these words that resound from the Guardian deeply enough, one will notice while looking back upon oneself that what is perceived while looking back is the first beginning of self-knowledge. This beginning, then, is a preparation for real self-knowledge that reveals cosmic spiritual knowledge to us, knowledge of that being that is one with our own human being. Insights come up that can still be acquired on this side of the threshold to the spiritual world. Insights rise up that show the impurities of our thinking, feeling, and willing in pictures that are true—but horrifying—to us. At the abyss between the sense world and the spiritual world, perceptions of three beasts are experienced rising up from the gaping abyss.

What we must feel at the abyss of existence, between the world of Maya and the world of real being, is shown to the soul by the fourth mood.

> Yet, beware of the abyss!
> For its beasts would soon devour you
> If in heedless haste you passed me by.
> Your cosmic age has set them within you
> As the enemies of knowledge.
>
> Behold the foremost beast; its crooked back,
> Its bony head, its parched form,
> Dull blunt blue appears its skin.

> Your fear of creative spirit being
> Begat this monstrous foe within your will;
> Only courage on the path of knowledge will overcome it.

My dear friends, we must be clear and face the fact that we have no courage for knowledge in our souls. Instead of courage we have cowardice. Fear of knowledge prevents most people in our time from getting close to the insights of the spiritual world.

> Behold the second beast; it bares its teeth
> In its distorted countenance, and tells lies with scorn.
> Yellow, streaked with gray, is its loathsome shape.
> Your hatred of the spirit's revelations
> Begat this weakling in your feeling;
> Your fire for knowledge must tame it.

This is the second beast we carry within us, the one that sows doubt in our souls and all kinds of feelings of uncertainty about the spiritual world. It lives in our feelings because our feelings are weak and cannot be aroused to true enthusiasm. True knowledge has to rise above the lower and more common enthusiasm that is aroused by all sorts of life from outside. This is a cheap arousal! Inner enthusiasm and inner fire will become the fire of knowledge that can overcome the second beast.

> Behold the third beast with cloven snout;
> Glassy is its eye, its posture slouching.
> Dirty red its form appears.
> Your doubt in the power of spirit light
> Begat this spectral form within your thinking;
> Your creative work in knowledge must make it yield.

We must find courage and fire to bring activity to our thinking. When we are creative in our ordinary consciousness we create with arbitrariness, and what we create is not real. When we properly prepare ourselves for it, the spiritual world streams into our creative thinking. And then, courage for knowledge, fire of knowledge, and creative knowledge in our soul gives birth to our real existence in the spiritual world.

> Only when you have overcome these three
> Will your soul develop wings
> To soar across the deep abyss
> That severs you from the field of knowledge
> Where the dearest longings of your heart,
> Aspiring to wholeness, wish to consecrate themselves.

These moods can carry us to the point that we feel in the right way what we as human beings must kindle in ourselves as true human beings, as really living human beings who may enter the spiritual world. It is a fact that in ordinary life, in the most commonplace of things, people experience life in all its seriousness. They understand that life is not just a game. Yet, what should lead us to true knowledge doesn't push as hard as outer life pushes. What ought to lead us to knowledge must be made active in our souls. We make a game of this too easily. We even persuade ourselves that we are earnest about this game. But we do a great deal of harm to ourselves and to others when we play with striving for the spirit and do not bring absolute earnestness to our spiritual striving.

Such earnestness need not be expressed in a sentimental way. That is not what we need. Earnestness can, in certain situations in life, call for humor. But even then, the humor must be serious. What is stressed here as earnestness does not indicate mere sentimentality, false piety, or a lofty gaze in contrast to playing around. What is meant is true spiritual striving and steadfastly living the spiritual path with persistence and perseverance (...).

In esoteric life it is impossible to live with what is so prevalent in normal life: to interpret the lie as truth. In esoteric life the truth is what works, rather than the interpretation. Only the truth, nothing but the truth, works in esoteric life. It is possible to color something with vanity, but the coloring you give it makes no impression on the spiritual world. The unvarnished truth is what works in the spiritual world.

From this you can gather how different spiritual realities are. Of course, they are at work today beneath the surface, as they always were. But how different they are from what outer life presents to us: a patchwork of the many lies of life. Today very little of what lives between people is really true. To repeatedly realize this belongs to the beginning of our work in the life of the Class. Only from a mood created in this manner can we find the inner strength to participate in what will more and more develop here in the Class as we proceed from lesson to lesson, finding our way into the spiritual world.

Only then will we become aware of what must come about in our thinking, feeling and willing, so that: thinking may overcome the specter of thought; feeling overcome the mocker; and, willing overcome the bony spirit, so that these three beasts will be conquered. For these three beasts are our own enemies of cognition, of knowledge. They are reflected to us as in a mirror, but we meet these three as real beings at the yawning abyss of existence.

Everything that hinders us from true knowledge is deeply rooted in our human essence—initially in our thinking. Ordinary human thinking is mirrored in the thought-specter of the third beast that was clearly described in form and appearance:

> Behold the third beast with cloven snout,
> Glassy is its eye, its posture slouching.
> Dirty red its form appears.

This is the picture of ordinary human thinking—thinking about things of the outer world, which is unaware that such thinking about the things of the outer world is but a corpse. Where did the being live whose corpse is this ordinary thinking?

Yes, my friends, today when we think according to the guidance given us in school and by life itself—from morning when we wake up until evening when we go to sleep— we think with a thinking that is a corpse. This is natural for our civilization and our age. But this thinking is dead! When was this thinking alive? Where did it live?

It lived before we were born. It lived when our soul was in its pre-earthly existence. Imagine it like this. A human being exists on the physical Earth in a physical body with a living soul, which is alive by virtue of this soul, until death. After death the living being of soul becomes invisible. Only the corpse, the dead form of the living human gestalt during life, remains visible. You have to imagine that thinking was alive in the same way. Thinking was a living, organic, growing, weaving being before the human being came down into earthly existence. After that it becomes a corpse buried in the tombs of our own heads and in our own brains. Just as a corpse in the grave would like to claim, "I am a human being," so says our thinking when it is buried as a corpse in our brain and thinks about the external things in the world. It is a corpse. It is perhaps depressing for people to realize that their thinking is a corpse. It is true all the same, and esoteric knowledge has to adhere to the truth.

After cautioning our souls to be watchful of the three beasts, the Guardian of the Threshold continues. These words now resound in our hearts:

> The third beast with its glassy eye,
> Is the evil counter-image
> Of thinking, that in you denies itself,
> And chooses its own death,
> Forsaking spirit powers who,
> Before its earthly life, sustained
> Its life in fields of spirit.

I will say it again:

> The third beast with its glassy eye,
> Is the evil counter-image
> Of thinking, that in you denies itself,
> And chooses its own death,
> Forsaking spirit powers who,
> Before its earthly life, sustained
> Its life in fields of spirit.

The thinking we use to achieve so much here in the sense world is, for the world of the gods, the corpse of our soul. We have died in our thinking at the present time by coming down to Earth. The death of thinking has been coming about since the year AD 333, in the middle of the fifth post-Atlantean epoch. Since then thinking has gradually become dead. In earlier times vitality still poured into thinking; it was a heritage of pre-earthly thinking. The Greeks, the Orientals, felt alive when they were thinking. They felt the presence of the spirit, of the gods, in the weaving of thinking. The Orientals, the ancient Greeks, they knew that when they were thinking a god was living in every thought. This has now been lost; thinking has become dead. Now we must follow the warnings given by the Guardian for our age:

> Yet, beware of the abyss!
> For its beasts would soon devour you
> If in heedless haste you pass me by.
> *Your* cosmic age has set them within you
> As the enemies of knowledge.

This cosmic age began three hundred and thirty-three years after the origin of Christianity, in the fourth century AD, after the first third of the fourth century. It is evident today that everything that proceeds from thinking is filled with powers of death and not of life. The dead thinking of the nineteenth century has brought dead materialism to the surface of human civilization.

Now with feelings things are different. Ahriman, the great enemy of humanity, has not been able to kill feeling as he has killed thinking. Feeling is still alive in the present age. Yet, people have pushed feelings from the realm of consciousness largely down into the half-unconscious. Feelings rise up in the soul. Who has their feelings as fully under control as their thinking? Who has clarity about what lives in their feelings like the clarity they have in their thoughts?

My dear friends, take one of the saddest phenomena of our time, saddest before the spirit. When people think clearly they are citizens of the world because they know quite well that thinking is what makes human beings "human," even if in the present epoch it is dead.

However, in feeling human beings are separated into nations. Especially today unconscious feelings rule in the worst possible way. At the present time, conflicts arise everywhere from undefined feelings that only allow one to feel that they belong to a particular human group.

All the same, world karma places us in a specific human group. Our feelings serve world karma when we are placed in this group, class or nation. It is not through thinking that we are so placed. Thinking, if not colored by feeling or will, is the same the world over. Feeling varies according to the different regions of the world. Feeling is half-unconscious. It is alive, but in the unconscious. This is how the ahrimanic spirit uses this opportunity to stir up the unconscious parts of feeling because it cannot influence the life of feeling directly. Ahriman does this to confuse truth and error. This is how our emotional prejudices are colored by ahrimanic influences and ahrimanic impulses.

Feelings must rise up in our soul in their true form if we want to enter the spiritual world. We must be able to practice self-knowledge with regard to feeling. By repeatedly looking back at our own being, we must be able to tell ourselves what kind of person we are as a feeling human being. This is not easy to achieve. It is easy to achieve with regard to thinking. If we want to obtain clarity about ourselves it is relatively easy to do with thinking. We don't always do it, but it is easier to admit to ourselves that we are not exactly a genius, or that we've fallen short with our clarity of thought. Vanity and opportunism mostly prevent us from obtaining clarity in our thinking.

But as to our feelings, we do not really even get to face ourselves before our soul. We are actually always convinced that our way of feeling is the right one. We must look very deeply into our soul if we want to see ourselves as feeling human beings. Yes, we must do this. Only by conscientiously facing ourselves as feeling human beings can we raise ourselves above the hindrances that the second beast has set before us on the path to the spiritual world.

If we don't practice self-knowledge from time to time and face ourselves as feeling human beings, then in reality we always develop a mocking face toward the spiritual world. In the same way that we are unconscious of our unhealthy feelings we are also not conscious that we mock the spiritual world. We clothe our scorn in all possible forms, although we really do scorn the spirit. And those of whom I spoke before, those who are not earnest, they are the cynics, the sarcastic ones. They may, at times, feel ashamed of themselves for expressing this derision inwardly in thought, but they are in reality scorning the spiritual world. How can anyone who merely plays at spirituality not be inwardly mocking? The Guardian of the Threshold speaks to them:

> The second beast with mocking face
> Is the evil counter-force
> Of feeling, that hollows out your very soul
> And makes for emptiness of life;
> Whereas enlightening spirit-fullness
> Was given you before you were on Earth
> From the might of spirit-sun.

The first beast is the mirror image of our will. The mirror image of our will addresses what lives in our will. But the will is not merely dreaming, it is not just half unconscious. The will is completely unconscious.

It has often been described to you, my dear friends, how the essence of will lies deep in your unconscious. And deep in their unconscious people search with day consciousness for their karmic path in life. Every karmic step people take in life is measured, but they know nothing about it. It all happens unconsciously. Our preceding Earth lives work strongly into our karma as a living force. Destiny brings us two milestones in life: our turning-points, or life-decisions, and our life-doubts. Here lies the path of error, the mistakes of the individual who pursues a life path of self-seeking. In thinking, a person seeks the path that *all* people seek. In feeling, one seeks the ways that *his group* seeks. For example, in feeling we recognize whether a person comes from the north, west, east or south of Europe. But we must enter into the deep, unconscious impulses of the will to recognize a person not as a generic human being, nor as a member of a group, but instead as a distinct human individual. The will works deep down in the unconscious. The first beast points to these erroneous paths of the will.

The Guardian speaks with earnest warning:

> The first beast's ghostly skeleton
> Is the evil creative might
> Of will that estranges your own body
> From all the forces of your soul
> And offers it to adverse powers
> Who want to rob the world's being
> In future times from Divine Being.

Spiritual powers are at work in our will. In truth, they want to steal our body away from us during Earth existence and with it, steal a part of our soul. They want to build an Earth existence with it that is unable to evolve further into Jupiter, Venus and Vulcan. They want to separate the Earth from the Divine's intentions for the Earth so that the Earth would be robbed of its future. Human beings would then be united with this Earth—an Earth stolen from the gods by certain powers living and working in one's will—living even in the will through which a person seeks their karma, their destiny.

The first beast is well-suited to represent what lives in the will as in a mirror image: the bony head, the parched body, the dull blunt blue skin and the curved back. The ahrimanic spirit works in the will in all searching for one's karma. That spirit can only be overcome by courage for knowledge…cognitive courage. And so, with the words just given you, the Guardian of the Threshold speaks about the first beast.

I will read it again.

> The first beast's ghostly skeleton
> Is the evil creative might
> Of will that estranges your own body
> From all the forces of your soul
> And offers it to adverse powers
> Who want to rob the world's being
> In future times from Divine Being.

Second Lesson

In these words spoken by the Guardian of the Threshold there resounds the warning he calls to the human spirit who is seeks insight, who seeks knowledge.

Dear friends, let these words live intensively and deeply in our souls. And let us listen often to what the Guardian speaks:

> The third beast with its glassy eye,
> Is the evil counter-image
> Of thinking, that in you denies itself,
> And chooses its own death,
> Forsaking spirit powers who,
> Before its life on Earth, sustained
> Its life in fields of spirit.

Once again you must grasp the harmonious working of the several verses.

[The first verse of the mantra is written on the blackboard.]

> *The third beast with its glassy eye,*
> *Is the "<u>evil</u>" counter-<u>image</u>*
> *Of <u>thinking</u>, that in you <u>denies</u> itself,*
> *And chooses its own death,*
> *Forsaking spirit powers who,*
> *Before its life on Earth, sustained*
> *Its life in fields of spirit.*

Above all, feel what each verse contains by itself. The second verse points to feeling:

> The second beast with mocking face
> Is the evil counter-force
> Of feeling, that hollows out your very soul
> And makes for emptiness of life;
> Whereas enlightening spirit-fullness
> Was given you before you were on Earth
> From the might of spirit-sun.

[The second verse is written on the blackboard].

The second beast with mocking face
Is the "<u>evil</u>" counter-<u>force</u>

—*Counter-force*: no longer *image*, but now *force!*—
[*Image* and *force* are double underlined, and then more is written.]

Of <u>feeling</u>, that <u>hollows out</u> your very soul
And makes for emptiness of life;
Whereas enlightening spirit-fullness
Was given you before you were on Earth
From the might of spirit-sun.

For the second time, feel here [in the first verse] *denies;* feel here [in the second verse] *hollows out*. Feel strongly the nuances in the verses by the fact that one time you have *denies* and the other time, *hollows out*.

The words of the Guardian are directed to our will:

The first beast's ghostly skeleton
Is the evil creative might
Of will that estranges your own body
From all the forces of your soul
And offers it to adverse powers
Who want to rob the world's being
In future times from Divine Being.

[The third verse is written on the blackboard]:

The first beast's ghostly skeleton
Is the "<u>evil</u>" creative <u>might</u>

—We have neither *image* nor *force*, but *might*: you should feel the progressive intensification—

Of <u>will</u> that <u>estranges</u> your own body

—Here you have a progressive intensification. First it was something more intellectual—*denies*. Then you have something that stirs things up in the inner life: *hollows out*. Finally, you have what takes the inner life away altogether: *estranges*—

[More is written.]

> *From all the forces of your soul*
> *And offers it to adverse powers*
> *Who want to rob the world's being*
> *In future times from Divine Being.*

Feel how the word *evil* resounds through all three verses. [In each verse, the word *evil* is emphasized by quotation marks and double underlining.] Feel the progressive intensification in these verses. Feel the distinction among *thinking, feeling,* and *willing*.

If you rightly feel how all these verses are connected through the one recurring word *evil* then, my dear friends, each of these verses becomes a mantra in its inner meaning. They can become your guide for each of the three stages into the spiritual world.

> The *third* beast with its glassy eye,
> Is the evil counter-image
> Of thinking, that in you denies itself,
> And chooses its own death,
> Forsaking spirit powers who,
> Before its life on Earth, sustained
> Its life in fields of spirit
>
> The *second* beast with mocking face
> Is the evil counter-force
> Of feeling, that hollows out your very soul
> And makes for emptiness of life;
> Whereas enlightening spirit-fullness
> Was given you before you were on Earth
> From the might of spirit-sun.
>
> The *first* beast's ghostly skeleton
> Is the evil creative might
> Of will that estranges your own body
> From all the forces of your soul

And offers it to adverse powers
Who want to rob the world's being
In future times from Divine Being.

If you always grasp the harmonious working of these three verses [the words third, second, and first are underlined on the blackboard] and never fail to connect the three of them by means of the one decisive word to form an inner soul organism, if you never call these three verses to life without including this word *evil* [the word *evil* is underlined for a third time], then my dear friends, these three verses will become your guide upon your path past the Guardian of the Threshold into the spiritual world. We shall learn to know the Guardian of the Threshold more closely in the following lessons.

(…)

Third Lesson

Dornach, February 29, 1924

My dear friends, we begin today with the already familiar words that the Guardian speaks at the threshold. He indicates the direction into the spiritual realm and describes what human beings can feel at the threshold of the spiritual world on passing the Guardian:

> From the far reaches of the beings of space,
> Who experience their being in light;
> From the beat of the course of time,
> Which finds its expression in creation;
> From the depths of the heart's experience,
> Where the world fathoms itself in your Self:
>
> There resounds in the speaking of the soul,
> There shines forth from the thoughts of the spirit,
> Working from divine, healing powers,
> Weaving in cosmic, formative forces,
> The Eternal Word of existence:
> O Man, Know Thy Self!

The point is, anyone who seeks entrance into the spiritual world should first follow this path in their thoughts. When a person on this path experiences in thought what the initiate experiences in reality upon entering the spiritual world, it is not incorrect to say that the thinker—if honestly and earnestly living in thought—would share the same experience that is revealed to the soul when actually entering the spiritual world...even if the reality of the spiritual world is only experienced as an ideal reflection.

We should not decide to leave entry into the spiritual world to those who seek initiation, to those who want to live with their soul in spiritual existence, just as some other people live with their senses in physical existence. One should really say it differently. When someone approaches what is presented as the path into the spiritual world through thinking, when what is encountered in the spiritual world is experienced in thought, then the thinker, whose thoughts are not superficial, would have a complete feeling and a full experience of what stirs and moves at the entrance to the spiritual world when coming from the world of semblance or illusion, the sense world that can only be comprehended by the intellect—the world of Maya.

Therefore, my friends, what I will tell you today is not only for those who seek a transformation of your hearts and minds that will place you in the spiritual world. This is also for those who want to experience this transformation in thought only. Basically, this is what all of you want; otherwise, you wouldn't be here.

The following must be said. When one makes observations in the sense world (life consists of such observations), these observations engage the will. One goes from observation to action, and actions work back upon one's feelings. Human beings move from observation to action. One experiences emotions when feeling is enthusiastic, combined with action and thought-filled observation. Since this is a natural state on Earth for a physical human being between birth and death, one stands, to some extent, on safe ground. People seek this safe ground when it is not there. When people need to believe something, they look everywhere for facts to support that belief and look for experiences to prove it. In ordinary life a person doesn't like to accept what is not proven by outer experience. One feels on safe ground because one can say: this is true because I have seen it; this is real because I have touched it.

This very certainty is part of human life by virtue of the world and the order present in it. Because of this certainty, a person discriminates between truth and illusion, truth and semblance, truth and dream. This is necessary for one's normal life between birth and death. People speak about semblance, or illusion, when verification or proof can't be provided by life itself. Only by being able to speak in normal life about truth and semblance, or about reality and appearance, are people led through life with certainty.

Dear friends, please imagine for a moment that you live your life in the world of the senses between birth and death without ever having the certainty to say whether you are encountering truth or illusion. Imagine that you have no way to discern if a person standing before you and telling you something is a real person or a semblance of one. Imagine that you could not distinguish whether an event you meet is only a dream or is a fact of the real world. If this were the case, just think what uncertainty, what terrible uncertainty, would come into your life!

This is precisely how you would feel, while either dreaming or facing reality, if life at every step withheld from you the capacity to discern reality from illusion. It is the same for a pupil at the threshold of the spiritual world. The first important experience a pupil has when standing at the threshold of the spiritual world is becoming aware of the fact that the spiritual world lies beyond that threshold.

At first we see only darkness streaming to us from the spiritual world. But then in the first experience where, here or there, more light may appear—and when the Guardian of the Threshold lets resound the words we heard last time—with this first experience, with all that we have achieved in the physical, sense-perceptible world and gained with our intellect, we are totally incapable of distinguishing between a real spiritual being, a real spiritual event, and a dream.

The very first experience you have when facing the spiritual world is when semblance and reality are entwined and the distinction between them is very problematic. This has to be borne in mind especially by those who are not in a regular spiritual training, but who nevertheless have experiences through elemental forces. Such elemental forces rise up for a variety of reasons, such as a shattering event, an illness, or because of other things. Above all, the situation has to be attended to when impressions come up from the spiritual world through such elemental forces.

Such people should not say to themselves prematurely, "Here is the spiritual world." For it may well be that what appears here and there in a flash is nothing more than an illusion. Consequently, the faculty to discern between truth and error, between truth and illusion, is the very first thing we have to learn independently of everything we experience in the physical world, so that we may enter the spiritual world in the right way. We must achieve a quite new ability to distinguish between reality and illusion.

At the present time people do not care much for what enters our life from the spiritual world. In our civilization people only care about what can be touched and what can be seen with our physical eyes. In our time when people want to rely solely on the outer security provided by the life between birth and death, it is extremely difficult to acquire the faculty of discriminating between truth and error, between reality and semblance, in the spiritual world. The utmost seriousness is necessary in these matters.

Why is this so? You see, when you, as a physical human being, confront the outer world, you have thoughts about the outer world and, at the same time, you receive impressions with these thoughts. The impressions of the physical world enter the thoughts and support them. You don't need to do much work to live in reality. Reality simply accepts you as part of physical reality.

It is quite different in the spiritual world. You must first grow into the spiritual world. In the spiritual world you must first obtain the right feeling of your *own* reality, and then you will gradually acquire the faculty for discriminating between truth and error, and between reality and semblance.

In the physical world, the moment you sit upright on a chair and don't fall to the ground you know that the chair is real, not imagined. The chair sees to it that you regard it as real.

None of this is present in the spiritual world. Why is it like this in the physical world? It is like this because in the physical world your thinking, feeling and willing are carried by your physical body as a unity. You are a threefold being: a thinking human being, a feeling human being and a willing human being. But, these three are held together by the physical body as one.

Yet the minute you enter the spiritual world you immediately experience your threefold being. Your thinking goes its own way; feeling goes another way; and, your willing goes still another. This separation, this division into three, occurs the moment you enter the spiritual world. You can think thoughts in the spiritual world that have nothing to do with your will, but then these thoughts are illusions. You can have feelings that have nothing to do with your will, but these feelings will contribute to your destruction, not to your advancement.

It is essential to comprehend that the minute a person approaches the threshold of the spiritual world it seems like their thinking flies out to far cosmic spaces, and their feeling goes back in time beyond their memory.

Notice the last thing I said. You see, memory comes right up close to the threshold of the spiritual world. Suppose you experienced something ten years ago. It rises up again in your memory. The experience is there. You are pleased, and rightly so, if you are able to call up a vivid memory in the physical world. Yet, for anyone who enters the spiritual world, it is as if they had to strike through their memory and go back farther than their memory can reach. At any rate, one goes farther back in memory than is possible in earthly life. One goes back to the time before birth.

When you enter the spiritual world you immediately feel that what you are feeling does not stay with you. In any case, thinking goes out into the present universe and disperses into worldwide space. Feeling leaves the world altogether. And if you want to follow it, you have to know where you are now. If you have reached the age of fifty, you may have gone back in time more than fifty years; you may have gone back seventy, ninety, one hundred, or one hundred fifty years. Feeling takes you from time, from the time that you experienced here on Earth from childhood on. As to the will, when you take hold of it in earnest, it takes you even farther back into your past lives on Earth. This is what happens directly, my friends, when you actually come to the threshold. The physical body no longer holds you together. You no longer feel contained by your skin. You feel dismembered.

You feel as though your thinking, which until now held you together with your feelings, would stream out into cosmic space and become cosmic thoughts. You experience yourself going back in time with your feeling directly into the spiritual world where you lived between your last death and your present life on Earth. And with your will you feel yourself in your past life on Earth.

This very dismemberment of the human being—described in my book *How to Know Higher Worlds*—causes difficulties on entering the spiritual world. Your thoughts expand and what you were able to hold together on Earth goes over into the wider universe. Thoughts become almost imperceptible while this is happening. You must acquire the faculty of continuing to perceive these thoughts as they go out into the cosmos.

Your feeling is no longer permeated by thoughts because your thoughts have gone away. The only thing to do is to turn with reverence and devotion in a mood of prayer to those beings you were together with between death and birth, before you came to Earth. If you have learned such feelings of reverence for the spiritual world during your life, you will not find it impossible.

Great difficulties arise for a person the moment they give themselves up to the will that wants to go to a past life. A great force of attraction arises in the soul for all that is of a lower nature in your being. What I've described before works very strongly here, namely the difficulty of discriminating between semblance and reality. A powerful tendency to surrender to illusion arises in people at this point. I will describe it.

When a person begins to meditate, when a person meditates on the subject of the meditation with true, inner devotion, they would like the meditation to proceed in a comfortable way. During meditation one does not want to be torn from the comfort of life. The desire to be as quiet as possible and not be torn from comfort is a powerful cause of illusion. If you honestly dedicate yourself to meditation, then by necessity feelings arise from the depths of your soul asking how many evil possibilities exist within you. It is impossible to do otherwise than to go deep down into yourself through meditation, to truly and deeply feel that all the possible things you could do, or are capable of doing, are down there. But the instinct not to admit this to yourself is so strong that you give in to the illusion that deep down you are actually a quite well-meaning person.

The genuine experience of meditation is not like this. Real meditation shows you how you can be filled with all possible vanities in overestimating yourself and in underestimating others. Or again, it shows you how you value the opinions of other people not because you respect them as people who have something worthwhile to say but, instead, you value them because you like basking in the sunshine of their opinion. But these are the least of the things you might discover. A real, honest meditant will see what instincts are alive in their soul and all that these instincts are capable of doing. Indeed, the lower nature of the human being appears to a great extent before the soul's inner eye. Honesty must be present in meditation. If honesty is present, then what your will is predisposed to is mirrored in the words spoken to us already. All these things are mirrored in the words:

> Behold the foremost beast, its crooked back,
> Its bony head, its parched form,
> Dull blunt blue appears its skin.
> Your fear of creative spirit being
> Begat this monstrous foe within your will.

Because this is so, the powerful tendency of human beings to prefer self-illusions and to suppress the essential impressions arising in meditation, causes people to feel incited to mock and ridicule the spiritual world. We will learn to stand honestly in the spiritual world by confronting these opposing forces. The sight of the second beast appears at the threshold:

> Behold the second beast: it bares its teeth
> In its distorted countenance, and tells lies with scorn.
> Yellow, streaked with gray, is its loathsome shape.
> Your own hatred of the spirit's revelations
> Begat this weakling in your feeling.

Then, if we are unable to reach out and are powerless to follow the thoughts contained in our head—to following them as cosmic thoughts—the third beast appears to us from our inability to lift our human thoughts up to cosmic thoughts.

> Behold the third beast with cloven snout,
> Glassy is its eye, its posture slouching.
> Dirty red its form appears.
> Your doubt in the power of spirit light
> Begat the spectral form within your thinking.

The less we give ourselves up to illusions about this triad that mirrors our own being, the more we shall find the true human being within us who can receive the light from the spiritual world, the true human being who is able, as far as possible on Earth, to solve the riddle given to us in the words "O Man, Know Thy Self!" From self-knowledge springs true knowledge of the world, which then can lead us through life in the right way. This threefold dismemberment that one experiences—where thinking goes its own way, feeling goes another way and willing yet another—which until now was united by what is external, this threefoldness could be expressed in the words the Guardian of the Threshold speaks to the spiritual pupil. These words were given to us in the previous lesson.

> The third beast with its glassy eye,
> Is the evil counter-image
> Of thinking, that in you denies itself,
> And chooses its own death,
> Forsaking spirit powers who,
> Before its earthly life, sustained
> Its life in fields of spirit.
>
> The second beast with mocking face
> Is the evil counter-force
> Of feeling, that hollows out your very soul
> And makes for emptiness of life;
> Whereas enlightening spirit-fullness
> Was given you before you were on Earth

From the might of spirit-sun.

The first beast's ghostly skeleton
Is the evil creative might
Of will that estranges your own body
From all the forces of your soul
And offers it to adverse powers
Who want to rob the world's being
In future times from Divine Being.

These words are spoken by the Guardian as a warning, so that we will recognize how not to enter the spiritual world. At the entrance to the spiritual world we must get used to a different way of judging, a different way of feeling, a different way of willing—different from what prevails in the physical world. Consequently, it is necessary that we really grasp this threefoldness in ourselves. We must turn our gaze inward with great strength and become aware of what our thinking really is, what our feeling really is, and what our willing really is. We must become aware of what they must all become before crossing over the threshold of the spiritual world, even if this crossing over is only in thought. This is how it is. The gods have required us to overcome ourselves before bestowing on us the bliss of knowledge.

Therefore, immediately after these discouraging, and perhaps horrifying, words that came down from the Guardian, which I have spoken to you about repeatedly, the Guardian speaks further, telling us what we must do. At this point, our first few Class Lessons become practical instructions that tell us what now has to enter into our thinking, feeling and willing so we may enter the spiritual world in the right way. Once again, the verse that should flow into us must be threefold, so that we can live with it. And because we live with it, we start on the path to the spiritual world. When we eat, drink, see and hear, something in us is set in motion. In the same way, these words should move us when they are spoken by the Guardian who stands with his earnest countenance before the spiritual world. In the first verse he says:

> See how thinking weaves in you;
> Experience, then, world-illusion.
> Selfhood hides itself from you;
> Dive down into the semblance.
> Ether's essence wafts in you;
> Selfhood's being should revere
> Guiding beings of your spirit.

Let us take the verse apart. The human being, while living in the sense world between birth and death, feels a sense of Self in the physical body. People know that their legs carry them through the world. They know that their blood circulation gives them life. They know that breathing awakens life in them. They trust their breathing, the circulation of their blood, and the movements of the legs that carry them through the world. A person is a physical being on Earth by accepting and surrendering to the Earth. In the same way that a person in the physical world surrenders to physical matter that enables them to live on the Earth—in breathing, the movement of the limbs, and in circulation—in the same way that we surrender to these functions, we have to surrender our souls to the guiding powers of the spiritual world when we want to be part of the spiritual world and wish to enter it with knowledge.

Just as I must say that in physical existence your blood has to circulate and your breathing must function to have good health, I have to advise anyone who wants to stand properly in the spiritual world that the soul must now be sustained and guided by its own spirit's guiding being.

[Beginning with the final words of the first verse, it is now written on the blackboard.]

Guiding beings of your spirit.

My friends, you have surrendered to your blood by force of nature. You have surrendered to the movements of your limbs by a force of nature, and your breathing, too. In the spiritual world you cannot surrender in the same way to the guiding beings of your spirit. You have to arrive there with inner activity. The guiding beings of your spirit cannot be reached in the same way you reach your breath through the movement of your lungs. You can reach the guiding beings of your spirit to the extent that you are able to learn *reverence*.

[*revere* is written on the blackboard above "guiding beings of your spirit," as follows:]

revere
Guiding beings of your spirit.

—To revere from the deepest core of your Selfhood's being.

["Selfhood's being" is now written as follows in front of *revere*.]

Selfhood's being   revere
Guiding beings of your spirit.

Selfhood's being should revere
Guiding beings of your spirit.

[While speaking the last two lines the missing words are added, so that the two final lines now appear in full on the blackboard.]

Selfhood's being should revere
Guiding beings of your spirit.

Here you have a situation where you will have to stand in the spiritual world, given in the words that the Guardian speaks.

How do you stand within them? You don't stand within them as you stand with your legs on the physical ground. You don't stand within them as you live in the physical warmth of your blood. You don't stand there by taking in a breath. You stand there within them as much as you feel yourself in the half-spiritual ether beings, inasmuch as the ether's essence, the ether being, wafts in you.

[The third line from the bottom is written on the blackboard.]

Ether's essence wafts in you;

You feel as though you were yourself a little cloud in the spiritual world with the spiritual wind blowing around you. You feel carried around by this weaving wind, as if your Selfhood, your own "I," reveres the guiding beings of your spirit who come to you in this weaving wind. Now we now told to enter deeply into this, but what does this mean, anyway? As long as we remain here in our meditation with all that has been described, we *live* in semblance, we live in the world of appearance. We must now enter into this world of appearance with full consciousness so that this weaving wind, this reverence for our guiding spiritual beings is, at first, "*semblance.*"

[The fourth line is written on the blackboard].

Dive now down into the semblance:

Why should we do this? We only have an undefined feeling of our "I" in our earthly life. We describe our "Selfhood" with the word "*I,*" but it is an undefined, dim feeling that hides itself from us.

[The fifth line from the bottom is written on the blackboard.]

Selfhood hides itself from you:

We don't know much about it. And what we do know, what we take hold of in thoughts we are aware of, is not world-being. It is world-semblance, world-illusion…Maya.

[The sixth line from the bottom is written on the blackboard.]

Experience, then, world-illusion,

All this comes to us when we obey the requests of the Guardian of the Threshold.

[The seventh from the bottom or the first line from the top is written on the blackboard.]

See how thinking weaves in you:

Everything becomes for us our own weaving thoughts.

Here we have the first mantric verse that should give us the strength in our thinking to comply with the demands of our Selfhood. At the start it can stand before our soul in these words.

Third Lesson

> See how thinking weaves in you;
> Experience, then, world-illusion.
> Selfhood hides itself from you;
> Dive down into the semblance.
> Ether's essence wafts in you;
> Selfhood's being should revere
> Guiding beings of your spirit.

This is what is asked of us—to look back into our thoughts. If you close yourself off from the outer world and observe how your thoughts flow and weave within you, and if you respond to the requests contained in these seven lines, you have fulfilled the first request from the Guardian.

Now you have to approach your *feelings* with the words the Guardian speaks.

> Perceive how feeling streams in you;
> How semblance mixes there with being.
> Your Self to semblance feels inclined;
> Immerse yourself in seeming being.
> And world soul forces dwell in you;
> Your Selfhood, it should deeply ponder
> Powers of life within your soul.

Just as in the first mantric verse we enter into thinking, so with the second verse we enter into the world of feeling.

[The first line of the second verse is written on the blackboard.]

> *Perceive how feeling streams in you;*

Turn away from thinking and try to look back into your feeling life. In thinking, nearly everything is just an illusion, a semblance. When we descend into our feelings, semblance and being are mixed together. We become aware of this at once:

> *How semblance mixes there with being.*

But now our own "I," or Selfhood, does not want to come into being. It is accustomed to the outer semblance of the sense world. It does not want to come into being. It inclines toward semblance; it is drawn toward illusion. It still is attracted to, has an urge for, the world of the senses:

> Your Self to semblance feels inclined;
> Immerse yourself in seeming being.

What appears at the core of our feelings is seeming being... illusion's being. It is a mixture of both semblance and being.

> "Immerse yourself in seeming being."

If we devote ourselves to the meaning in these four lines, this is the path where we already begin to feel that things are getting serious. We immerse ourselves into real being:

> And world soul forces dwell in you;

In the first verse, Selfhood, as it submerged itself in thinking, was called upon to "revere." Now Selfhood must "deeply ponder." Thoughts must be carried down into feelings. Now we come up against something that assures us of real being:

> Your Selfhood, it should deeply ponder
> Powers of life within your soul.

It is no longer "semblance"; now the "powers of life" are there. While our own being, our own "I," would incline to semblance, the gods give us the firm rock of being, the foundation of existence, at the core of our feelings.

It is good to consider again correspondences such as these to make the verses into real mantric verses:

> <u>"revere"</u>
> <u>"ponder deeply"</u>

—in the third verse we shall find a further enhancement—

> <u>"semblance"</u>　　　　you experience.

Third Lesson

Here [first verse] we find merely semblance, or illusion. And here, in the [second verse] we have:

> "*semblance*"   mixing with "being."
> "*guiding beings*"   [first verse] of your spirit
> "*powers of life*"   [second verse]

Our feeling follows the beings who guide us through the ether, who are powers of life and who lead us back into pre-earthly existence.

If you want to make this into a real mantra, you have to also consider something else.

Now read the first verse:

> See how thinking weaves in you;
> Experience, then, world-illusion.
> Selfhood hides itself from you;
> Dive down into the semblance.
> Ether's essence wafts in you;
> Selfhood's being should revere
> Guiding beings of your spirit.

Here you clearly have to deal with a trochee, a trochaic mood that I ask you to consider. Emphasize the first syllable strongly and the next syllable weakly [macron and breve showing the trochaic meter are written above the first two syllables at the beginning of each of the seven lines]: this one feeling strong, this one feeling weak, and so on. This is the true ether weaving of the soul where only reverence for higher beings needs to sound. Then you will be carried into the spiritual world.

Things become different in the second verse.

[Breve and macron show the iambic meter: ˘ ¯ are written above the first two syllables of each of the seven lines. While doing this, the verse is spoken with appropriate emphasis.]

> Perceive how feeling streams in you;
> How semblance mixes there with being.
> Your Self to semblance feels inclined;
> Immerse yourself in seeming being.

> And world soul forces dwell in you;
> Your Selfhood, it should deeply ponder
> Powers of life within your soul.

The way the soul experiences these words, trochaic [first verse] and iambic [second verse] gives the soul the suitable impetus, or momentum. In the first verse you have a distinct trochaic character, while the second verse is iambic in character.

It is not merely a matter of getting intellectual content into the soul, even if the soul only makes its way into the spiritual world in thought. It is important for the soul to get into the right breathing and the right rhythm of the cosmos. If you use the iambic rhythm when striving toward cosmic thought, you have misunderstood the Guardian of the Threshold. If you use the trochaic verse instead of the iambic verse to find your way into the world of feeling, you will have again misunderstood the Guardian.

The third thing we must enter into is the will. The Guardian also gives us directives in a verse for the will. Now that the first two have passed before our soul, we shall find it easy to understand the third verse.

[The first three lines of the third verse are written on the blackboard.]

> *Let work the impulse of will in you;*
> *It rises up from worlds of illusion*
> *Creative in its very essence.*

—What gives substance and content to the will surges up from the will.—

> *To this devote all your life,*
> *For filled it is with cosmic spiritual might.*
> *Your very being should now grasp*
> *World creative might in your spiritual "I."*

Feel again the intensification: [The words of the third verse that are in quotes are written on the blackboard.]

"revere:" you are far away, you look up, and revere from without;

Third Lesson

"ponder deeply:" you approach in thought while you are entering;
"grasp:" this is the greatest enhancement, you come close and take hold of it.
"guiding beings"
"powers of life" and now:
"world creative might." This word stands at the beginning of the sentence, corresponding to the reality of the direct working of the forces of the will.

You will experience these three as mantric verses when you are attentive to the trochaic in the first verse and the iambic in the second verse. Here, however, in the third verse, you have two emphasized syllables. Here we do not begin with a rising syllable or a descending syllable, but we start with two equally-emphasized syllables. [Macrons showing the spondaic meter ‾ are written above the first two syllables at the beginning of each of the seven lines. While doing this the verses are spoken with the appropriate emphasis.]

> L̄ēt work the impulse of will in you;
> Īt r̄ises up from worlds of illusion
> C̄r̄eative in its very essence.
> T̄ō this devote all your life,
> F̄ōr filled it is with cosmic spirit might.
> Ȳōur very being should now grasp
> W̄ōrld creative might in your spiritual "I."

Here you have the spondaic meter.

This needs to be observed. You must tear yourself away from the mere intellectual meaning of the words and take notice of the trochaic, iambic and spondaic rhythms. The moment we leave the intellectual meaning and devote ourselves to the rhythms, at that moment we have the possibility of leaving the physical world and actually entering the spiritual world. The spiritual will not be comprehended if we use words meant for the sense-perceptible, earthly world. It will only be comprehended if we seize the opportunity to carry these words in meter into the weaving of cosmic existence.

Thus, we let the threefold self-contemplation of thinking, feeling and willing work on our soul. What is necessary for the soul will then emerge from this experience. Just as the soul experiences eating, drinking, breathing, and the circulation of the blood in the body, the soul will experience what rhythm is able to weave in these words.

> See how thinking weaves in you;
> Experience, then, world-illusion.
> Selfhood hides itself from you;
> Dive down into the semblance.
> Ether's essence wafts in you;
> Selfhood's being should revere
> Guiding beings of your spirit.
>
> Perceive how feeling streams in you;
> How semblance mixes there with being.
> Your Self to semblance feels inclined;
> Immerse yourself in seeming being.
> And world soul forces dwell in you;
> Your Selfhood, it should deeply ponder
> Powers of life within your soul.
>
> Let work the impulse of will in you;
> It rises up from worlds of illusion
> Creative in its very essence.
> To this devote all your life,
> For filled it is with cosmic spiritual might.
> Your very being should now grasp
> World creator might in your spiritual "I."

With the words alone it is as if you have only the blood, while with the words and the corresponding rhythms, you have the blood in circulation. Look for the inner sense and meaning of these rhythms. Let them work in the life of your soul, and you will see how you come closer to the first warning of the Guardian, words I spoke to you at the beginning of these lessons.

Third Lesson

Where on Earth foundations, color upon color,
Life, creative life, manifests itself;
Where from earthly substance, form on form,
The lifeless world is fashioned;
Where sentient beings, powerful in will,
Warm themselves with joy in their existence;
Where you, yourself, O Man, acquire
Your body from earth, air and light:

There you enter with your own true being
Deep into night-enveloped cold and darkness;
From the dumb expanse you ask in vain,
Who you are and were and will become.
For your own being the light of day fades into
Soul's night and spirit-darkness;
With anxious seeking you turn your soul
To the light that takes its strength from darkness.

And if we want to turn to the light that comes from the darkness, we will find it if we seek it on this threefold path. We will find it if we permeate ourselves with this life-blood of the soul, the soul that wants to be on the path to true spiritual knowledge...knowledge of God.

Fourth Lesson

Dornach, March 7, 1924

My dear friends, in the preceding lessons we considered the encounter with the Guardian of the Threshold. We have to understand this encounter with the Guardian of the Threshold more and more. We have to comprehend what is meant by this encounter with the Guardian so deeply that the full earnestness of it is always present in our souls. For with the Guardian we have entered a realm that is essentially different from other realms of spiritual life, from what our present civilization calls spiritual life or our relationship to spiritual life. Meeting the Guardian of the Threshold is actually the first event that happens to human beings when they come into a relationship with the spiritual world with true sincerity and earnestness. A real relationship with the spiritual world cannot happen without understanding the meeting with the Guardian of the Threshold. The spiritual world exists only on the other side of the threshold. And if we receive communications from the spiritual world, they can only be received in such a way that they can be taken as communications that prepare the ground for our relationship with the spiritual world.

My dear friends, to begin with I would like to tell you a story about what is to come before your souls today, a story that stems from an old esoteric tradition. Once there was a pupil who was going to be received into the Mysteries. This pupil completed the first stages of his training, and when a certain level of maturity had been reached, he entered into a relationship with the spiritual world. Please don't imagine that he immediately achieved the capacity that, perhaps, most people today conceive of as clairvoyance. The pupil entered this relationship only when his inner life—the appropriate or correct feelings of his soul—were developed to receive messages from the spiritual world. At this point his teacher said to him: "Listen. When I speak to you, the words I say are not merely human words. What I have to tell you is only clothed in human words. What I have to tell you are the thoughts of the gods...and the thoughts of the gods are initially spoken to you in human words. Accordingly, you must realize that I am calling upon all that lives in your soul. You must bring all of your thinking, all of your feeling and all of your willing to the words I speak to you on behalf of the gods. You must bring all the enthusiasm in your soul to what I tell you—all of your inner warmth and inner fire. You must bring all of your conscious alertness, an awakened alertness that is as strong as you possibly can unfold in your soul life.

But there is one force in your soul I do not call for, that I do not call upon at all, and that is your memory, your faculty of recollection. I will be satisfied if you don't remember what I am saying to you now. I'll be content if tomorrow you have already forgotten what I'm telling you now. Because what you normally call your memory, what other people call your memory, is only meant for earthly concerns and not for the concerns of the gods. And when you appear before me again tomorrow and I speak to you again, calling upon your thinking, feeling and willing and all your enthusiasm, all your warmth and inner fire, calling upon your fully awakened alertness, at that point all these forces in your soul should be ready to receive what will be brought to you then. Your soul must be new and freshly alive tomorrow, and the next day, and so on. Your soul should be fresh and alive each day.

In saying I do not call upon your memory—your faculty of recollection—at the same time I'm not saying that tomorrow you should retain nothing of what is spoken to you today. I'm only saying that you should not retain it *in your memory alone*. You must wait and see what your memory makes of it. But the innermost feelings of your soul are what will bring you to me tomorrow in a new and refreshed state. These innermost feelings should preserve what is spoken to you today. You see, memory—the faculty of recollection—is there for learning. But what esoteric teaching expresses should not be for mere learning, it is for life itself. Consequently, every time esoteric teaching comes to you, it should be a new experience without needing to rely for help upon your pictorial and conceptual memory.

This is a fact. We should approach esoteric truth without ever thinking, "Oh, I know that already." This is because the essence of esotericism lies not in knowing, but in direct experience. Esoteric truth should be grasped and nurtured in our innermost soul, at the deepest levels of our soul life where memory lives. When you consider this, my dear friends, then you will see that there is a lot to learn in the near future about how to grasp true esoteric life. This has to be taken very seriously. The moment we receive an esoteric truth, understanding it requires a new relationship to thinking, feeling and willing from what we are accustomed to in our everyday consciousness.

In everyday consciousness thinking, feeling and willing are intimately connected with each other. We can take a very trivial example and convince ourselves by this trivial example how closely connected thinking, feeling and willing are in ordinary life. Imagine you know someone, anyone with whom you have had a close or more distant relationship. Your experience together is permeated with feeling and is stored in your memory. When you meet each other again, these stored memories lead you to certain impulses of action and determine your behavior toward this person. You continue to live with your thoughts and feelings for this person until one day someone says something that reminds you of the person. Calling up the thought of this person causes the same feelings you once held for the person to rise up in you again. If it was love, then love rises up. If it was hatred, then hatred rises up. If you intended to undertake something together, then what you wanted to undertake rises up in your mind. You cannot separate your feelings and willing from your thoughts about this person.

Anyone who continues to live in this kind of soul attitude cannot really understand esoteric truth. You understand esoteric truth in the right way if you are capable of doing the following. You know a person with whom you have a particular relationship and certain aspects of this person are very antipathetic to you. On being reminded of this person, it is possible for you to imagine the person without any antipathies rising up in your soul. If you can do this, you are truly able to *think* about the other person. Try to imagine, my dear friends, the difficulty of just *thinking* about your enemy and not allowing feelings of animosity to rise up. This attitude can nonetheless be practiced if we have an understanding of artistic things. Ask yourself if you are you capable of taking in with pure imaginative thought the despicable characters described by Shakespeare. I would feel strong antipathies for these characters if I met them in real life. But, I can confront them artistically in an objective way; I can *think* them possibly just because they are such excellent scoundrels. In the artistic realm it is possible to see Shakespearean scoundrels on stage without manifesting the overwhelming urge to jump on stage and thrash them. Thus, it is possible to separate thinking from feeling in the artistic realm.

To become a true esotericist we must be able to achieve the same thing in life. If something is spoken from esotericism and if it is to truly find its way into the soul, it must be possible at that moment to separate thinking from feeling. This won't happen by itself. At first, when we think intensely about esoteric content—its nature being far removed from any personal feeling—we are unable to comprehend it at all unless we take hold of it in pure thought. If we are not listening to esoteric teaching like a sack of straw and letting it pass us by with indifference, then we must develop feelings and will impulses apart from what thoughts give us. Feelings must be developed because esoteric life should not remain in an ice cold realm only poured over our intellect. Instead, esoteric life should steep us in radiant enthusiasm. This enthusiasm, this world of feelings, would have to come from somewhere quite different, if it doesn't come from pure thought.

You see, we have to be clear that when we speak from esotericism in the correct way, which is spoken from the realm of the gods, we must warm up our feelings in the right way and bring spiritual realities to our feelings, rather than merely to our thoughts.

This is why in the First Lesson of this First Class I spoke about how the School speaks, signifying the real spirit that lives in the School. It is necessary for us to recognize that the School has not been created by any personal intention but has been willed and established from the spiritual world. If we see the School in this context, then the School's very existence will give us the enthusiasm we need.

We must understand something else as well. My dear friends, people speak to us in words in ordinary life and in ordinary science. When we take in the thoughts communicated with these words, they reach us because they are carried by the words. The esotericist must also use words because it is necessary to speak. But the esotericist uses words as an opportunity to make us aware of how the spirit in its reality streams in upon us and wants to pour itself into the hearts of human beings.

Therefore, in an esoteric school it is necessary for the pupil to develop over time an inner sense of listening to what lies behind the words. When this inner sense is developed with respect to esotericism, we will acquire what has been held sacred in esoteric streams throughout the ages, namely: the power of silence, the sacred power of silence. This sacred silence is connected with something else we cannot do without in esotericism: the deepest levels of human humility. Nothing esoteric can be approached without the deepest human humility. Why? The innermost being of our soul, the deepest essence of our soul, is called upon when we are summoned to listen for what lies behind the words. Our memory is not called forth, but the innermost being of our soul is. Here it matters how much ability we have to listen behind the words. While it is good for our own soul to hear as much as possible, we would do well not to regard what rises up in our soul as the final truth that could be brought into the world as unconditionally valid. We will need a long time—especially when we hear what lies behind the words—before we come to terms with ourselves. We should, therefore, develop the inner mood that esotericism first has to live in the wordless weaving of the soul before it can be regarded as fully mature.

Thus it is that in esoteric life we must go further back, beyond the meaning words have in ordinary life, to meanings that lie in deeper layers of the soul. My dear friends, this is what came to us in the last Class Lesson when we brought mantric verses before your soul, where rhythms were the essence. The trochaic rhythm is essential in the first verse; the iambic rhythm in the second verse; and the spondaic rhythm in the third. We learn to feel, through the trochaic rhythm in the first verse regarding our thoughts, how we descend from a mountain into a valley. We feel it correctly when we feel our soul descend from the heights of heaven to the valleys of Earth. This is how we feel our way into the mood of our weaving thoughts. That is why the verse is trochaic, beginning with a strong syllable and then going down to a weak one. The trochaic rhythm brings about a kind of blood circulation in the soul that takes place in spiritual space. We are not just standing there speaking something in thought when we bring such a mantra to life in our soul. We move together with what moves spiritually in the spiritual world when human thoughts weave in our soul. This is how the first verse is related to the weaving of thoughts.

> See how thinking weaves in you;
> Experience, then, world-Illusion.
> Selfhood hides itself from you;
> Dive down into the semblance.
> Ether essence wafts in you;
> Selfhood's being should revere
> Guiding beings of your spirit.

The gods have truly raised us to their heights by giving us thoughts. And we descend when we experience our thoughts weaving in our soul. We descend from the heights, where the gods have placed us, into the valleys where we encompass and comprehend earthly things, by their bestowing thoughts upon us.

It is different with feelings. Our attitude of soul, our soul posture, as it were, is correct if we feel ourselves standing below in the valley while wanting to ascend with our feelings to the gods as if on a spiritual ladder. Feelings bring us in the opposite direction, moving from below upward.

That is why the mantric verse is iambic; first the weak syllable begins and then it rises to a strong syllable. We should experience this:

> Perceive how feeling streams in you,
> How semblance mixes there with being.
> Your Self to semblance feels inclined.
> Immerse yourself in seeming being;
> And world soul forces dwell in you.
> Your Selfhood, it should deeply ponder
> Powers of life within your soul.

It is different again when we come to the will. When we come to the will we must become conscious of how human beings are actually divided beings. We must come close to the gods in feeling. And when we are halfway there, we must be able through the strength of our feelings to give birth to impulses of will. This will only happen if we meditate in a spondaic rhythm, beginning with one strong syllable followed by another:

> Let the impulse of will work in you;
> It rises up from worlds of illusion,
> Creative in its very essence.
> To this devote all your life
> For filled it is with cosmic spirit might.
> Your very being shall now grasp
> World creative might in your spiritual "I."

As I said to you last time, what matters here is that we not only take hold of the meaning of the words, but we take hold of what lives in the movement of the words and what carries our soul along in the movement. In doing so we no longer depend only upon ourselves. We grow into the world.

Words understood merely by their meaning leave us only with ourselves. What matters in esoteric life is that we come more and more from ourselves as we grow together with the world. Only by growing from ourselves shall we be able to bear the separation of thinking, feeling and willing. Our body-bound ego holds our thinking, feeling and willing together in everyday consciousness. When our thinking, feeling and willing are outside of us, they must be held together by the gods. But for that we must first find our way into divine existence. There we must grow together with the world. We must really learn to develop a mood where we can honestly say to ourselves in all seriousness: here is my hand; I look at it. Over there is a tree; I observe it. I look at my hand: that is me! I look at the tree: that is me! I look at a cloud: that is me! I look at a rainbow: that is me! I listen to thunder: that is me! I look at lightning: that is me! I feel myself one with the world.

It is quite easy to achieve this abstractly, but that is dishonest. To achieve it concretely—meaning honestly—people must overcome many things in their inner lives. The desired goal will be achieved only if one does not shy away from overcoming these things. The esotericist must ask the question: I look at my hand; it belongs to me. What would my life (which began a few decades ago) have become if I didn't have a hand? My hand has been necessary for all that I've become. But let's consider a tree. The trees standing before us today had their origins on the Ancient Moon existence and have grown from the whole Moon organism. The entire Moon organism could not have existed unless the first beginnings of trees were formed from it. The beginnings of my thinking also originated at that time from the entire Moon existence. I would not be able to think today if trees did not exist. My hand is only necessary for my present-day Earth life. Trees are necessary above all for me to become a thinking being. Why should my hand be more valuable to me than, say, a tree? Why should I count my hand as belonging more to my body than a tree? I will come to a point where what I call the outer world counts even more as belonging to my inner life than my body's internal organs. We have to learn to feel this in all depth and honesty.

Today we would like to place three mantric verses before our souls through which this feeling of union, of being at one with the entire outer world, can gradually imprint itself deeply upon our souls.

How do we stand in relation to outer existence? We look down to the Earth and we feel dependent on it. The Earth gives us what we need for our outer life. We look out into the wide spaces around us. The sun rises over here in the morning and sets over there in the evening. Light sweeps over the Earth. It comes from the widths of space and goes back into the widths of space. We look up, and at night the stars in the sky speak mysteriously to us. Our relationship to the world is determined by this threefold perspective. I look down to the Earth, I look around in space, and I look up to the sky. Let us do so with the most intense awareness, as expressed in the following mantric verses:

> Feel how from the depths of Earth
> Forces press into your being,
> Into members of your body.
> You will lose yourself in them
> If you give your will over
> Powerlessly to their surging.
> Dim and dark they make your "I."

[The first verse is written on the blackboard.]

> *Feel how from the depths of Earth*
> *Forces press into your being,*
> *Into members of your body.*
> *You will lose yourself in them*

—In the forces—

> *If you give your will over*
> *Powerlessly to their surging.*
> *Dim and dark they make your "I."*

Yes, my dear friends, it is a fact that we do not connect in full consciousness to what binds and chains our human essence to the Earth. We look down on the Earth and we know: crystals are formed in the Earth; the Earth carries us in space; and, it exerts the force of gravity that attracts a stone and makes it fall to the Earth. We know, too, that the Earth grounds us. We think about all of this. But we don't think about the urges, instincts, desires and passions that live in us and that we consider our lower nature.

Those, too, belong to the Earth. Therefore, when we look down and ask, "What does the Earth create in us?" we ought to remember: everything that wants to drag us down below our human level lies there. Everything that wants to darken our "I," everything that wants to drive us down into the subhuman, lies down there. We have to bring this to awareness. We are connected to the Earth in such a way that, in spite of all the beauty and majesty that spreads out before us, it is the Earth that drags human beings down into the subhuman. By honestly admitting this, we can develop ourselves into true human beings.

Then, if we develop ourselves in a proper human fashion, we will come to a place where we not only turn our gaze downward, but also turn our gaze outward to the widths of space. We shall look out onto all that encircles the Earth and takes in with its encircling our own being, our own human nature. There something begins, even at the physical level, that in a way lifts us above the subterranean forces that pull us down. A person can become evil through the forces found in the depths of the Earth. But this does not happen so easily through one's breath, which also belongs to the forces orbiting the Earth. Even less so does that happen through the sunlight that encircles the Earth. But then we consider breath and light as spiritually insignificant. Yet, divine beings live in our breath, they live in the light. We must be aware that divine powers are at work especially in light, working differently than the forces that work in the subterranean depths. We bring this to consciousness in the second mantric verse.

[The second verse is written on the blackboard.]

> *Feel how from the worldwide spaces*
> *Godly powers send spirit radiance*
> *Lighting up your inmost soul.*
> *Find yourself in them with love.*
> *Wisdom weaving they then create*
> *You as a Self within their spheres,*
> *Strong for spirit works of Good.*

We are not always aware that it is possible to love the light that spreads over the Earth, be it the light of the sun or the light of the stars. We are not always conscious of this. But when we are aware that we can love sunlight, we can love it with the same warmth as we love a friend. Through this we also learn how the gods encircle the Earth with a garment of light. Sunlight becomes the garment of the gods who wander over the Earth in garments of light. What we experience as light becomes true wisdom for us. The gods bring wisdom to our hearts and into our souls. Indeed, after making this differentiation in our feelings, we have now risen higher. We have, indeed, risen up.

First we have developed the right feeling for the forces of the subterranean depths. We have learned to feel that part of our nature belongs to the subterranean forces. We have raised ourselves up to a higher place in our being, a place that belongs to the gods who traverse the Earth in a garment of light. These divine beings do not want to leave human beings in the earthly realm, but want to receive them within their own sphere while they are still on Earth, so that they can continue living in their realm after going through the gate of death. The gods do not want to leave us alone on Earth; they want to draw us into their circle. They want to make us into beings that can dwell among them. The forces from the depths of the Earth want to tear us away from the forces of the gods.

Therefore, we heard here in an earlier mantra:

> The first beast's ghostly skeleton
> Is the evil creative might
> Of will that estranges your own body
> From all the forces of your soul
> And offers it to adverse powers
> Who want to rob the world's being
> In future times from Divine Being.

We must feel this when we place ourselves in the world, when we identify ourselves with the world and feel united with it.

But we have not taken account of our full humanity. We have not brought to consciousness our entire human nature if we are unable to look upward as well. Down into the depths we must look. Into the wide spaces around us we must look. Up into the heights we must look. We must stir up what is mixed together in our everyday consciousness: depths, widths and heights. Then we must differentiate between our awareness of the depths, our awareness of the widths and our awareness the heights.

[The lines of the third verse are written on the blackboard.]

> *Feel how in the heights of heaven*
> *Selfhood selflessly can live,*

We can feel this, my dear friends, when we look up to the heights in full consciousness. Imagine you are standing in an open field and looking up to the heights of heaven at the starlit sky. You could also do this in full daylight, but nighttime provides a better opportunity. By standing in this open field we feel ourselves one with that world. We feel: that is you. But from that one, single point where we stand on the Earth, considering it so precious that we always refer to it as our own self, we find it dissolves away when we look up into that vast expanse. It expands to encompass the entire hemisphere. If we feel this rightly, then our narrow Selfhood ceases to be and becomes selfless, because it infinitely spreads out into the wide expanse of heaven above us.

> *Feel how in the heights of heaven*
> *Selfhood selflessly can live,*

[Writing continues:]

> *If in spirit-fullness it will follow*
> *Powers of thought and striving to the heights,*

Whoever has genuinely felt how, with the streaming sunlight that encircles the Earth, the gods in their garment of light enter human souls with every inhaled and exhaled breath...whoever then looks up at the heights of heaven, selfless in their Selfhood, will consciously develop further what finds expression in the following lines.

> Feel how in the heights of heaven
> Selfhood selflessly can live,
> If in spirit-fullness it will follow
> Powers of thought and striving to the heights,

[Writing continues:]

> *And will bravely then receive the Word*
> *That rings forth from heights above with Grace*
> *Into the true essential nature of Man.*

Thus speak the heavenly heights. And so, just as we can grow together in love with the gods who encircle the Earth in a garment of light, so we can grow together with the words that resound from the heights if we develop this inner sense to strive upward with powers of thought into the heights of heaven.

My dear friends, you will only be able to rightly achieve these feelings of being conscious of the depths, widths and heights if you take the contrasting verses of the three beasts vividly into your soul and compare them with today's verses.

You come before the Guardian of the Threshold. Vivid images of this experience ought to live in your soul. The Guardian shows you the third of the three beasts, whom we spoke about in the previous lessons. The description of the third beast resounds in you:

> The third beast with its glassy eye,
> Is the evil counter-image
> Of thinking that in you denies itself,
> And chooses its own death,
> Forsaking spirit powers who,
> Before its earthly life, sustained
> Its life in fields of spirit.

This is what draws us downward. We tear ourselves away from it by saying to ourselves with courage in our soul:

Fourth Lesson

> Feel how from the depths of Earth
> Forces press into your being,
> Into members of your body.
> You will lose yourself in them
> If you give your will over
> Powerlessly to their surging.
> Dim and dark they make your "I."

Here the two verses appear only slightly different in comparison, whether you look at the beast or look at what tears you away from the beast. Consider how the one mantra sounds similar to the other, both describing what tears us down, but only one describing the actual beast, while the other depicts how we become conscious of what pulls us down.

But, when we go to the second beast, let us consider what saves us from the second beast. Then let us put both mantric verses together, side by side. Their moods are completely different. The one features the horrible description of the second beast while the other appeals to the gods who draw near to us in their garments of light. Let us hear these two mantric verses side by side. Listen how different they are in style and mood.

> The second beast with mocking face
> Is the evil counter-force
> Of feeling that hollows out your very soul
> And makes for emptiness of life;
> Whereas enlightening spirit-fullness
> Was given you before you were on Earth
> From the might of spirit-sun.
>
> Feel how from the worldwide spaces
> Godly powers send their spirit-radiance
> Lighting up your inmost soul.
> Find yourself in them with love.
> Wisdom weaving they then create
> You as a Self within their spheres,
> Strong for spirit works of Good.

First, in describing the third beast we must place ourselves in this mantra ["Feel how from the depths of Earth."] We must place ourselves right beside the third beast. Initially, we are incapable of tearing ourselves away. We are challenged to be aware of where this beast wants to lead us. When we turn to the second beast with support from the second verse ["Feel how from the worldwide spaces"], the verse already leads us far away from the beast, whose loathsomeness is characterized by its mocking face.

Now we come to the first beast who wants to prevent us from ever making human life sacred by looking up to the heights of heaven. This beast is characterized by its own style. We feel how we wrest ourselves away from it by turning to the mantric verse that directs us to look into the heights of heaven:

> The first beast's ghostly skeleton
> Is the evil creative might
> Of will that estranges your own body
> From all the forces of your soul
> And offers it to adverse powers
> Who want to rob the world's being
> In future times from Divine Being.

Now, if we want to burn what is said in this verse and rise in the flames, the other verse stands there in contrast and must be the comforter. It bestows grace upon us through our own courage in contrast to the first beast:

> Feel how in the heights of heaven
> Selfhood selflessly can live
> If in spirit fullness it will follow
> Powers of thought and striving to the heights,
> And will bravely then receive the Word
> That rings from heights above with Grace
> Into man's true being.

Fourth Lesson

Please take note that last time we learned how to receive an inner rhythm when we want to enter with our own being into the weaving of the radiant being of the world. Today, we must familiarize ourselves with how the things that come to us from this esoteric school are inherently connected and how we have to go back every time to what went before. We are not going back to the meaning of the words, because words will always remain with the Earth. We have to go back to the inner mood. We find that this inner mood comes to us from the whole and also from the details.

So, let us take the first verse: "Feel how from the depths of Earth." Our attention is directed to the depths of the Earth. And the other verse draws our attention to "The third beast with its glassy eye." The two stand side by side.

In the second verse's "Feel how from the worldwide spaces" we feel how the gods draw near to us in garments of light. Here we are lifted up above what ridicules the divine in the world. "The second beast with mocking face" is truly extinguished through bright sunlight, if we are ready to take hold of sunlight in its spirituality.

The third verse's beginning "The first beast's ghostly skeleton" makes us rigid. We only get warm when we free ourselves from this rigidity by turning our gaze upward to the heights of heaven. Then we can say: when you behold the third beast with its glassy eye, stand firm and feel what the depths of the Earth want of you.

When you see the second beast's mocking face, lovingly receive the light of the sun.

When you are frozen rigid by the first beast's bony head, enkindle the warmth of your true humanity by lifting your warm heart toward the heights of heaven.

So we shall gradually feel our way into spiritual life and this spiritual life will grow ever more akin to our soul.

(...)

Feel how from the depths of Earth
Forces press into your being
Into members of your body.
You will lose yourself in them
If you give your will over
Powerlessly to their surging.
Dim and dark they make your "I."

Feel how from the worldwide spaces
Godly powers send their spirit-radiance
Lighting up your inmost soul.
Find yourself in them with love.
Wisdom weaving they then create
You as a Self within their spheres,
Strong for spirit works of Good.

Feel how in the heights of heaven
Selfhood selflessly can live
If in spirit fullness it will follow
Powers of thought and striving to the heights,
And will bravely then receive the Word
That rings forth from heights above with Grace
Into man's true being.

Fifth Lesson

Dornach, March 14, 1924

My dear friends! We have seen the changes that take place in a person when they learn to know the Guardian of the Threshold. That one can approach the spiritual world and comprehend it at all is dependent on knowing the being of the Guardian of the Threshold. We have seen in particular how our inner life—thinking, feeling, and willing—undergoes an essential change in the realm of the Guardian of the Threshold. It became especially clear to us in the last Class Lesson how, in a certain way, thinking, feeling and willing go in various directions when we first enter the spiritual world. They enter into a different relationship in the spiritual world than normally exists in human consciousness on Earth.

We have seen that one becomes aware of how strongly one's will is connected to the Earth. Thinking, feeling and willing immediately separate in the soul as soon as one approaches the spiritual world. Willing then lives in the soul with much greater independence than previously. The will now reveals that it is related in a high degree to the terrestrial forces that pull us downward. Feeling proves akin to the forces that hold the human being in the circumference of the Earth, which are filled with weaving light that makes the day bright in the morning, and then disappears again from human sight in the evening. Thinking is the force that leads us upward to the heavens. Consequently, the minute one comes before the Guardian of the Threshold, the Guardian makes one aware of how they belong to the entire world: through willing, to the Earth; through feeling, to the Earth's circumference; and through thinking, to the powers that range above.

My friends, this is what must become clear to us upon entering the spiritual world, that through spiritual life one grows together with the entire world. In our ordinary consciousness we stand in the world so that powers are at work outside of us in the mineral, plant and animal kingdoms, and also in the physical human kingdom. The forces of nature that we access through our senses do not, at first, show any kinship with human beings. As humans, we stand apart from nature, and when we look inside ourselves, we perceive our thinking, feeling and willing. We become aware that thinking, feeling and willing are distinct from external nature; we are aware that they stand by themselves. We feel a deep chasm between our own being and the world of nature spread out around us.

But this chasm must be bridged. For this chasm, which in our everyday consciousness we are only aware of in its external aspects, is the threshold itself. To be able to perceive the threshold requires that we stop accepting the unconsciousness that throws us back upon ourselves when we look inward, and points to the world of nature that is foreign to us when we look outward. This chasm needs to be understood not only as being important for human life, but also for the life of the entire universe.

You see, a bridge must be built over this chasm, this abyss, the minute one enters the esoteric path. In a sense we must grow together with nature. We must stop saying to ourselves: out there is nature, and nature really has nothing to do with morality. We don't ask the minerals about morality, something that greatly interests our soul. We don't ask the plants or animals about morality. In our materialistic times we have even stopped asking human beings about morality, because nowadays only human physicality is taken into consideration.

In turn, when we look into the human being one sees a normal consciousness where passive thinking visualizes the world in pictures, a consciousness that, however, is powerless in itself. Thoughts, which allow us to recognize objects in the world, are at first something we own, although these thoughts have no power. Our feelings comprise our inner life. To a certain extent we stand separate from the world with our feelings. Our will connects us to the outer world. It communicates itself to outer objects, but in doing so the outer objects receive something that is foreign to them.

A great realization must come upon us when we become aware of the abyss that lies between one's "I" and nature, when we come close to the Guardian of the Threshold. Something truly great. This great realization has been expressed in words since ancient times, words that must be understood anew in every age. The words are: "Nature must appear to be divine and human beings must become magical, can be magical." What does this mean that "nature must be able to appear divine?"

Nature must be able to appear divine. The way nature first appears to the senses, how the intellect understands it, is certainly not divine. We would prefer to put it this way, that "divine being is hidden in nature." Nature only shows us its external aspect. At best we first see a kinship between nature and our inner life in our dreams. We can perceive how an irregularity in our breathing process in one direction or another can cause dreams to be either happy or fearful and filled with anxiety. We can recognize how an over-heated room brings a kind of moral content into the dream. Dreams draw nature closer to our soul life.

Nevertheless, we also know that in dreams our consciousness is submerged. Dreams cannot bring the spiritual to us directly. Rather, we must see how nature presents itself to an awakened consciousness instead of to a sleeping consciousness.

Dear friends, in the natural world we have, to begin with, the relationship of the human physical body with what is solid in nature, with what bears a terrestrial character. Then there is the relationship between the human etheric body and what bears the characteristics of water. These relationships, between the human physical body with the earthly and the human ether body with the water element, lie deep beneath what people first experience.

The breathing process that takes place in the air lies closer to us. And rising upward from the breathing process a region begins where one can feel one's self related to nature when first approaching the spiritual.

When we look at the breathing process, we find the airy element where we live and have our being. [On the blackboard is written:] *Air*. Above *air*, we have the quality of warmth. [On the blackboard above *air* is written:] *Warmth*. And above *warmth*, we have the essence of light: warmth ether and light ether. [On the blackboard above "warmth" is written:] *Light*.

If we go still higher we come to a region that is not so close to us, which we must speak about later. Human beings live and move in the airy element. This can be shown by an outer consideration. We need only look at dreams to see how certain kinds of dreams are dependent on irregularities or abnormalities in breathing. We don't notice our breathing process while we are awake because, as a rule, we don't pay attention to what takes place on its own in the normal course of life.

Consider the element of warmth. Living in warmth is essential to human beings. This fact can be demonstrated by an outer observation. Suppose we touch ourselves with a cold object, something colder than our body, for example, with a cold knitting needle. We distinctly feel each cold spot separately, even if the needles are held very close together. We are very sensitive to cold. The difference is not as noticeable if we touch ourselves with something that is warmer than our body. We can hold two cold needles close to each other and distinctly feel the coldness of each. If we hold two warm needles close together, we sense these two spots as a single spot. We have to hold them farther apart to perceive them as separate and distinct. We are, in fact, far more sensitive to cold than to warmth. Why is this? We tolerate warmth much better than cold because we ourselves are beings of warmth. Warmth is our own nature. We live and have our being in warmth. Cold is something foreign to us. We are very sensitive to cold.

It is more difficult for ordinary consciousness to understand light. Today we would like to approach these things esoterically, so that what I have indicated as the meaning of air and warmth to normal consciousness may already be sufficient. But in ordinary experience we feel the air as something external and natural. We also feel warmth as something that touches us from the outside, just as we feel light as something that comes to us from the outside.

Fifth Lesson

The minute one experiences the sudden jolt that brings one close to the Guardian of the Threshold, in that moment one perceives how intimately one is related to what otherwise may seem alien and external. I have often pointed out how, basically, in every moment of our lives, for normal consciousness as well, our relationship to the world can be perceived through our relationship to air. Air is outside of us. The same air that is outside of us is inside of us a moment later, and then is outside of us again. But we aren't aware of this. Just as we carry our muscles and bones inside us, but only become conscious of their origins in embryonic life and their demise in death, so we are barely aware that we always carry an air-being within us. We continually carry air within us, releasing it out and receiving it back again, so that we become one with the entire weaving, living being of the air element where we, as terrestrial creatures, live our lives.

This is no longer the case the minute we enter spiritual realms. At that moment we begin to feel how with every exhalation, with every breathing out, we fly out on the wings of the exhaled air into the wide expanses of existence where the exhaled air disperses. And we feel how by breathing in we take into us the spiritual beings who live in the circulating air. The spiritual world flows into us when inhaling; our own being goes out into the environment when exhaling.

This is not only true with respect to air but is also the case to an even greater extent with warmth. As the beings of air are one with the Earth's atmosphere [two white circles are drawn on the blackboard, picture number 1], so we are united to an even higher degree with the warmth that surrounds and penetrates the Earth [Red]. When we approach the spiritual world we really experience the spirit entering us when breathing in. Our own being streams out into the wide expanse of space while breathing out. We experience a spiritual interweaving by inhaling and exhaling air. We feel ourselves more intensely when living in the element of warmth. We feel how we become more human when warmth increases and less human when warmth decreases. At that point warmth ceases to be merely something natural. At that point we say to ourselves: if we recognize the inner soul nature of warmth, the spiritual reality of warmth, we feel it closely related to our humanity. We feel it is inwardly connected to our being human. We feel through increasing warmth that the spiritual beings who live and work in warmth are saying to us: "Through warmth we give you your humanity. Through cold we take your humanity away from you."

And we now approach "light," the light where we move and live. Except that we don't notice light because with our everyday, normal consciousness we have no idea that the inner weaving of light is contained in our thinking. We have no idea that every thought is "captured light"—both for those with sight and those who are blind. Light is something objective. Not only those who can see light receive light, but also the physically blind receive light when they are thinking. The thoughts we hold fast within us, the thoughts we inwardly capture, are present within us as light.

And so we can say: if we approach the Guardian of the Threshold, he cautions us in the following way:

> O Man, when you think, your being is not inside of you, it is in the light. O Man, when you feel, your being is not within you, it is in the warmth. O Man, when you will, your being is not inside of you, it is in the air. O Man, stay not within yourself! Do not think that your thinking is only inside your head. Consider your thinking to be none other than your experience of the light that undulates and weaves through the world. Consider that your feeling is nothing other than the weaving, living element of warmth. Consider your willing to be nothing other than the overall moving and living element of air working within you.

We must be very conscious of the fact that in the presence of the Guardian of the Threshold we are divided into the elements of the universe, that we can no longer hold ourselves together in the usual dark and chaotic fashion of our ordinary consciousness. This is the great experience that initiate knowledge gives to human beings: that they cease to take seriously the idea that they are enclosed within their own skin. For that is nothing more than a sign that we are human beings. For spiritual consciousness, what is enclosed within our skin is an illusion, because a human being is as large as the universe. Your thoughts extend as far as

Fifth Lesson

the light; your feelings range as wide as the warmth; and your will is as broad as the air.

If a being with a sufficiently developed consciousness were to descend to Earth from another planet, it would speak to people in quite a different way than people address each other in ordinary consciousness on Earth. This being would say: "The light that envelops the Earth is differentiated [a cloak of yellow light is drawn around the air and warmth circles on the board.] Many individual and differentiated beings exist within the light. One must imagine that in the light that weaves and surrounds the Earth, that in this single space, many beings are present. As many are present as there are people on Earth. They cover themselves in the terrestrial world of light." And so, for this visitor from another planet, all human thoughts exist within this mantle of light, this weaving light. All human feelings are contained in the Earth's mantle of warmth. All human willing is to be found in the Earth's atmosphere, in its mantle of air.

Then this being from another planet would continue and say: "Here a being is differentiated in a purely qualitative way. Its presence here, that it exists, is indicated by the fact that it has a body—body A. There is another being in the mantle of light, which is also indicated by the presence of body B, and so on. [Two spots, A and B, are drawn within the yellow on the board.] The presence of bodies are the outer signs that they are there, that they exist. The real human beings are all within one another in the light, warmth and air that surrounds the Earth.

For one who really stands before the Guardian of the Threshold, this is no speculation. It is an experience. Spiritual progress consists in being able to grow together with the surrounding world. It is of little use to speak theoretically about these things. It is not profoundly mystical to say you are "at one with the world" if you merely think you are, if you don't begin inwardly and actually to experience how when you are thinking you are living in the light of the whole Earth. By doing so, by becoming one with the light of the Earth, you go out of yourself, you go out through all the pores of your skin into divine spiritual existence. You become one with the very being of the Earth itself and with other members of the Earth's being. This must be understood in all seriousness by anyone who strives for a relationship with the spiritual world.

We see that light must first affect us morally. We must become aware of how we are related to light and how light becomes related to us in our esoteric experience of the world. But then, the moment you step over the threshold, it becomes clear that light assumes a quality of being, it becomes *being*, and it has to wage a hard battle with the forces of darkness. Light and darkness become real. Something now occurs to a person so that they say to themselves: "If I merge my thinking completely with light, I will lose myself in the light." The minute I merge my thinking with light, then light beings take hold of me and say, "You, human, we will not release you from the light again. We will keep you in the light." This expresses the will of the light beings. They want to draw human beings to them forever through their human thinking. They want to make them one with the light; they want to tear human beings away from all earthly powers and to weave them into the light. Beings of light are all around us who, in every moment of our lives, would like to tear us away from the Earth and weave us into the sunlight that sweeps over the Earth. These light beings, who live in the surroundings of the Earth, say to us: "You humans should not remain with your soul in your body. With the first rays of the morning sun you should shine down upon the Earth itself, and should set with the evening red of sunset. You should encircle the Earth as light!"

These light beings will be found tempting us ever and again. The minute one crosses the threshold one becomes aware of these light beings who want to pull us away from the Earth, who try to convince us that it is not worthy of us to remain chained to the Earth, weighted down by gravity. They want us to be absorbed into the sun's radiance. For ordinary consciousness it is true that the sun shines above us while we humans stand below and let the sun shine down upon us. For the more developed consciousness the sun in heaven is the great tempter who wants to unite us with its light and pull us away from the Earth, who whispers in our ears:

Fifth Lesson

O Man, you don't need to stay on the Earth. You can become a being in the rays of the sun yourself. Then you'll be able to shine down upon the Earth yourself, and bring blessings to it. Then you won't need to be shone upon and blessed from without.

This is what we encounter when we meet the Guardian of the Threshold. Nature, which was previously quiet outside us and made no claim upon our normal consciousness, now has acquired the power to speak to us morally. Nature appears to us as a tempter, just like the sun. What was previously quietly shining sunlight now speaks to us in an enticing and tempting manner. And when the enticing, tempting beings who want to pull us away from the Earth appear in the sunlight, we then first realize that something spiritual lives and moves in sunlight. For these beings wage a continuous battle with what constitutes the interior of the Earth. They are in constant battle with darkness.

If we then go to the extreme—which is quite possible, because the experience of meeting the Guardian of the Threshold is a serious and profound one for the human soul—when we realize how enticing the sunlight is with its light beings, then, if we remember that we are supposed to be human beings, we want to become free from them. We ought to never lose this memory. Although we continue to live physically on the Earth, if we lose this memory we become, to a certain extent, paralyzed in our soul. But when we become aware of how enticing sunlight is, we then turn to the opposite side and seek peace from these temptations in darkness, which light continually fights against. As we swing from light into darkness we fall into the opposite extreme. So, this Self who wanted to surge into the bright, shining sunlight is now threatened in the darkness by loneliness, by being separated from all other beings. We human beings can only live in the zone of equilibrium between light and darkness.

Such is the mighty experience we have before the Guardian of the Threshold, where we are faced with the temptations of light and the impending power of darkness. Light and darkness become moral powers; they exercise a moral power over us. We humans must realize that it is dangerous to look at pure light... and dangerous to look at pure darkness. We are only reassured when at the threshold we see how the divine beings of the middle—the good gods of moral progress—tone down the light to a paler yellow and to a less-radiant red. We are reassured when we know we can no longer be lost to the Earth if we do not perceive just the light that enticingly dazzles, blinding us, but when we become aware of color. In the spiritual world color is subdued light; it is dimmed light.

It is equally dangerous to surrender to pure darkness. We become inwardly free in the spirit land if we if do not confront pure darkness directly, but stand before the lightened darkness that appears as violet and blue. In the spirit land yellow and red tell us: "The temptations of light will be unable to wrest you away from the Earth." Violet and blue tell us: "Darkness will not be able to bury your living soul in the Earth. You will be able to hold off the effects of Earth's gravity by yourself."

Those are the experiences where the natural and the moral grow together as one, where light and darkness become real beings. We won't become aware of the true nature of thinking unless light and darkness become real beings for us. Therefore, we should listen to the words the Guardian of the Threshold speaks when we stand before him with our thinking—thinking that has become independent of, and separated from, our inner soul life.

> Light battles with darkness
> In that realm where your thinking
> Would like to penetrate spirit-being.
> You find, toward light aspiring,
> That spirit takes your Self away.
> You can, if lured by powers dark,
> Lose your Self in matter.

This means becoming aware of the duality into which one has been placed. We must find balance and harmony between these polar opposites in our thinking.

[The verses are written on the blackboard:]

*Light battles with darkness
In that realm where your thinking
Would like to penetrate spirit-being.
You find, toward light aspiring,
That spirit takes your Self away.
You can, if lured by powers dark,
Lose your Self in matter.*

We must strongly receive into our thinking everything that can be born from these words. We must learn to feel how light can only be tolerated when it is toned down to *color,* even when looking at outer light and outer darkness. Then with spiritual perception we must seek to find how thinking is involved in the battle between light and darkness. We must find how thinking is carried away when it comes close to the light, how it is absorbed and interwoven in the light. We must perceive how thinking is extinguished when it comes close to darkness. Our thinking dies away when we want to enter into matter, into dark matter. Our thinking is extinguished. One really lives, then, in spiritual life.

And my dear friends, to experience this we must have courage, inner courage. If we say to ourselves that we don't need courage, if we deny that we need courage, then we are completely ignorant about the true situation. We might think that courage is needed to have a finger cut off, but that courage is not needed to allow our severed thinking-stream into the whirlpool it is seized by, when it finds itself at the threshold in the midst of the battle between light and darkness. Thinking always stands within this battle. Cognition alone signifies that we become aware of what is...always.

In every waking moment we stand with our thinking in such danger that certain spiritual beings who live on neighboring heavenly bodies know that, as far as humanity is concerned, in every age, in every century, it is possible for light to defeat darkness, or for darkness to be victorious over light.

Yes, my dear friends, in our ordinary consciousness life seems to be as free from danger as a sleepwalker is before their name is called out...so they don't fall down. For those who look deeper into life, a battle exists. And they cannot say with certainty whether a hundred years from now light or darkness will be the winner, or whether the human race will have a life worthy of human dignity or not. But they know full well why such catastrophes have not happened in human evolution until now.

I could use yet another image. If you see a tightrope walker walking on their rope, you are aware that they could fall to the left or right at any moment. But that you are such a tightrope walker in your soul—that each individual human being can fall down in their soul to the right or to the left—there is no awareness of this in ordinary life because we do not see the abyss lying at either side. Nevertheless, the abyss is there.

This is the blessing that the Guardian of the Threshold bestows on us, that he does not let us see the abyss until we are prepared for it by his warnings. That was a secret in all the Mysteries in all ages. The abyss was shown to human beings and thereby they were able to achieve the strength necessary for knowledge of the real world.

As it is in life with respect to thinking, so it is with warmth with regard to feeling. Whoever approaches the Guardian of the Threshold with their feelings becomes aware that they are entering the battle between warmth and cold. They become aware how warmth always entices one's feelings, for warmth wishes to absorb them. In the way the luciferic beings of light would, as it were, fly away with us from the Earth to the light, in the same way the luciferic warmth beings would absorb our feelings into the general cosmic warmth. All human feelings would thereby be lost for humanity and would be absorbed into the general warmth of the world.

This is indeed an enticement, a temptation, because of the presence of what those who receive initiation science perceive when they come before the threshold with their feelings. They become aware of warmth beings who want to give them a superabundance of the element they actually live in—warmth. They want the warmth to absorb all of a person's feelings. We are made aware of this as we approach the threshold. Warmth beings are there. One becomes warmer and warmer; one becomes total warmth; one flows over into the warmth. It is an immense bliss and a temptation at the same time. Everything flows continuously through you. One must be cognizant of all this because unless one knows that this temptation lurks in the warmth, it is impossible to gain a free and unobstructed view into the spirit land.

The enemies of the luciferic beings of warmth are the ahrimanic beings of cold. ahrimanic beings of cold attract those who still are aware of the danger of dissolving in the bliss of warmth. Aware of the dangers of warmth, they would like to plunge into health-giving cold. But then they find themselves in the other extreme where cold can harden them. Then, if coldness approaches a person in this situation, in this state, the result is endless pain, infinite pain...a pain just like physical pain. Physical and psychological, matter and spirit—they all become one. One experiences how cold seizes one's entire being, tearing it apart in immeasurable pain.

What we really ought to understand from the Guardian of the Threshold's warnings regarding feelings is that we human beings are continuously engaged in the battle between cold and warmth.

[The second verse is written on the blackboard:]

> *Warmth battles with cold*
> *In that realm where your feelings*
> *Would like to live in spirit-weaving.*
> *You find, in loving warmth,*
> *Your Self scattered in spirit-bliss.*
> *You can, if coldness hardens you,*
> *Crush your Self in suffering.*

We dive down with our will into a world that seems quite near to us. Indeed, it is very near. It is the world of air, the world that sustains our breathing. We have no idea how intimately connected the human will is with the air we breathe, for our will depends upon our breathing. Air, dear friends, contains life and death, both life-giving oxygen and deadly nitrogen. It is there, I would say...so near that you could touch it. The chemist says with a terrible and untrue abstraction that air consists of oxygen and nitrogen. As long as we remain in ordinary consciousness one may say "oxygen and nitrogen." Once we arrive at the Guardian of the Threshold it becomes clear that oxygen is the outer manifestation of the many spiritual beings who give life to humanity. It also becomes clear that nitrogen is the outer manifestation of spiritual beings who bring death to humanity. This death includes the death that, by developing our soul and our thinking, works as a partial death and breaks us down every minute of our waking life.

A battle is being fought in the air. Luciferic oxygen-beings do battle there with ahrimanic nitrogen-beings. As long as one has not come to the threshold, air consists of abstractions, what the chemist calls oxygen and nitrogen. But at the threshold air becomes a battle between Lucifer and Ahriman, with oxygen as the outer mask of Lucifer, and nitrogen the outer mask of Ahriman. A battle rages in the air but is hidden from everyday, illusion consciousness. We enter this battle when we cross the threshold.

And here again, danger exists. If we wish to lay hold of what lives in the oxygen spirits, what lives in the life element, if we wish to unite our wills with creative spiritual activity, if we want to be inspired by the oxygen spirits to bold and courageous action, the danger is that all our actions may be swept away by this spiritual activity... that we even cease to be human beings. The danger is that what strength we had by way of willpower for the spiritual world is claimed by the luciferic world for itself.

If we then turn to the other side, the nitrogen powers tempt us. ahrimanic nitrogen powers tempt us with what lives in the air element as death. This is not the death we see happening in the physical world, which we are not involved with. Once you get involved with death, once you begin to see death as something to unite with, one can never free one's self from it. While we are inside the life element, spiritual beings want to take hold of us so that their deeds may absorb our deeds—the deeds of human beings. On the other side we are thrown in the opposite direction, into the realm of the ahrimanic nitrogen beings, and into the nothingness of life. We would like to unfold our activity in this death element, in this nothingness. But instead of being active, we are cramped. We become cramped within our Self.

Again, we are placed between the two poles that require us to become aware of our will, to become conscious of our will.

[The third verse is written on the blackboard.]

> *Life battles with death*
> *In that realm where your own will*
> *Would like to reign as creative spirit.*
> *You find, when grasping life,*
> *Your Self will vanish in spirits' might.*
> *You can, if subdued by death's own power,*
> *Encramp your Self in nothingness.*

My dear friends, if you now say: "I would rather run from such knowledge! Why should I expose myself to face the Guardian of the Threshold, when this knowledge is otherwise mercifully hidden from humanity? Can it help people to become aware of these terrible truths?" It is obvious that this objection arises from our human love of comfort, our love of ease. Asking the question, "What should I do with these truths?" means that you would rather not know the answer.

But, my dear friends, the task of the present time is that we enter reality. We should not cowardly shrink from reality but penetrate reality and unite with what actually constitutes our own being. We can only bury our heads in the sand and ignore such truths during our brief life on Earth. We should not be allowed to do so any longer. For we are now entering a new age where human beings can only thrive after death, if during their life on Earth they've already acquired awareness of what they will experience after death.

How will it be, then, after death? When we've passed through the gate of death, and before our consciousness is extinguished and we look back upon our life, during our retrospect we become aware that spiritual beings whisper into this process and give it a soft undertone. We look back after death—during the first few days after death while the ether body dissolves into the cosmic ether—we look back, and while watching the pictures of the Earth life we have just lived, certain spirits whisper into this process.

> Life battles with death
> In that realm where your own will
> Would like to reign as creative spirit.
> You find, when grasping life,
> Your Self will vanish in spirits' might.
> You can, if subdued by death's own power,
> Encramp your Self in nothingness.

We know now that this is reality. Either of these things can happen if we do not find the middle way but wander instead to the right or left. And again, when we go through the period of sleep after death (which does not last very long), we enter a state of consciousness where we journey backward through our life on Earth. This experience lasts one third of the time we lived on Earth, as described in anthroposophic lectures. As we become conscious while living our lives in reverse, spiritual beings counsel us again and again at certain milestones and speak these words to us.

> Warmth battles with cold
> In that realm where your feelings
> Would like to live in spirit-weaving.
> You find, in loving warmth,
> Your Self scattered in spirit-bliss.
> You can, if coldness hardens you,
> Crush your Self in suffering.

Mindful of this, I have often advised many who have asked me what they should do for the dead who were close to them in life. I tell them they should address the dead with thoughts that say: "May my love reach out to you. May it warm your cold and moderate your warmth!" This is because warmth and cold play a significant role during the time when reviewing your life in reverse. But we are also told in the verse that warmth and cold play this role all the time. These are simply realities.

When we then pass over from the retrospective experience of our life to when we are set free in the spirit land—where we prepare for our next life—then spiritual beings appear once again at significant milestones and counsel us, calling to us unceasingly:

Fifth Lesson

> Light battles with darkness
> In that realm where your thinking
> Would like to penetrate spirit-being.
> You find, toward light aspiring,

This "aspiring," this striving, is a true reality, for we are capable of veering off to the right or to the left.

> That spirit takes your Self away.
> You can, if lured by powers dark,
> Lose your Self in matter.

My dear friends, when human beings still had instinctive clairvoyance, someone going through the gate of death could still understand these words that were spoken at the three stations of life after death. In the age human beings had to pass through in order to achieve freedom, it was less and less possible to understand what was called to them after death. And now we live in an age when people are unable to understand these words, unless their meaning is pointed out to them during their life on Earth...words that are called to them in the language of the spirit.

This is what can happen to one who lives toward the future. One has to pass through a world where these words are called out, but are not understood...and one must suffer all the agony of not understanding. What does this mean, the "agony of not understanding?" It signifies that an overwhelming fear grows up in the soul, a fear of losing connection with the creative spiritual powers. At the end of the day it signifies a fear of losing one's human origin to alien powers instead of reaching those powers one owes one's existence to.

My friends, penetrating esoteric life means not just instruction; it is no mere theory. It means taking life seriously. Immersing yourself in esotericism doesn't mean immersing yourself in doctrines or theories but immersing yourself in life. The life our senses perceive is just an outer manifestation, a revelation, of the spiritual world that lies behind it at every moment. We will not enter the spiritual world if we close ourselves off to what lies behind these words. If we enter deeply into these words in meditation, our thinking, feeling and willing will become strong. They will be capable of grasping the living spirit…the spirit human beings must take hold of.

(…)

Light battles with darkness
In that realm where your thinking
Would like to penetrate spirit-being.
You find, toward light aspiring,
That spirit takes your Self away.
You can, if lured by powers dark,
Lose your Self in matter.

Warmth battles with cold
In that realm where your feelings
Would like to live in spirit-weaving.
You find, in loving warmth,
Your Self scattered in spirit-bliss.
You can, if coldness hardens you,
Crush your Self in suffering.

Life battles with death
In that realm where your own will
Would like to reign as creative spirit.
You find, when grasping life,
Your Self will vanish in spirits' might.
You can, if subdued by death's own power,
Encramp your Self in nothingness.

Sixth Lesson

Dornach, March 21, 1924

My dear friends! In today's considerations we will approach the very truths that one can learn from the Guardian of the Threshold. The unceasing warnings that the Guardian of the Threshold offers us concern the awareness of how to make spiritual progress in your soul if you become conscious of your true relationship with the world.

To become conscious of your true relationship with the world you must first begin to know the world around you as you observe it in the kingdoms of nature. The realm of nature lies outside of your own being. We learn to know the animal kingdom, the plant kingdom and the mineral kingdom. Our relationships to the plant, animal and mineral realms stimulate us. They offer us the opportunity to know and admire them, to use them for our own purposes, and so on. You learn to know the whole world as your outer world. But in your everyday consciousness you are hardly aware of how you yourself have grown from this world, of how deep your relationship is to the entire world.

Nevertheless, we cannot feel the relationship with these kingdoms of the world merely by gazing about. We must advance to a true knowledge of the self, to a self-knowledge that feels like it belongs to this world. And if we wish to develop self-knowledge that truly feels it belongs to this world, then we ought not to rest content with looking at things as they appear externally. We must go back to what is revealed between things, to what is revealed behind things.

Since the beginning of this most recent phase of human evolution people seldom look at what is revealed behind things. People only look at the external aspects of the three kingdoms of nature. But you know, my dear friends, that behind the kingdoms of nature we have to recognize real being, the real essence, of what we call the world of the elements.

Then we can say: "Our feet stand upon the Earth; they are planted on solid ground."

[Written on the blackboard:] *Earth*. The solid Earth supports us under our feet; it also gives its substance to the animals, plants and minerals and to our own physical body. And when we lift up our gaze from the ground beneath our feet and look around us at approximately eye level, we see that air is not the only element present, for air is always permeated with water. It is true that our way of life as human beings has become such that we feel water as a fine solution in the air around us and we have to condense it for use in our own organism. Although this is the case, it is nonetheless true to say that we live in the water element.

[Above *Earth* is written:] *Water*. And human beings also live in air, because we breathe the air.

[Above *Water* is written:] *Air*.

The minute we observe these elements we can no longer speak of them as we speak about the other beings in the kingdoms of nature that we see in front of us in clear outline. We see individual beings in nature, we see solid bodies in sharp contour. But of the solid as such—the earth element—we are able to say only that we *live* in it. We are too connected to the earthly to particularly distinguish ourselves from it; we don't distinguish the part that belongs to ourselves. We can distinguish a table or a chair that is external to us, but we don't perceive what is inside us in a clearly defined manner. We do not see our lungs or heart as distinctly defined objects. Only when we make them external objects do we see them that way, as in the study of anatomy. Just as we are related to our own body, so to a larger extent are we also related to all the elements. We live in earth, water, air and warmth. They belong to us. They are too close to be grasped as something sharply outlined in the world.

Sixth Lesson

Let us this one time lay out before us what is around us, and at the same time, what is within us, as elemental world, so that we can regard it as the content of the outer world and as our own content. Here we have what we call "earth," what we call "water," what we call "air," and what we designate as "warmth."

[Above *Air* is written:] *Warmth*. When we rise from the denser substances further into the etheric, from "warmth," which is already etheric, we then come to "light"

[Above *Warmth* is written:] *Light*. And then we come to what we have always called, in a dry and abstract way, the "chemical ether" and its effects. Because it brings about the ordering of the world, the formation of the world, this time we want to call this great chemical activity of the cosmos "cosmic formation" or "world organizing power." It is difficult to find the right expression for it.

[Above *Light* is written:] *Cosmic Formation*. Then we wish to designate what is highest in the etheric and call it "cosmic life," "life ether," or "world ether"

[Above *Cosmic Formation* is written:] *Cosmic Life*.

My dear friends, you will have seen from the previous lesson that people living on Earth are not related to these elements in the same way. Indeed, people only live in "warmth" so as to be completely connected with it.

[*Warmth* is written on the blackboard and a red cross is marked beside it.] For spiritual progress it is necessary to be fully conscious of such things.

Just think for a minute how directly, how instantaneously, you feel warmth and cold as your own. You are strongly affected by the difference between warmth and cold. By way of example, you are already less directly affected by what goes on in the surrounding air. You notice whether the air is good or bad only indirectly, by its effects upon your organism. It is similar with the effects of light. All the same, we human beings are very closely related to air and light.

[Two yellow *X*'s are marked next to *Air* and *Light*.] We stand extraordinarily close to these.

Although we are related to the watery element, one of the denser elements, we are relatively distant from it. Nevertheless, human life is deeply related to the watery element.

[A blue cross is marked next to *Water*.]

My dear friends, imagine for just a moment that you are having a vivid nightmare and observe how your perspiration and the secretions of your bodily fluids are influenced by such dreams. Note how the element of water plays a significant role in sleep. Human beings live in the watery element. The fluids that permeate our environment are of great significance for us, although they do not have such a direct influence on us as warmth does. As soon as our environment becomes cold or warm, we feel this condition as part of ourselves. *We* become cold; *we* become warm. For example, when we enter into a fog we do not notice with our ordinary consciousness that fog has an equally significant, albeit indirect, influence on our human nature. It is like this: when we are wrapped in a fog, or mist, our own watery element merges, so to speak, with the watery element of the external world. And then we feel a delicate transition from the watery element in ourselves to the watery element in the world. We feel it differently than when our watery element transitions into a dry atmosphere. In this transition we feel how we are connected to the entire cosmos. Dry air makes us feel more inward, more human; with moist air we feel dependent on the cosmos. But we have no training today to observe such things. In a lecture cycle given in The Hague I spoke in greater detail about our dependence on the elements. These dependencies exist. Part of esoteric life means becoming aware of them in a practical way.

Still deeper in the subconscious, I would say, lies our relationship to the element of earth.

[A blue cross is marked beside *Earth*.]

What does anyone know about their relationship to the earth element? We know that salt is salty and that sugar is sweet. These experiences belong to the earth element. But of the particular metamorphoses that salt and sugar undergo in our organism, how we are related to the

Sixth Lesson

cosmos while dissolving salt or sugar in our organism, how cosmic forces work in from the cosmos when the sweetness of sugar or the saltiness of salt courses through our body...we notice only a slight reaction to these things caused by their sweet and salty taste. Profound processes take place here. The entire universe has, so to speak, opened its doors to certain forces when we dissolve sugar on our tongue and transfer it into our organism.

Again, it is the case that, while these denser elements have an indirect effect upon human beings, the more dilute, more refined etheric elements of cosmic formation and cosmic life also have an indirect, hidden influence upon human beings.

[Blue crosses are marked next to *cosmic formation* and *cosmic life*]

The most obvious influence upon human beings comes from warmth, the element in the middle. The influences of light and air are also powerfully evident for our normal consciousness. But hidden in the unconscious are the influences of water and earth from the one side, and cosmic life and chemical organization of the world, chemical formation of the cosmos, from the other. That is also why, during our life on Earth, we ought to be conscious that as human beings we live in the middle elements [*air, warmth, light*], and that we are unconscious of our relationship to water, earth, cosmic formation and cosmic life.

Thus it always was the case when instinctive consciousness—with a hint of clairvoyance—was still alive, that students of the Mysteries received at a certain level of their development this solemn warning: trust in fire, trust in air, trust also in light, but beware when you come to the lower regions, to water and earth. When you come to the upper regions beware of cosmic forming and cosmic life. Since our connections to these things are steeped in the unconscious, the temptations of Lucifer will arise in cosmic forming and cosmic life and the temptations of Ahriman will rise up in earth and water.

[The list is completed by adding the words *Lucifer* and *Ahriman*. See also picture 2]

Cosmic Light	X [blue]	⎫
Cosmic Formation	X [blue]	⎬ Lucifer
Light	X [yellow]	
Warmth	X [red]	
Air	X [yellow]	
Water	X [blue]	⎫
Earth	X [blue]	⎬ Ahriman

Esoteric teaching in the mysteries always led human beings to understand how to find the right relationship to these elements, how to feel connected to them in the right way. One who ascends to imaginative life feels precisely this relationship with the elements. We look outside of us with our normal consciousness and recognize the animals, plants and minerals as things that are outside of us. If we learn to know the elements and how they relate to us, we should not merely look into the world outside, but we must also learn to feel and experience what is in us and in the world at the same time.

Then, when we have advanced to imaginative knowledge, we shall be able to feel our kinship with the earth element. If we have developed this feeling in the right way, at that point we make a profound confession. Making this confession to yourself is actually the on-going, real and true human self-knowledge. We realize that we are first only human when we are released, as it were, from the world, released from our connection with the Earth where we stand isolated and alone, where plant, animal and mineral existences are outside of and foreign to us. We no longer feel our humanity when through imaginative knowledge we comprehend our connection with the Earth. We feel our animality; we feel a close connection with all the animal nature spread around us.

And if you feel at one with the watery element on Earth, you realize: you are related to the world of plants. Something in you is asleep, something is dreaming…just like the plants. And we feel mineral existence in ourselves when we become aware of our relationship to air. We feel as if something mineral fills us throughout our entire skin.

Sixth Lesson

As soon as we enter the world of the elements with imaginative knowledge, we feel related to animals, plants and stones. We feel differently toward these kingdoms of nature when we feel that we belong to them. We feel our inner connection with these kingdoms in the following way.

We look out at the animal kingdom and observe the sluggish animals who take one slow step after another. We see active animals in the flying birds. We observe that everything in the animal is in motion, so that from their own being, from their inherent nature, they fill the world with movement. Then we say to ourselves: everything that stirs from the innermost being of animal nature, from animality...that same thing is revealed in our own will. We feel the relationship of our own will to the animal world.

But at the same time we feel something else; we become afraid of ourselves. This is precisely what one would like to see happen to everyone who enters esoteric life—to feel fear of one's self. One should not to remain stuck in that fear, but should transform it into a higher faculty of soul. But this is already the case if one is aware that, actually, our human form is only present in us through the fact that we stand alone, that we stand separate, and that the kingdoms of nature are outside of us. We can see them outside of us. Then we feel: the Earth as it really is does not make us human beings; it makes us animals. Here we are animals. By virtue of the Earth, we are animals. Since the earthly is always present, so also the danger is ever present that we sink down into animality. And if we don't interpret this as abstract, theoretical knowledge (as is common today), but if we feel it, we become afraid that at any minute we are capable of descending into animality. Yet, precisely this fear stimulates us to rise above our animal nature, to step out of this elemental life and emerge into a life—a life that surrounds us externally as an alien world—but a life that leads us to our humanity at the same time. Understanding our relationship to the world with true feeling leads us to genuine esoteric life.

Again, when we feel our relationship to the water element we become aware that by virtue of water we would not be human beings; we would be plants. My dear friends, as I have often explained, our feeling life is essentially dreaming; our feelings show a constant tendency to be plant-like.

Try to immerse yourself in your most delicate feelings, your most intimate feelings, then you will be able to experience the plant-like nature of feelings. Then you will feel that you are not only threatened by the danger of falling into animality, but that you are also threatened by the danger of living like a plant, of living with an immobilized consciousness as if you were asleep and dreaming. This stagnant feeling that resides in the depths of your unconscious must be changed into a feeling that awakens you to human existence. The fear of animality must be changed into the courage to raise ourselves up as human beings. The feeling of living a paralyzed, plant-like existence must be changed into a call to awaken ourselves, to summon up the inner strength to make ourselves into people who are fully awake in the world.

Furthermore, if we become aware of how we live in the air element, we see how all thinking is actually nothing more than a refined breathing process... except that people don't know this. Thinking is refined breathing. The thoughts we live in are actually a refined breathing process. Breathing in, holding it in, and then breathing out, work in a coarse way upon the blood circulation and in a finer, contrasting way upon the vibrations of the brain. Breathing is thinking in the physical world. Sublimated breathing is thinking.

One who has advanced to Imagination no longer believes in the abstract thinking that lives tenuously in the brain. Someone who has advanced to Imagination feels the in-breath, the expansion of the breath, in their brain. They feel how the breath expands. If the breath expands in this way and closes in upon itself, then closed concepts are formed, closed ideas. If the breath surrounds something else with undulating waves, then ideas that move arise. What we describe as the forming of mental pictures, as thinking, is only a refined breathing process surging and modulating through us.

In the same way that you feel "I breathe in; I draw a breath up into my brain and let it strike my ear," so you feel that you hear a tone as a sound that lives in you as thought. I let the breath strike my eye and it lives in me when I see color. The inner language of breathing works in me as ideas and mental pictures. When the highly refined breath strikes the sense organs it makes mental pictures. But if you become aware of this, if you become more aware of yourself as a thinker and a breather, so to speak, then you feel this breathing process as something refined into thinking—a thinking that fills you like an organized mineral, like an organized stone.

You know that oxygen is changed into carbon dioxide inside human beings. The uptake of carbon dioxide by the finer branches of breathing appears in the human head like carbon dioxide is being captured. It is a mineralizing process. The more one is in a position to perceive inwardly the capture of carbon by oxygen, the more one is conscious of this mineralizing process. We take up carbon, the coal substance, into ourselves. Carbon is the Philosopher's Stone. But carbon is the Philosopher's Stone only when it is inside human beings.

Read how the old instinctive clairvoyants described the Philosopher's Stone. You will find they said that the Philosopher's Stone can be found everywhere. It can be made everywhere, only people don't know it. You can find it where it exists; it can be found in the Earth. How to make carbon by burning wood is clearly described. The Philosopher's Stone can be made everywhere. It is carbon. It is in the shafts of coal mines...[gap in the shorthand report]...one feels inwardly made into stone...[gap in the shorthand report]...through a mineralization process, through living in the air, similar to the way we feel plant-like by living in water, to the way we feel our animal nature when living in the Earth.

This is what the Guardian warns us about: that we should become aware of our relationship to the kingdoms of nature. Therefore, we receive these admonitions from the Guardian of the Threshold as meditations spoken to us. And if we work with these verses with profound feeling and in earnestness, we will begin to perceive the relationship of the earth element to the will, of the water element to feelings, and of the airy element to thinking and to the forming of mental pictures, as I have just described.

[Writing on the blackboard]

> *To earthly nature you descend*
> *When unfolding your force of will.*

This remains entirely unconscious in normal consciousness. Every time we will anything we descend into the earth element, but our ordinary consciousness knows nothing about it. The moment we become aware of this descent we change ourselves from being human to being animal; we change from humanity to animality. We appear to ourselves as some kind of animal...at least one sees such as an etheric form. We may not exactly become an elephant or a bull, but something like it comes from the will that allows us to express something bull-like, elephant-like or eagle-like, and so on.

[Writing continues on the blackboard]

> *When as thinker you tread the Earth,*
> *Then power of thought will show to you*
> *Yourself in your animal nature;*

My dear friends, such admonitions of the Guardian of the Threshold should not be taken as concepts or theories. They are to be experienced by the whole human being. If we see which way our will is tending, if we perceive our own animality, we become afraid of ourselves. This fear of ourselves must be transformed into courage of the soul; then we shall make progress. Then we shall enter the spiritual world.

[Writing continues on the blackboard]

> *Fear of Self*
> *Must change to courage in your soul.*

Here we have the first descent into the realm where ahrimanic forces are powerfully at work. Our proper bearing is indicated by the warning just given by the Guardian of the Threshold:

> To earthly nature you descend
> When unfolding your force of will.
> When as thinker you tread the Earth,
> Then power of thought will show to you

> Yourself in your animal nature.
> Fear of Self
> Must change to courage in your soul.

As a rule, the best thing we can attain to for our spiritual progress results from something that drags us down. If we succeed in overcoming what drags us down—like the fear of our own animal nature—if through our own inner activity we can transform it into courage, then this transformation will become an impulse toward a noble, human quality, one we need in order to make spiritual progress.

We learned to descend into the watery element through the following admonition spoken by the Guardian of the Threshold:

> With watery nature do you live
> Merely through feeling's dreamy weaving.
> Send wakening through your watery being.
> Your soul will then emerge
> In plant-like dull existence;
> Paralysis of Self
> Must lead to wakefulness.

If we really descend into the watery element with full consciousness, the transformation of the sleepy, dreamy weaving of feeling into its opposite will become an awakener within us.

[The second verse is written on the blackboard:]

> *With watery nature do you live*
> *Merely through feeling's dreamy weaving.*
> *Send wakening through your watery being.*
> *Your soul will then emerge*
> *In plantlike dull existence;*
> *Paralysis of your Self*
> *Must lead to wakefulness.*

If we feel a relationship to air, then we already feel this relationship in our ordinary consciousness because with air one descends less deeply into the unconscious. Yet, a trace of ahrimanic temptation remains in this descent. When we live in our memories and recollections we live mainly in the inner activity of breathing. If we refine our normal breathing into thinking about what is in our surroundings, then there is hardly any danger. But when memories arise and the breath works from within, there is still an element of danger, even if this danger is among the easiest to observe. The Guardian of the Threshold gives us the following admonition when making this descent from thought into sensing, where we mostly deal with our memory images:

[The third verse is written on the blackboard]

> *In fleeting air you dream your thoughts*
> *Merely in forms of memory-pictures.*
> *Take hold of the airy being with your will.*

Dear friends, we can do this if we join one thought to another with the same inner activity, with the same intensity, that we otherwise use for outer actions. We are accustomed to exert ourselves when moving a chair from one place to another, but we are not accustomed to move a thought from one place to another. We would like to arrange our thoughts according to the pattern of outer appearances, to think just in the way things present themselves to us. We'd like to have a book to show us the sequence of thoughts; we'd like a newspaper to show us the sequence of thoughts; and, we are at ease, our minds are at rest, when this happens. It is as if you expected that all you had to do to exert your will is to first be stimulated by a force outside of yourself, by an objective power—as if a spirit should stand before you and move one of your legs in front of the other so that you could walk, or move your arm so that you could lift a chair. With respect to thinking, we are just like we would be if we relied on one leg being placed after the other so that we could walk.

[Writing on the blackboard continues, after the last line has been repeated "Take hold of the airy being with your will."]

> *Your soul will threaten you with pain,*
> *Rigidified and cold as stone.*

Sixth Lesson

This is what it means to become mineralized.

You don't know how hard our normal, ordinary thinking is if you don't know what Imagination is. Normal thinking is as hard as stone. Once we have entered the spiritual world we feel that our thinking has edges and corners. Thinking even hurts when it occurs in an especially abstract form. If you have learned to live a spiritual life, you can no doubt live with thoughts that spring from human feelings or from human impulses. You can even live with fits of hatred or anger expressed in thought. But, we feel inwardly wounded as if by edges and corners when the abstract thoughts of our present-day civilization enter our organization. You won't be aware of the suffering caused by today's thinking if you don't know the sentence: "Your own soul will threaten you with pain, rigidified and cold as stone." You'll have no idea of the pain. But when you consciously descend into the realm of memories, into the realm of wafting air where your breath is captured by mental images, then things will be as I have described. But, this inner death in thinking, this death from cold, must set us on fire to develop the counter force, the inner strength, required to summon up a living, vital spirit in our thinking.

[Writing continues on the blackboard]

> *But Selfhood's death from cold*
> *Must yield to spirit's fire.*

These are the three admonitions about the lower realm, the world of the lower elements. The Guardian of the Threshold speaks these words to those who approach the threshold to show how, if they seek true knowledge, they must become aware of their own relationship to the three kingdoms of nature. One must become aware of their own animal nature through their relationship with the Earth-being and thereby aware of the nature of the animals in the environment. One must become aware of their own plant-like nature through their relationship with the being of water, and thereby aware of the nature of the plants in the environment. One must become aware of their own mineral nature, their own nature of stone, through their relationship with the being of air, and thereby aware of the minerals in the environment.

The negative qualities of fear, paralysis and death have to be developed in the process, but they must be transformed into the positive spiritual qualities of courage in the soul, wakefulness of the soul, and vitalizing fire.

This is also what the Guardian of the Threshold calls up in those who cross the threshold. First, inner feelings of fear of descending into animality; then, the feeling of powerlessness in plant-like paralysis; and then, the longing to engender a vitalizing fire in your soul to oppose the cold rigidity of stone.

Thus sounds the threefold warning of the Guardian of the Threshold:

> To earthly nature you descend
> When unfolding your force of will.
> When as thinker you tread the Earth,
> Then power of thought will show to you
> Yourself in your animal nature.
> Fear of Self must change
> To courage in your soul.
>
> With watery nature do you live
> Merely through feeling's dreamy weaving.
> Send wakening through your watery being.
> Your soul will then emerge
> In plant-like dull existence;
> Paralysis of Self
> Must lead to wakefulness.
>
> In fleeting air you dream your thoughts
> Merely in forms of memory-pictures.
> Take hold of the air being with your will.
> Your soul will threaten you with pain,
> Rigidified and cold as stone.
> But Selfhood's death from cold
> Must yield to spirit's fire.

Sixth Lesson

Down here [lower part of the list on the blackboard, see page 356, picture 2] we come into the realm of Ahriman where we are warned by the Guardian of the Threshold how we can save ourselves from Ahriman's art of temptation. Similarly, we enter the other direction; [upper part of the list on the blackboard, see page 356, picture 2] we enter into light, cosmic formation and cosmic life, while standing on the Earth and seeking an esoteric life.

When we take light into ourselves we are usually not aware when it enters our eyes and how it becomes united with our breath; only warmth lies in between. We are usually not aware how the breathing of air unites with light [middle part of the list on the blackboard, see page 356, picture 2] so that a mental picture arises above the sense perception. We live in light when we form our thoughts just as on the opposite side we live in air and breathing in the lower realm. We derive our thoughts from light. We do not know that thoughts can only live in us when they are illumined by light, when our breathing is illumined by light.

For someone who has progressed to Imagination, thinking is a delicate exhalation of breath that is inwardly illumined, vibrated through and penetrated by light.

There go the rarefied waves of breathing [waves are drawn on the blackboard, see picture 2]. They light up in the light [yellow]. In Spiritual Science we describe everything that works in through the senses as light. Light is not only what works through the eyes but also what works in sound; light is what works in the sense of touch, as far as we perceive it. All sense perceptions are described as light. But, when we become aware of how thinking, how having thoughts, is refined breath that undulates and weaves though the light, it is really just as though we were looking out over the surface of the ocean and saw the sunlight shining on the waves [red on yellow is light reflection]. We see this not from the outside but as if we are in it and feel the light weaving on the waves; we feel the light glistening on the waves. Such is every perception when it is experienced inwardly.

Now, Lucifer's temptation comes about because this experience is something beautiful. It stirs up immense pleasure and a tremendous feeling of wellbeing. A true inner passion overcomes us. We easily fall prey to the enticements and temptations of Lucifer, who wants to pull us away from the Earth and into the beauty of the world where he rules. Lucifer tries to take us away from the earth element and then raise us into the angelic-spiritual realm so that after each time we sleep we no longer want to return to our physical body. Luciferic temptations occur here, in contrast to ahrimanic temptations that take place in the denser elements.

Now we must make sure that we listen to the admonitions of the Guardian of the Threshold and not enter this realm without the firm resolve never to forget the needs of the Earth. Then our bond with Earth existence, which we must pass through, will be made firm. This is why the admonition of the Guardian of the Threshold sounds as follows:

> Of light-shine's power you retain
> Mere thoughts within your inner self.
> When light-shine thinks itself in you
> An untrue spirit-being will arise
> In you as Selfhood's vain delusion.
> But mindfulness of earthly needs
> Maintains you as a human being.

[This verse is written on the blackboard]

> *Of light-shine's power you retain*
> *Mere thoughts within your inner self.*
> *When light-shine thinks itself in you*

That is to say, when through Imagination we become fully connected to the light and when thoughts are no longer abstract, but play as light upon the waves of the breath—

> *An untrue spirit-being will rise*
> *In you as Selfhood's vain delusion.*
> *But mindfulness of earthly needs*
> *Maintains you as a human being.*

Sixth Lesson

If we rise further into the etheric element, luciferic temptations become even more intense. Here the temptations are not only the concern of our thoughts, which are comparatively easy to find our way through. But here we also must consider the dull element of feeling, for in feelings we retain the substances from the cosmic forming that works and weaves in the cosmic chemical ether. If one now rises with imaginative knowledge and really feels oneself in this cosmic chemistry, then one must live within all the substances; one must enter into all the combining and separating. This is very different from a comfortable, philistine laboratory where a chemist stands at a table with everything happening outside in the laboratory. One becomes a cosmic chemist interwoven with the chemical processes. A person so interwoven with cosmic formative forces feels the luciferic temptation as a form of inwardly fainting. At first, he is brought into a kind of inner bliss that he is capable of being a spirit. If he is forgetful of what the Earth needs, he doesn't want to go back to the Earth. Now he becomes faint and is no longer in command of his humanity, his humanness. He must protect himself from faintness of soul by approaching this world only after acquiring true love for all that is valuable on Earth, only after acquiring love for all earthly values.

Of world-formation you retain

—So speaks the Guardian of the Threshold—

Mere feelings in your inner self.
When cosmic form then feels itself in you
Your faint experience of the spirit
Will choke you in your Selfhood's being.
But love of values of the Earth
Will save your human soul.

[This verse is written on the blackboard]

Of world-formation you retain
Mere feelings in your inner self.
When cosmic form then feels itself in you
Your faint experience of the spirit

—Which in effect comes from Lucifer—

> *Will choke you in your Selfhood's being.*
> *But love of values of the Earth*
> *Will save your human soul.*

We can reach our cosmic goal only if we become angels at the right time. Contemporary humanity will rise to the level of the Angels during the Jupiter existence. Lucifer's temptation is that he wants to make us into stunted angels already during Earth existence, to become immature angels at the wrong time. Human souls would then be lost as stunted angelic souls. Therefore, we should listen to the Guardian of the Threshold's warning:

> But love of values of the Earth
> Will save your human soul.

The temptation we experience when we ascend to the last element of cosmic life, to the all-prevailing cosmic life, is the strongest of all. From this element we sustain our will, which, as I've often said, is sleeping in us. If the will is awakened in our imagination, we become aware—in contrast to the narrow life enclosed within our skin—of how we share in this cosmic life. And at that very instant of sharing in cosmic life, we are dead. To live consciously in the all-pervading cosmic life is to experience death as an individual being. Universal life kills us when it takes hold of us. The experience is comparable to the way an insect flies into a flame from craving for the light and, in that moment, dies. In the same way one's individual life dies into the general cosmic life when entering it consciously with their spirit. As the insect, compelled by an indescribable bliss, flutters into the flame, flickering up for a single instant, so one dies as an individual being and goes with their spirit out into the universal cosmic life.

We dare not go into this element even in thought unless we have first developed in ourselves a will surrendered to God, a will devoted to the spirit and to the Earth. This means that we must be fully conscious that we are to carry out the intentions of the spiritual world on Earth. If we permeate ourselves with this God-surrendered will, glowing inwardly with love, we will not let ourselves be seduced. We will not allow ourselves to become degenerate angels. Then, for the time necessary for humanity to be human beings, we will remain human beings. Therefore, the Guardian of the Threshold warns us:

> Of cosmic life you do retain
> Mere willing in your inner self.
> When cosmic life takes full hold
> Consuming spirit bliss will kill
> Your experience of Self.
> But earthly will, devoted to spirit,
> Lets the divine in us hold sway.

[This verse is written on the blackboard]

> *Of cosmic life you do retain*
> *Mere willing in your inner self.*
> *When cosmic life takes fully hold*
> *Consuming spirit bliss will kill*
> *Your experience of Self.*
> *But earthly will, devoted to spirit,*
> *Lets the divine in us hold sway.*

The threefold admonition of the Guardian of the Threshold sounds on the subject of the upper region, regarding the element of the ethers [see the list on page 92]:

> Of light-shine's power you retain
> Mere thoughts within your inner self.
> When light-shine thinks itself in you,
> An untrue spirit-being will arise
> In you as Selfhood's vain delusion.
> But mindfulness for needs on Earth
> Maintains you as a human being.

Of world-formation you retain
Mere feelings in your inner self.
When cosmic form then feels itself in you,
Your faint experience of the spirit
Will choke in you your Selfhood's being.
But love of values of the Earth
Will save your human soul.

Of cosmic life you do retain
Mere willing in your inner self.
When cosmic life takes fully hold
Consuming spirit bliss will kill
Your experience of Self.
But earthly will, devoted to spirit,
Lets the divine in us hold sway.

My dear friends, you have been introduced in these lessons to the practice of knowledge, to the practice of cognition. What was given in this manner must not be taken as a description of something theoretical. You will experience it as heartfelt life if you have developed the right prerequisites, the proper preconditions. The material given in these lessons are instructions from the Guardian of the Threshold himself. They originate directly from conversations with the Guardian of the Threshold. It is not the intention of these Class Lessons to give out theories. The intention is to let the spiritual world itself speak. That is why we spoke in the First Lesson of how this School must be regarded as being established by the spiritual world itself.

This is the essence of all Mystery Schools, that people appointed by the spiritual powers of the world speak in them. The essence of the Mystery Schools must so remain. This is the reason for the strong warning to be earnest, which every member of this Class must enkindle and maintain within themselves. Actually, no one can be a member of this School, or have a genuine spiritual life, without developing earnestness. This, my friends, is what I, as your earnest advisor, would like to direct your attention to once more. Take the School as being directly constituted by the will

Sixth Lesson

of the spiritual world itself, which we merely seek to interpret correctly for our time. This is the age we entered when the period of darkness was over and light had come once again. At first this light finds poor expression on Earth because people still hold onto the old darkness. Yet, the light is here. Whoever knows in their heart that the light is here will also grasp the nature and will of our spiritual School in the right way.

(...)

Seventh Lesson

Dornach, April 11, 1924

My dear friends! (...) Our studies in these Class Lessons have been primarily concerned with what can be communicated about meeting the Guardian of the Threshold. The encounter with the Guardian of the Threshold signifies the first experience of truly achieving authentic suprasensory knowledge. Today, I would like to add something more to what we have considered so far.

Before one can say their encounter with the Guardian of the Threshold has been successful, a person must have experienced what it means to live with their essential humanity outside of the physical body, to live only in their "I" and astral body. When one's being is enclosed in the physical body we can only perceive our surroundings through the tools of the physical body. Only the sense world can be perceived through the tools of the physical body. The sense world is a reflection of the spiritual world, but at first it doesn't reveal what is being reflected; it doesn't reveal what that reflection means.

Generally speaking, it is not difficult to get out of our physical body. We do it every time we go to sleep; we are outside our body then. Our consciousness is reduced to unconsciousness when we are asleep and outside our body. Only illusory—or perhaps not so illusory—dreams rise up from the unconscious. But for the attainment of higher knowledge it is necessary that we go out of our physical body with full conscious awareness. This is so we can perceive the world around us while we are outside our physical body, just as we perceive the physical world with the help of our physical senses while we are inside our physical body. Then, when we are outside of the physical body, we perceive the spiritual world.

At first, when outside of our body, we are fast asleep; we are unconscious. Under ordinary conditions one is not informed about what can be perceived when outside the body. And the reason we can't perceive anything is precisely because, at first, we are protected from approaching the spiritual world unprepared.

What happens to someone who has been sufficiently prepared to approach the spiritual world? If they are found to be prepared as described in the previous lessons, when they come to the abyss between the sense world and the spiritual world [red drawing on the blackboard, see picture 3], the Guardian of the Threshold takes up the true human being, he takes your true essence out. One's true human essence can then spread its wings and cross the abyss [yellow is added] with the means indicated in the last mantric verses. Now you are able to see your own physical, sense-perceptible being from the other side of the threshold.

My dear friends, the first great impression of real knowledge occurs when the Guardian of the Threshold can say to us: Look! See! On the other side of the threshold you are as you appear outwardly in the physical world. Here with me you are what you are according to your innermost being.

And then, important words sound again from the Guardian of the Threshold. These significant words from the Guardian are called out to those on the other side of the abyss. This makes us realize how differently things appear on the other side of the abyss. We look at ourselves differently. We see our self as a trinity [green is added]. We look at ourselves as a trinity, a threefoldness that is expressed in the soul through thinking, feeling and willing. Actually, three human beings are contained in every human being: a thinking human being, a feeling human being and a willing human being. They are only held together as one by the physical body in the physical world. What a human being sees at this moment resounds from the lips of the Guardian of the Threshold:

> Behold the Three,
> They are as One,
> When you bear in Earth existence
> The stamp of being human.

—or one might say, *the stamp of the human form*. These words have to be translated from occult language—

> Behold the Three,
> They are as One,
> When you bear in Earth existence
> The stamp of being human.
>
> Experience the cosmic form of your head.
> Feel the cosmic beat of your heart.
> Think the cosmic strength of your limbs.
>
> These are the Three
> The Three that live as One
> In Earth existence.

[The mantra is now written on the blackboard.]

> *Behold the Three,*
> *They are as One,*
> *When you bear in Earth existence*
> *The stamp of being human.*
>
> *Experience the cosmic form of your head.*
> *Feel the cosmic beat of your heart.*
> *Think the cosmic strength of your limbs.*
>
> *These are the Three*
> *The Three That live as One*
> *In Earth existence.*

The Guardian of the Threshold indicates what the three look like when separated from each other as soon as we leave the physical body. He indicates how they appear in relation to the physical body. The Guardian of the Threshold shows us our physical body. He shows us our head, heart and limbs and then says: "When you actually see the cosmic truth revealed by the human head, you see an image of the heavenly cosmos. You must look into the distant expanse of space where the world seems to have limits, where in reality it is bounded by the spirit (the world is not as simple as pictured by physics). We must look up and in doing so remember how the roundness of your head is a true image of the heavenly world. We bring this to consciousness in the mantric words:

"Experience the cosmic form of your head."

—And we join these words to this sign [this sign is drawn at the beginning of the line.]

We pause at this line of the mantra to picture the upward direction to ourselves. Everywhere around the Earth the direction leads upward to the vast reaches of the cosmos around us.

"Feel the cosmic beat of your heart."

The rhythm of the world moves through the heavenly cosmos and sounds to us like cosmic music. When we feel the human heart beating, it seems like the heart beats only as the result of what goes on inside the human organism. The truth is that the heart beats as an echo of cosmic rhythms whose cycles range not merely over thousands of years, but over millions of years. Therefore, the Guardian says we must pause again at the words "Feel the cosmic beat of your heart." Feel in your heart what works downward as well as upward—[This sign is drawn at the beginning of the line]—and unites what is below [triangle pointing up] with what is above [triangle pointing down.]

"Think the cosmic strength of your limbs."

This cosmic strength, this force, is concentrated in the force of gravity and in other terrestrial forces working up from below. We must look down with our thinking because our thinking is only capable of understanding earthly things. Then we shall understand what streams up from the Earth and works within us. Here again we should pause at the words "Think the cosmic strength of your limbs" and consider the triangle pointing downward. [This sign is drawn at the beginning of the line.]

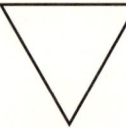

▽

If we call this mantric verse to life and let it work on us, we shall feel the way the words of the Guardian ought to work upon our heart and soul at the present time.

> Behold the Three,
> They are as One,
> When you bear in Earth existence
> The stamp of being human.
>
> Experience the cosmic form of your head.

—Speak this sentence while making the sign in front of your head.

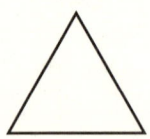

△

Feel the cosmic beat of your heart.

—Speak this sentence while making the sign over your chest.

⧖

Think the cosmic strength of your limbs.

—Speak this sentence while making the sign downward.

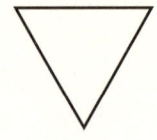

▽

> These are the Three
> The Three that live as One
> In Earth existence

After letting this mantric verse work on our soul, we should try to silence our senses; close our eyes and hear nothing with our ears...we should try to perceive nothing. Feel yourself surrounded by darkness, and in that darkened silence try to live in the atmosphere created by the sound of the words. We are transported in this way to the sphere where initiation can be experienced in all its reality, where we meet the Guardian of the Threshold. This is one way to take your first step across the threshold.

But we must also let the Guardian's further words work upon us in all earnestness. For the Guardian's further words show us that the minute we cross the threshold everything changes from how it is in the sense world. In the sense world we think that our thoughts—our mental images—live inside our head. So it is...for the sense world. Nevertheless, a little bit of will is always mixed in with the thinking of the head. This is perceptible even to ordinary consciousness, for when we move from one thought to another we must exert as much will as when we move an arm or leg, or want anything. Yet it is a very gentle and refined will that leads one thought into the next. That's the way it is in the world of the senses: a wide range of thinking and a little will, a touch of will, are connected with the head. But as soon as we cross the threshold and approach the Guardian the opposite is true: only a little thinking and a vast amount of will are connected with the head. And in this will, which is otherwise asleep in us, we feel the spirit working from the cosmos, working from the heavens, and forming the human head into a spherical image of itself in every detail.

Therefore, when we have arrived on the other side of the threshold, the Guardian of the Threshold calls out these words to us:

[A new mantra is written on the blackboard.]

> *Spirit of the head,*
> *You can <u>will</u> it*

We see now that will is something quite different than it was before. Previously our senses were the mediators of our sense impressions. We had no awareness that will passes through our eyes and ears, that it pervades our warmth, that will passes through all our senses. Now we see that all the varied shades of color the eyes experience, all the various tones the ears can hear, all that we perceive as qualities of warmth and cold, roughness and smoothness, smell and taste, and so on—all of this is will in the spiritual world. [Writing continues.]

> *And _will_ becomes for you*
> Heaven's weaving of manifold forms in the senses.

If we have recognized this by seeing our head from the other side of the threshold—how the will goes through the head, and how the senses represent the will—then we are shown further how the heart bears the soul within it. We can feel the soul in our heart just as we can will the spirit in our head. Now we see that thinking is not a quality of the head but a quality of the heart, of the soul in the heart. Now we recognize that thinking belongs not to an individual human being but it belongs to the whole world. Then we experience the life of the world that circulates through us as music—the music of the world. We experience World-life as World-music.

[The next verse is written on the blackboard.]

> *Soul of the heart,*
> *You can _feel_ it*
> *And _feeling_ becomes for you*
> *The seed for awakening cosmic life in $\frac{thinking}{willing}$*
> *You live in worlds of appearance.*

—This is not the world of appearance that has no being, but the world of appearance where the being of the world is shining.

[The lines that sum up the first and second verses are written on the blackboard. The first verse is spoken once again.]

> Spirit of the head,
> You can will it;
> And will becomes for you
> Heaven's weaving of manifold forms in the senses.

—Now we sum this up with the line:

> *You weave in worlds of wisdom.*

So, we also sum up what is related to the soul of the heart, to feelings, in the sentence:

> *You live in worlds of appearance.*

Just as we recognize the senses as will, so now we recognize, with regard to cosmic existence, thinking as feeling when we behold "the three that are one only in the sense world."

The Guardian of the Threshold continues with a third verse. [The third verse is written on the blackboard.]

> *Strength of the limbs,*
> *You can think it;*

Now we have a complete reversal. Whereas normally we have the idea that thinking is concentrated in the head, here will is concentrated in the head. Feeling remains in the heart just like it is felt in the sense world, because the inner power of the heart goes directly over into the spiritual world.

> *Strength of the limbs,*
> *You can think it;*

—Thinking is now brought into connection with the limbs, the very opposite of what is found in the sense world.— [The writing continues.]

> *And thinking becomes for you*
> *Purposeful human striving of the will.*
> *—thus, will becomes thinking—*
> *You strive in realms of virtue.*

This is why we've been told by the Guardian of the Threshold about the phenomenon of complete reversal in the spiritual world. Whereas we normally distinguish willing, feeling and thinking in human beings from below upward, now we see the human being from the other side as threefold. We see: will above in the head; feeling in the middle region; and, thinking below in the limbs. We now discover: that the will, concentrated in the head, is the weaving cosmic wisdom we live in; that feeling is cosmic appearance where all spiritual beings radiate and shine; and, that thinking, perceived in the limbs as human striving, can live as virtue in human beings. The three appear before spiritual vision as:

> *Spirit* of the *head*
> *Soul* of the *heart*
> *Strength* of the *limbs*

[The words *head*, *heart*, and *limbs* are underlined in white, and the words *spirit*, *soul*, and *strength* are underlined in red.]

This is how the mantric structure of the verse is built up. We must be conscious of its inner consistency, its internal congruence. Further, we must be conscious that, if we allow this verse to work on us, we are approached by

> *Heavenly weaving*
> *Cosmic life*
> *Cosmic striving*

[underlined in yellow] so that the words of the Guardian are brought before our spiritual eye where, after we cross over to the world beyond the threshold, "the Three come into being from the One."

> Spirit of the head,
> You can will it
> And will becomes for you
> Heaven's weaving of manifold forms in the senses.
> You weave in worlds of wisdom.

Seventh Lesson

> Soul of the heart,
> You can feel it
> And feeling becomes for you
> The seed for awakening cosmic life in $\frac{\text{thinking}}{\text{willing}}$
>   You live in worlds of appearance.
>
> Strength in the limbs,
> You can think it
> And thinking becomes for you
> Purposeful human striving of the will.
>   You strive in realms of virtue.

These feelings must pass through the soul if true knowledge is to be attained. This is the advice given by the Guardian of the Threshold, as he now says to us:

> Enter:
> The door is open!
> You will become
> A true human being.

[This is written on the blackboard.]

> *Enter:*
> *The door is open!*
> *You will become*
> *A true human being.*

These words—admonishing and encouraging us at the same time—have sounded for countless millennia at all gateways to the spiritual world.

> Enter:
> The door is open!
> You will become
> A true human being.

Imagine, my dear sisters and brothers, that you say to yourself for the first time: "I will take these words of the Guardian of the Threshold seriously. I will admit that I was not yet a human being. I will admit that I will become a human being through insight into the spiritual world." Imagine, my dear sisters and brothers, that you say a second time: "No, the first time I did not take these words seriously enough. I will say that I need not one but two steps up from my present condition to become a true human being." Now, imagine that you say this to yourself a third time: "I will admit that I need three steps higher from the point where I am now, where I am not truly human, to become a true human being."

The first resolve you make to yourself is to be earnest. The second one is to be more earnest. But the highest level of earnestness must be reserved for the third level of resolve. And if you are capable of arousing this threefold earnestness in the depths of your soul, you will get a feeling for what it means to become truly human through knowledge. Then you will return—as we will return today in this Class Lesson—to the Guardian's first admonition that ought to live as a transformative verse in our soul:

> Behold the Three,
> They are as One,
> When you bear in Earth existence
> The stamp of being human.
>
> Experience the cosmic form of your head.
> Feel the cosmic beat of your heart.
> Think the cosmic strength of your limbs.
>
> These are the Three
> The Three that live as One
> In Earth existence.

My dear sisters and brothers, these words have sounded in the hearts of all who have striven for knowledge since human life has been on Earth.

There was a pause in this striving—a caesura—since the dawn of the fifth post-Atlantean cultural epoch. In accordance with the will of the divine spiritual beings who guide humanity, this pause has come to an end.

It will be up to you to bring forth again in human hearts in a worthy manner everything the wise guides of humanity have employed, since human life has been on Earth, to lift up human hearts to perceive what works as spirit in the world, and to perceive what works as spirit in the human being—the crown of creation.

Eighth Lesson

Dornach, Good Friday, April 18, 1924

My dear friends! (...) Today I would like to start—please don't take notes at this stage; just listen to the words—by speaking the mantric verse that resounds in the human soul, in the heart, as the great challenge to strive for true knowledge of yourself. It has sounded throughout time, first starting in the Mysteries, but the Mysteries received it from the stars, from the writings of the great cosmic script. This challenge rings forth from the entire cosmos: "O Man, Know Thy Self!"

If we look up to the fixed stars, to those that stand with a particularly distinct script in the zodiac, which, through their grouping in certain forms (the constellations) bring the great cosmic script to expression, then the content of the Cosmic Word is first revealed to those who understand this script: "O Man, Know Thy Self!"

If we look up to what the planets reveal through their movements—to begin with the sun and moon—but also the other planets associated with the sun and moon, then the heart and soul of the cosmos are revealed by the movements of the planets. The essence of the Cosmic Word—powerful of soul and with cosmic strength—is revealed through the constellations in the same way.

Through our experience with the elements that surround us on Earth, where they interact with us through our skin and our senses, where they enter into and work upon our body through earth, water, fire and air, through these the will-impulse is poured into these words.

And so we can let the Cosmic Word work upon our souls through this mantric verse:

Eighth Lesson

O Man, Know Thy Self!
Thus sounds the Cosmic Word.
You hear it with strength of soul,
You feel it with might of spirit.

Who speaks so powerfully through the world?
Who speaks so tenderly within your heart?

Does it work through the far-spread rays of space
Into your senses' experience of life?
Does it sound through the weaving waves of time
Into the evolving stream of your life?

Is it you, yourself, who,
By sensing space, by experiencing time
Begets this word,
Feeling yourself estranged in the psychic void of space,
Because you lose the force of thought
In the annihilating stream of time?

My dear friends, my dear sisters and brothers, no knowledge exists that does not penetrate through to the spiritual world. Everything we call knowledge that is not found in the spiritual world, or has not been given by those capable of researching the spiritual world, is not real knowledge. We must make it clear to ourselves when we look at the world around us, at the realms of nature, that we are looking at what reveals itself in color upon color, in gleam and glitter, what lives in the sparkling stars above, in the warm, shining sun, what springs up from the depths of the Earth below—all this magnificence, majesty and beauty is permeated by wisdom. We would be doing a grave wrong to disregard this beauty, magnificence, power and wisdom. If we wish to become an esotericist, if we want to penetrate to real knowledge, then we must also have a sense for what surrounds us on Earth. We must have a free and open feeling for it. For during our earthly life between birth and death we are obliged to derive our strength from the Earth's forces and to return the fruits of our labor to the Earth.

But, true as it is that we must participate in the external realms that surround us—color upon color, sound upon sound, warmth upon warmth, star upon star, cloud upon cloud, nature being upon nature being—it is also true that when we look at all this majesty, power, magnificence, wisdom and beauty that our senses convey, we still do not find who we are ourselves. Just at that point, when we have a correct sense of the majesty, beauty and grandeur of our surroundings here on Earth, we realize that the source of our inner being is not found in this light-filled realm called Earth. It is found somewhere else. Full recognition of this fact causes us to seek that state of consciousness where we are brought to what is called "the threshold of the spiritual world." This threshold, which lies directly in front of an abyss, must be approached. There we must remember: in all that surrounds us during our Earth existence between birth and death, the primal source of humanity is not to be found.

Then we must know: at this threshold stands a spiritual figure called the Guardian of the Threshold. The Guardian of the Threshold takes care, in a beneficial way, that we do not come to the threshold unprepared, without having experienced deeply in our soul those feelings just spoken about.

But when we are really prepared for spiritual knowledge with inner earnestness—whether we gain it through clairvoyant consciousness or through our healthy common sense understanding (both ways are possible)—then in both cases we must either have a vision of, or have knowledge about, the Guardian of the Threshold. Only then is it first possible for the Guardian of the Threshold actually to reach out with helping hands and let us to look across the deep abyss. There, on the other side of the threshold where the human being originates, where the origin of our innermost being is found, at first, only darkness is found...uttermost darkness.

My dear friends, my dear sisters and brothers, we seek the light in order to behold the origin of our own being in the light. Yet, at first, there is only darkness all around. The light we seek must radiate from the darkness. And it will only radiate from the darkness if we become aware of how the three fundamental impulses of our soul life—thinking, feeling

Eighth Lesson

and willing—are held together during Earth existence by our physical body. Thinking, feeling and willing are joined together during physical Earth existence.

If I were to draw a diagram showing how they are connected, I'd have to draw it like this: [the middle sketch in Picture 4] first thinking [yellow]; then thinking reaches into feeling [green]; then feeling extends into will [red]; so that the three of them are joined as one during our earthly life.

We must now learn to experience how these three separate from each other. If we increasingly take up the meditations recommended here by the School, and make them a vital content of our inner life, we will notice the following [drawing on the right side of Picture 4 is made]. Thinking [yellow] becomes free; it detaches itself from its connection with feeling. Feeling [green] becomes independent; it exists by itself. The will [red] also becomes independent and exists by itself. At that point we learn to perceive without the need for a physical body.

Our physical body has held thinking, feeling and willing together; it has bound them together [an oval is drawn around the middle drawing in Picture 4]. Here the physical body is no longer present, it is no longer at hand [right drawing of thinking, feeling and willing].

Through the meditations received from this School, you gradually come to feel as if you are outside of your body. You come into a condition where what was the world becomes the self and what was self becomes the world. When we stand here on Earth we feel like human beings. And when we become aware of what is inside us, we say: this is my heart, these are my lungs, this is my liver, this is my stomach. What we identify as our organs, as our physical organization, we call our own. Then we point upward: there is the sun, there's the moon, and there are the stars, the clouds, a tree, a river. We identify these as being outside us. We are inside our organs. We are outside those things we pointed to: the sun, moon, stars and so on.

If we have prepared our soul sufficiently so that our soul can live without its body—meaning our soul can perceive the spiritual universe outside of the body—the opposite consciousness, its reverse, then takes place.

Now we talk about the sun in the same way we talk about our own heart in Earth existence. We say of the sun: this is *my* heart. We say of the moon: this is the creator of *my* form. We speak about the clouds in the same way we talk about our hair. What people on Earth see as parts of the universe we now see as parts of our own organism. We point at them and say: Look! There is a human heart, a human lung, a human liver. These are something objective; this is the world. When we, as human beings, view the world from our physical body, we see the sun and the moon above and outside us. But when we look at the sun, moon, stars, clouds, rivers and mountains from the vantage point of the universe…they are inside us. So, when we see the human being as our outer world, the only difficulty lies in the spatial relationships. And this difficulty will be overcome.

This is how we see things as soon as we leave our physical body with our thinking. Thinking becomes one with everything manifested by the stars. Just as here on Earth we call the brain our own, and speak of it as our instrument for thinking, so there, when we are out in the universe and see the human being as something external to us, we begin to feel the stars of the zodiac as our brain.

And we experience the orbiting planets as our feeling. Our feeling now lives in the orbital paths of the sun, in the courses of the moon and the other planets. Indeed, the sun lies between what we experience in the stars as world thinking, and feeling [the sign of the sun is drawn between the yellow and green in the drawing on the right side of Picture 4]. And the moon lies between feeling and willing, which we also feel inside us [the sign of the moon is drawn between red and green]. Simply by meditating upon this figure, it contains the power to bring us ever closer to spiritual vision. Only we must realize that the words I've spoken here can really be inwardly experienced: leaving our physical body, expanding throughout the cosmos, feeling parts of the cosmos—sun, moon, stars and so on—as our own inner organs and looking upon the human being as our outer world.

At this point we must be very clear: our thinking, feeling and willing now change from the unity they are on Earth—due only to the

Eighth Lesson

Earth-bound physical body—to a trinity. We learn above all to experience this threefoldness when we observe thinking itself.

My dear sisters and brothers, the thinking we use on Earth between birth and death is just a corpse; it is not alive. Whatever we may think with our brain regarding the beauty, majesty and grandeur of this world around us, these thoughts are not alive. They were alive in pre-earthly existence before we descended into the physical world, when we were living as soul-spiritual beings in a soul-spiritual world. That's when the thoughts we have on Earth were alive. And our physical body is the tomb where the dying thought-world was buried when we descended to Earth. Here we carry the corpse of thought within us. We think about our sense-perceptible, earthly environment with these thought-corpses, not with living thoughts. We had living thinking within us before we descended into this physical world.

My dear friends, we need only permeate ourselves with these truths again and again, with force and inner strength, and we will develop a consciousness knowledge that *this is the truth*. We learn to know the human being in this manner. We so learn to know him that when we look at a person we can say: here is the human head [on the left side an outline of the head is drawn, Picture 4]. This head is the bearer and ground of earthly, corpse-like thinking. From it spring forth [in the sketch on the left, the long form downward is drawn] the dead thoughts that spread over everything perceived by our eyes, ears, our sense of warmth and our other senses. We are looking here at the kind of thinking that is only concerned with earthly things.

But we gradually learn to see through such thinking. Behind it, within the spirit-cell of the human head, a remnant still exists of the true, living thinking we lived in before descending to the physical plane. When you look at a person the first thing you see is their dead thinking [red in the front part of the head]. But living thinking lies behind the dead thinking [yellow part of the head] in the spirit-cell within the head. And this living thinking brought with it the power to shape our brain. The brain is not the generator of our thinking but is the product of pre-earthly, living thinking.

So, when we look at a person with a properly developed consciousness we see dead, earthly thinking revealed on the surface of their head. And, if we look behind the surface into the spirit-cell of the brain, we behold a living thinking that is actually a kind of will. This will, which we ordinarily perceive in our motor system, is really sleeping in us. We don't know how thought descends into our muscles and the like when our intent is to will something. If we observe what lives in us as will, then we see the will as thinking in the spirit-cell that lies behind the sense-orientated thinking. This will, which we now perceive as thinking, is the creator of our organ of thought. This type of thinking is no longer human thinking... it is cosmic thinking.

If we can understand the human being so that we look through their earthly thinking into the living thinking that first created the brain as the basis for earthly thinking, then sense-bound thinking flows away into the cosmic void. Eternal thinking, cosmic thinking, then rises up in us as will.

We bring all this to consciousness if we let these mantric words work upon us:

> See behind thinking's sensory light,
> How in the darkened spirit-cell
> Will ascends from the body's depths.
> Let lifeless thinking flow through the strength of your soul
> Into the cosmic void.
> And will now rises up
> As cosmic thought-creating.

My dear friends, this imagination must gradually arise before you. Dead thoughts stream forth from the head, thoughts that are oriented to the sense world. Behind it—at first in darkness—lies the true thinking that shines through the sense-bound thoughts, the true thinking that first created the brain when we descended from the spiritual into the physical world. True thinking is will. So we see how will rises up from the human being [white upward strokes], spreads out into the head and becomes

Eighth Lesson

cosmic thinking [white shape in the head], because the will that lives in thinking is already cosmic thinking.

Therefore, one should try better to grasp this material more and more. One should bring these mantric thoughts to life again and again in pictures that one can place in the soul with the following words:

[The first verse is written on the blackboard.]

> *See behind thinking's sensory light,*
> *How in the darkened spirit-cell*
>
> —*We must look <u>behind</u> thinking*—
>
> *Will ascends from the body's depths.*
>
> —*We must now become strong in our soul and let go of our normal sense-bound thoughts*—
>
> *Let lifeless thinking flow through the strength of your soul*
> *Into the cosmic void.*
> *And will now rises up*
> *As cosmic thought-creating.*

These seven lines actually contain the secret of human thinking in connection to the universe.

We must not pretend we can grasp these things with the intellect. We must let them live in our soul, feeling them as a meditation. These words have power; they are harmoniously constructed. "Thinking," "willing," "cosmic void," "willing," "cosmic thought-creating" [these words are underlined] are arranged with an inner thought-organization so that they can work on imaginative consciousness.

Just as we can look at the human head as a means to look at cosmic thought-creation, so we can look at the human heart as the physical representative, the imaginative representation, of the human soul. Similarly, as thinking is an abstract representative of the human spirit, we can look at the human heart as the representative of feeling. Here again, we can look into feeling as it applies to life on Earth between birth and death. But this time we don't look *behind* feeling, we look *into* feeling. [Drawing of a yellow oval on the sketch on the left]. As we perceive cosmic thought-creation in the spirit-cell behind ordinary thinking, so do we perceive in feeling, symbolized by the heart, something that flows through feeling that goes in and out of us from the cosmos. Cosmic life is what we perceive—cosmic life that becomes human soul-life.

If the first verse had to say "behind thinking's sensory light," so now the second verse has to say "see in feeling," which phrase must be harmoniously interwoven with the first verse:

> See in the soul the weaving of feeling,
> How in the dimness of dreams
> Life streams in from worlds afar.
> Let, through the peace of your heart,
> Human feeling waft away in sleep.
> And cosmic life becomes spiritually active
> As the power of man's true being.

[The second verse is written on the blackboard.]

> *See in the soul the weaving of feeling,*
> *How in the dimness of dreams*

Feeling is simply a conscious waking dream. We are not as conscious of our feelings as we are of our thoughts. We are conscious of feelings as in a dream. Consequently, feeling is similar to dreaming during waking life. Therefore, the verse says:

> See in the soul the weaving of feeling,
> How in the dimness of dreams

[Writing continues.]

> <u>Life</u>

In the first verse "will" streams upward from the body's depths. But now "life" streams into the weaving of the soul from the far distances of the cosmos.

Eighth Lesson

Streams in from worlds afar.

[Four horizontal arrows are added to the drawing.]

The point is, in the first verse we should let thinking flow into the cosmic void through strength of soul. Now we let the dreaming-feeling waft away and perceive in its place, within our soul's weaving- feeling, the cosmic life that streams into it. When the dreams of feeling waft away in sleep, when individual human feeling ceases, cosmic life can then stream into us:

Life streams in from worlds afar.

[Writing continues.]

Let, through the peace of your heart

In the first verse we need strength of soul. In the second verse we need complete inner peace and quiet. Then the dreams of feeling will waft away in sleep and cosmic spiritual life will stream into the human soul:

Let, through the peace of your heart,

[The writing continues.]

Human feeling <u>waft away</u> in sleep.
And <u>cosmic life</u> becomes spiritually active
As the <u>power of man's true being</u>.

The whole secret of human feeling is contained in these seven lines, as feeling becomes independent and separates from the unity to become part of a trinity.

We can look at our limbs where the will is expressed in the same way. But when we look at our limbs [Picture 4: white arrow in an elongated, downward form] we cannot say "look behind" or "look into," but we have to say "look over" or "look above;" for thinking streams down from the head into the will. In ordinary consciousness we don't see this, although thoughts stream down from the head into the limbs so the will can *be active* in the limbs.

When we perceive the will working in the limbs, when we see how the stream of will flows into every movement of our arms and legs, we also perceive that a hidden thinking lives in the will, a thinking that directly takes hold of Earth existence. Actually, it is our own being from former Earth lives that takes hold of Earth existence through our limbs so that we can live our present life on Earth. Thinking descends into the limbs. But when we see the will in our limbs, when we see how thinking descends into the will in our limbs, we are seeing thinking in the will [On the left sketch, red swath going down into the elongated form].

When we look with the eye of the soul at how thinking lives in our arms, hands, legs, feet and toes, and is hidden from our ordinary consciousness, then we must see that this thinking is light. Thinking streams as light through our arms, hands, legs and toes. And will, which normally slumbers in our limbs, is transformed. Thinking is revealed as the magical essence of will that moves us from earlier lives into our present Earth life:

> See above the bodily working of will,
> How thinking descends from the forces of the head
> Into slumbering fields of action.
> Let our will be transformed,
> Through the soul's perception, into light.
> And thinking now appears
> As will's magic essence.

It is magic. Unseen thinking acts magically in the will in our limbs. We first understand the human being when we know that, because we are asleep in our will, we don't perceive the thinking that works magically in our limbs as will. A person understands true magic who recognizes the thoughts that live through our arms, hands, legs and toes as magic.

[The third verse is written on the blackboard and the words "thinking," "transformed," "thinking," "will's magic essence" are underlined.]

> *See above the bodily working of will,*
> *How __thinking__ descends from the forces of the head*
> *Into slumbering fields of action.*

Eighth Lesson

> *Let our will be <u>transformed</u>,*
> *Through the soul's perception, into light.*
> *And <u>thinking</u> now appears*
> *As <u>will's magic essence</u>.*

The secret of the human will is contained in these lines, as it works creatively, like magic, from the cosmos into human beings.

Therefore, my dear friends, my dear sisters and brothers, let us consider this as a foundation upon which we will build in future lessons. Let us time and again meditate on these words, letting them flow through our soul.

> See behind thinking's sensory light,
> How in the darkened spirit-cell
> Will ascends from the body's depths.
> Let lifeless thinking flow through the strength of your soul,
> Into the cosmic void.
> And will now rises up
> As cosmic thought-creating.

> See in the soul the weaving of feeling,
> How in the dimness of dreams
> Life streams in from worlds afar.
> Let, through the peace of your heart,
> Human feeling waft away in sleep.
> And cosmic life becomes spiritually active
> As the power of man's true being.

> See above the bodily working of will,
> How thinking descends from the forces of the head
> Into slumbering fields of action.
> Let our will be transformed,
> Through the soul's perception, into light.
> And thinking now appears
> As will's magic essence.

Ninth Lesson

Dornach, April 22, 1924

My dear friends! Without taking any notes, we will first listen and feel in our soul the admonition to the human being that draws our attention to the ancient, sacred word of knowledge:

> O Man, Know Thy Self!
> Thus sounds the Cosmic Word.
> You hear it with strength of soul,
> You feel it with might of spirit.
>
> Who speaks so powerfully through the world?
> Who speaks so tenderly within your heart?
>
> Does it work through the far-spread rays of space
> Into your senses' experience of life?
> Does it sound through the weaving waves of time
> Into the evolving stream of your life?
>
> Is it you, yourself, who,
> By sensing space,
> By experiencing time,
> Begets this word,
> Feeling yourself estranged in the psychic void of space,
> Because you lose the force of thought
> In the annihilating stream of time?

My dear friends, we can look up at the far distant stars and rest our gaze upon all that shines and sparkles from the universe in the fixed stars that show us their variously formed constellations. When we immerse ourselves in all this majesty, which works on us from the far distances of the cosmos, we shall gain an ever-increasing inner strength. And we will especially need this inner strength to free our soul from our body. Especially then do we need to direct our gaze to the starry world so that we do it in a purely inward way. By "inward" is meant that we have looked at the stars ever so often and have kept a picture of this vision in our soul. Then we no longer depend upon seeing the external starry sky in order to activate in our consciousness the majestic image of the vault of heaven, with the stars shining down upon us. When this image arises from our own inner activity, if the soul has the power to create this image by itself, then the soul will first be able to free itself from the body through its strengthened forces.

Then we can turn our attention to all that streams down and shines into us from the planets orbiting the Earth, which carry with them all that lives and weaves in the Earth's wind and weather. And we can again make a conscious image in our soul of all this and fill it with feeling so that we experience how we are woven into the movement of the encircling spheres. We have here a second experience.

Then we can turn our attention to everything that chains us to the Earth, everything that makes us a heavy body among other heavy bodies, everything that makes us feel earthbound. We can call this up vividly in our soul, and it becomes a third experience.

From these three inner experiences we derive the following. First, what we have gained from the stars as a thought that now shines, weaving and living within itself. Second, what we have if we immerse ourselves in the orbit of our Earth on its path through the cosmos and all the meaning the planets say to us through their movements in space—when we, feeling ourselves at rest among the stars, feel ourselves set in motion by the cosmos itself. And third, we feel ourselves bound to the Earth; we are drawn by forces of the Earth itself. These three inner experiences will steadily and properly support the beginning of our entrance into the spiritual world. Today, everyone can make this beginning.

To be sure, the question can be asked: Why is it that so few people make this beginning? The answer must be that most people do not really want to experience anything as intimate as is required to enter the spiritual world. They reject such intimate experiences. They want their experiences to be more exciting. They want the spiritual world to meet them with all the same qualities as the sense world.

People today would be easily convinced of the reality of the spiritual world if, for example, a table were to appear before them from the spiritual world. But there are no tables in the spiritual world. There are only spiritual beings in the spiritual world and they must be perceived by what is spiritual in us. What is spiritual is what we can read in the stars, what we can feel in the movements of the planets, and what we can perceive of the terrestrial forces that hold us to the Earth and make us into earthly human beings.

Therefore, anyone who wants to understand this in the right way must learn to understand it inwardly. All anthroposophic content can be understood with common sense; but to understand this content inwardly means to transform the content into one's inner life. Whoever wishes to understand the transformation of spiritual content into inner life must decide to undergo such intimate exercises as are indicated here by these three feelings, or three experiences...call them what you will.

And today, my dear sisters and brothers, what flows from the spiritual world through this School to you wishes to express how, through an intimate exercise, we can become more aware of humanity's connection with the world, more aware than we are accustomed to perceive with our normal, outer consciousness.

First, we human beings should really make ourselves in later life into what we were to a high degree as a little child. As a child we live almost entirely in our sense organs; we are all eyes and ears. A child experiences everything that happens in its environment as if its entire body were a sense organ. That is why children imitate everything, because everything continues to resonate within them and strives to express itself outwardly again through their will.

A child retains this body-as-sense-organ characteristic only as long as we protect it from doing with its bodily senses what we do with these same senses later on as adults. A child develops this inner sense faculty for as long as we enfold it and protect it from exposure to the forces from the Earth. It is really quite a wonderful thing, while watching a human being grow up, how this sense-being is protected from the influence of terrestrial forces during the time when it is especially alive.

The moment a child stands on its feet and begins to move about, its movements become subject to terrestrial forces and the child has to find its own balance. In that very moment the intimate connections experienced by the child's sense-being come to an end. This is why we do not remember this first stage of human life, why we are quite unaware of what it really means to feel our whole being as a sense organ. But, if we want to experience the true human being more and more in ourselves, we must begin to experience our entire being as a sense organ once again. We must experience ourselves as an organ of touch, as one, great organ of touch throughout our entire body.

My dear sisters and brothers, when you take hold of something, it presses on you and you feel the pressure. Or you perceive its surface texture when you touch it. In actual fact, you are always touching something when you place your entire body on the Earth oriented from above downward. You are always touching the Earth with the soles of your feet, only you are so used to it that you don't notice it. When you begin to notice it, then you really feel yourself as a human being standing amid the forces of the Earth. Therefore, we find this admonition at the threshold of the spiritual world—

[The first two lines are written on the blackboard.]

> O Man, touch and sense through your body's whole being
> How earthly forces <u>support</u> your existence.

With this we allow the first stage of this inner experience to work in us.

Now we can feel ourselves again as human beings who sense things through touch. We can experience the touching itself; we can feel ourselves inwardly as human beings in whom this touching weaves and lives. If we raise ourselves up to feel this touching itself, then we do not perceive just the Earth forces but we begin to perceive the pulsating water forces in us, the fluid forces that, as blood and other sera, surge and weave throughout our body. Then we feel how everything fluid in us, all that surges and weaves as watery substance, is connected with the universal ether.

[Writing on the blackboard continues:]

> *O Man, live and experience in the whole sphere of your touch*
> *How water-beings <u>mold</u> your existence.*

If we only had Earth forces to sense our being through touch, we would appear like something that is continually falling to pieces. The water forces shape and form the human body from the cosmos. The Earth only influences what is solid in us. The whole, vast, etheric world influences what is fluid in us.

Then during the third stage we can enter more deeply into all that lives and weaves in what is fluid. We can feel this inwardly. For example, when we feel our breath, we shall discover how we are nurtured by the nature of breath, by the nature of air. We would be helpless children in this world were it not for the forces of the breath. The forces of breathing continuously flow through us, nurture us, and transform us from helpless children into human beings.

[Writing on the blackboard continues.]

> *O Man, feel and perceive in the whole weaving of your life*
> *How powers of air <u>nurture</u> your existence.*

Now that we have advanced to the third stage of inner experience, we can attain the fourth, where we feel inwardly warmed through, where we become aware of how our own warmth fills us and lives in our breathing and in all the air in us. Only through the air's weaving and living in us is the inner warmth generated that gives our body an inner life.

We can reach the warmth that lives within us with our thoughts. And here we touch upon a very significant secret of human nature.

Ninth Lesson

My dear sisters and brothers, you cannot reach with thought how Earth forces work upon and support you; you can only reach the Earth with the sense of touch. You cannot reach with thought, but only through inner experience, the way water forces form and mold you. You cannot reach with thought, but only inwardly experience, how the forces of air nurture you. You can be grateful that they nurture you. You can love them, but you cannot reach them with your thoughts. But through meditation you can go down into your own warmth with your thoughts and truly experience yourself inwardly as a being of warmth.

A doctor comes with a thermometer and measures the body's warmth externally, from the outside. Just as warmth can differ at different places on the body, so also is warmth different inside the various organs. We can direct our thoughts down to the individual organs and find there an entire inner organism of warmth with all its differentiations. We can reach into ourselves as a warmth organism with thought.

But then, once you've done that, you have a very definite feeling. This feeling, my dear sisters and brothers, will now be brought before your souls. Suppose you succeed in reaching into your differentiated warmth organism with your thoughts. Suppose you succeed in reaching the warmth of your lungs, of your liver and the warmth of your heart. These are, in reality, divine, spirit-created beings inside of you. You penetrate them with your thoughts. Now for the first time you know what thought is. Before this you didn't know what thought was. Now you know that when thought descends into warmth, it turns what previously was merely warmth into flames; it turns it into fire. For in ordinary life thought appears to you as inwardly imperceptible, as abstract thought. When you send thought down into your body, when it enters into your lungs, heart and liver, it appears as luminous and radiant. Just as light issued from your brow reaches downward, so does thought illumine your various organs, differentiating itself into manifold shades of color.

One cannot just say: "I think myself through according to the differentiations of my warmth." One has to say: "I enlighten myself through thoughts according to the differentiations of my warmth."

[Writing continues:]

O Man, think and perceive throughout your flow of feelings
How fire spirits <u>help</u> your existence.

Everything contained in these eight lines can be summed up by letting the experience work once more upon your soul with these words:

[Writing on the blackboard continues, and the elements are added to the corresponding lines.]

O Man, behold yourself in the kingdom of the elements.

Elements:	Earth
	Water
	Air
	Fire

Thus do you measure, radiate and strengthen yourselves with respect to the body. But note, just once, how this strengthening, this measuring, extends from a more physical feeling into a moral feeling.

Here we have the physical support for the human being. EARTH

Here we have the plastic, formative forces, which is still somewhat physical but permeated with the etheric. WATER

Here we have the powers that nurture, which already has a certain morality. As we ascend from water to air we can feel that the beings in the air are already permeated with a moral quality.

And then in fire we not only have beings who nurture us but who also help us. These are friends, comrades, beings who are similar to us.

Just as we feel through to our body in this way, so can we feel through to the soul itself. For this we must not concentrate on the elements, but instead we must concentrate on what pulls the planets that circle the Earth, what draws the currents of the air and the oceans and all that moves along with it. We feel our physical, bodily nature in its spirituality in the way I have explained, but we have to live through to our soul nature. Further details will be developed in later lessons. Today let us briefly write down what can be experienced by living through to our soul.

Ninth Lesson

[The writing on the blackboard continues.]

> *O Man, let hold sway in the depths of your soul*
> *The cosmic powers that guide the planets.*

This, too, can be summarized in the sentence:

> *O Man, come into being through the cosmic circling.*

We realize and experience the spirit in us when we lift up our spirit to the fixed stars that shine down on us in their constellations, forms and figures and thus become like a celestial script. If we preserve what is thus written in the starry heavens, then we shall become aware of our spirituality—a spirituality that doesn't address the human being personally, but speaks about the whole universe.

[Writing on the blackboard continues]

> *O Man, preserve in your spirit's creativity*
> *The heavenly revelation of the stars immobile.*

Summing this up:

> *O Man, create yourself through heaven's wisdom.*

Not through vague generalities, nor through vague sensations, will we be increasingly able to succeed in freeing our souls from our body and go out into the universe. We will be able to do all this, but only in the clear and specific way shown here, by grasping one element after another, by grasping the movement of the planets and the meaning of the stars. If we do this, we unite with the world.

If we do this, we shall soon notice that in carrying out the first part of such an exercise, we feel life within us—the life of the universe.

[Beside the first eight lines of the mantra is written]

> *Life*

Once we have carried out the second part of the exercise, we feel in love with the entire world.

[Beside the tenth and eleventh lines of the mantra is written]

Love

In carrying out the third part of the exercise, we feel a mood of piety. [Beside the thirteenth and fourteenth lines of the mantra is written]

Piety

Truly, an ascent from life through love to piety to a genuine religious experience of the cosmos can be undergone with the help of such mantras.

But then, if this is really undergone and if by means of such an exercise we finally end up in a mood of piety, the world ceases to be physical for us. Then we say to ourselves with complete inner truth: the physical aspect of the world is only semblance; it is only Maya. Everywhere the world is spirit, through and through. As human beings we belong to the spirit. If we feel ourselves as a spirit in the spiritual world, we are on the other side of the threshold.

However, once we are on the other side of the threshold we sense how here on this side of the threshold our body holds thinking, feeling and willing together through its own bodily force. We sense how the minute we are free from our body, our thinking, feeling and willing are no longer one but are three. They are no longer unified but are threefold. Then, if we unite with the terrestrial forces of earth, water, air and fire, we send our will to the Earth and become one with the Earth through our will.

In addition, because we feel love in our soul for the movement of the planets (meaning we feel love for the spiritual beings who live there), we experience the powers orbiting in cosmic space as feeling. If we are able to say: the Sun moves in cosmic space as feeling; Mercury moves in cosmic space as feeling; Mars moves in cosmic space as feeling; then, we have grasped feeling in its cosmic essence when it is separated from thinking and willing.

If we are able to take hold of thinking so that we can free our thoughts from physical existence, it is as though our thinking would fly far out to the stars and come to rest in the stars themselves. And when we have arrived at the other side of the threshold we can say to ourselves: my thinking is at rest in the stars; my feeling is moving with the planets; my willing unites with the forces of the Earth. Thinking, feeling and willing are distributed in the universe in this manner.

They must be joined together again. Here on Earth we don't need to join thinking, feeling and willing together because they are bound together as a unity due to our physical body. Thinking, feeling and willing would continually fall apart if they were not held together by the physical human being without our intending or willing it. But now on the other side of the threshold they are separated. Thinking, feeling and willing are separated so that thinking rests above with the stars; feeling is circling with the planets; and willing unites with the forces of the Earth below. Now we must—with strong, inner determination, by means of our own forces—bring these three back together again into a unity, the three that are far apart on the other side of the threshold.

To achieve this, which is possible through such mantras, we must experience thinking, feeling and willing in such a way that we are able to communicate to thinking, which has gone out to the stars, something of feeling and willing; so that we are able to communicate to feeling, which is orbiting with the planets, something of thinking and willing; and, so that we can communicate to willing, which is bound to the Earth, something of feeling and thinking.

We must look up to the stars and say to ourselves with devotion: my thinking is at rest up there. But I will bring the starry sky into movement in the same way that feeling moves the planets. In spirit I will slowly move the starry sky. I feel attracted to the starry sky; I want to go up there and be one with the star-filled heavens. In this manner I incorporate feeling and willing into thinking, which is bound to the stars. Then I look up to the planets and feel: my own feeling wanders with these planets. But I will try to hold fast to the moment I beheld the ever-moving planets, holding it as fast as the stars are held fast in their positions. And with my entire "middle man," the central part of my nature, through all that belongs to heart and lungs, I will become one with the entire planetary system. Then I have imparted thinking and willing to feeling.

If through this mantric formula I now become aware of how, as a human being, I am bound to the Earth, I ought to add feeling and thinking to my earth-bound condition. I should bring the Earth into movement in thought so that I orbit the Earth like a planet without perceiving its weight. Being earthbound becomes for me as if I carried the Earth along with me through cosmic space. Feeling is thereby mingled with will. Thinking is mixed with will when I move with the Earth in thought, but can also hold it still again, making the Earth into a fixed star through meditation and my own power of thought.

If I do such a meditation and repeat it again and again, I will gradually come to feel myself outside of my body within the cosmic-all. Now, my dear sisters and brothers, let this mantric verse work on you; it can work especially strong on your soul [the new mantra is written on the blackboard].

> *Bring into your thinking*
> *Feeling and will*
> *That irradiate the light-filled soul*
> *As pure reflection.*

—that is, as meditation, as contemplation—

> *And you are a spirit*
> *Among pure spirits.*

Second:

> *Bring into your feelings*
> *Thinking and will*
> *That weave throughout the soul*
> *With warmth as noble love.*
> *And you are a soul*
> *In the realm of the spirits.*

Third:

> *Bring into your powers of will*
> *Thinking and feeling*
> *That actively live in your soul*
> *As spirit-impulse.*
> *And you see yourself*
> *As a body from spiritual heights.*

The human body appears in its true form only when seen in this way.

These mantric verses express what is thus heralded from the spiritual world, what the initiate experiences in the spiritual world. And if inwardly experienced, they will guide us to the spiritual world.

Therefore, if you let these words work upon your soul, they will be a true guide into the spiritual world.

> Bring into your thinking
> Feeling and will
> That irradiate the light-filled soul
> As pure reflection.
> And you are a spirit
> Among pure spirits.

> Bring into your feelings
> Thinking and will
> That weave throughout the soul
> With warmth as noble love.
> And you are a soul
> In the realm of the spirits.

> Bring into your powers of will
> Thinking and feeling
> That actively live in your soul
> As spirit-impulse.
> And you see yourself
> As a body from spiritual heights.

Then, my dear sisters and brothers, when what lies in these mantric verses becomes ever clearer, when you return to these lessons again with ever greater understanding—meaning with enhanced cosmic experience—you will hear these words:

O Man, Know Thy Self!
Thus sounds the Cosmic Word.
You hear it with strength of soul,
You feel it with might of spirit.

Who speaks so powerfully through the world?
Who speaks so tenderly within your heart?

Does it work through the far-spread rays of space
Into your senses' experience of life?
Does it sound through the weaving waves of time
Into the evolving stream of your life?

Is it you, yourself, who,
By sensing space,
By experiencing time,
Begets this word,
Feeling yourself estranged in the psychic void of space
Because you lose the force of thought
In the annihilating stream of time?

Tenth Lesson

Dornach, April 25, 1924

My dear friends! Esoteric development—meaning real knowledge—requires one to find their way to understand what it means to live in a world where the senses and the entire bodily organization no longer act as mediators. This means living with your soul and spirit as a true human being in a world of soul and spirit.

Many different soul exercises—essentially meditative practices—enable us to gradually become capable of living in a world of soul and spirit. A picture will be given in these Class Lessons of what the human soul undergoes on the path from experiencing the world that is real for the senses to experiencing the spiritual world in a sense-free state. A picture will be given through several considerations and by summarizing these considerations in individual mantric verses, which then may be meditated by each person according to their possibilities and needs.

After some time has passed, the communications given in these Class Lessons—genuine communications from the spiritual world itself—will form a coherent whole. Those who have taken part in these lessons, which is also their karma for those who could be present, will have received a complete picture of the first stage of esoteric development.

From the various considerations given here it will become apparent how human beings can gradually rise above Earth existence and develop those inner feelings necessary to have experiences that will carry them into the vast reaches of the cosmos where the spirit comes to meet them. As long as people restrict themselves to connect with their sense-perceptible environment only through their senses and intellect, it will be impossible to make themselves light enough in soul and spirit so that the spirit-soul can grasp the truths accessible to humanity.

You see, my dear friends, I have often stressed the fact that healthy human common sense can understand what is presented in Anthroposophy if it makes enough effort to free itself from prejudice. Yet, common sense understanding is nowadays, in fact, a kind of litmus test to see if someone is truly karmically destined to participate in Anthroposophy.

You see, two possibilities exist. One is that a person hears about anthroposophic truths, lets this content work upon their souls, and they consider these truths to be self-evident. It is obvious that all the friends present here belong to this group. Those who don't belong to this group, but nevertheless wish to participate as a Class member, would not be honest in doing so. In esoteric life everything depends above all on honesty; everything depends that complete honesty permeates the human soul and spirit.

Another group of people finds what is presented in Anthroposophy to be fantastic, something belonging only to visionaries. This group shows by their behavior that they are unable, according to their karma, to sufficiently separate healthy common sense from their physicality and their senses in order to comprehend sense-free truths, sense-free knowledge.

Thus, the extent to which common sense is bound to our bodily nature determines the great divergence between people. If you can honestly say you possess a healthy common sense that understands Anthroposophy, then the moment your common sense understands Anthroposophy, it does so independently of your body. Healthy common sense that sincerely understands Anthroposophy is the beginning of esoteric striving. We should treasure the fact that healthy common sense is the starting point for esoteric striving. This should not be overlooked. For, if we start by understanding things through healthy common sense, and if we follow the instructions given in the appropriate schools, we shall make ever more progress on the esoteric path. You can apply one or another mantric verse given here, according to what suits you. But first, you must always bear in mind the explanations that indicate how the mantras relate to the inner life of human beings.

Today I wish to help again with one of the ways one can be loosened from one's body—even if the loosening is so slight that one doesn't even notice it, or appreciate it.

We should develop with deep inner feelings the ability to stand in the world and observe the minerals, plants and everything else in our environment. We should make ourselves fully aware—if only by thinking about it—of how our terrestrial environment is connected to us and how we, as earthly beings, are connected with our physical nature to everything around us as mineral, plant, animal and so on. Then we might ask ourselves in all honesty: what is it all for? Why do I take in terrestrial substances after I've been born? Why do I drag myself through life, from birth to death, only to end my life when my organism is incapable of assimilating earthly substances? Starting from such a life riddle—one's personal life-mystery—we must learn to feel how deeply connected we are with our physical environment. Then we shall more and more feel what can also become the starting point for esoteric life. Then we really feel that we are blind and groping in the dark in our physical, earthly life.

After all, my dear sisters and brothers, consider how people today are placed in earthly life. Consider how they are educated with the current methods, and then are called to this or that occupation by purely external circumstances. They don't understand the relationship of their work to the totality of human existence. Perhaps they don't know much more than they must work in order to eat. They don't even know that cosmic forces are contained in the plants they eat, forces that pass through their organism and, in a certain sense, undergo thereby a cosmic evolution. As a result of present-day materialism, not even a first glimmer of this can be achieved. Yet, to admit to ourselves that we are spiritually blind as long as we only look at earthly conditions, that we are living in the dark...to admit this is the beginning of true esoteric development.

Then we turn our gaze away from what surrounds us in earthly life and look up toward the star-filled heavens. This can be done either in thought or, if we really want the experience, we may do it in reality. We look up to the planets, we look at the stars and fill ourselves with the endless majesty of what comes toward us from the universe. We then say to ourselves: we are as connected to what shines down upon us from the cosmos as we are connected to all that surrounds us in our physical environment.

Looking at the star-filled heavens in this way we begin to feel that we no longer live in darkness, but are free from a life in darkness. Now we lift our soul-spiritual being up to the stars and to the pictures the starry constellations present. If we are really able to enter into this vision of the stars, then the starry heavens become an abundance of imaginations. You are familiar with the ancient pictures where people not only painted groups of stars but also brought the stars together to create symbols of real animals. Not only were the groups of stars in the Ram or the Bull drawn as groups, but actual symbolic pictures of the Ram and the Bull were represented.

Today, people think that the early inhabitants of the Earth did this arbitrarily—because the constellations were named that way and pictures were painted in that fashion. But in fact, it was not like that. In primeval times the shepherds in the fields looked at the stars not just with their physical eyes. While tending their flocks they fell into a dream consciousness, or fell asleep, and when their eyes were closed, their souls looked out into cosmic space. They didn't see the constellations as our eyes see them today. In fact, they perceived those pictures and imaginations that filled cosmic space, albeit a little differently from what is shown in later paintings.

We can no longer go back to what the simple shepherds experienced with instinctive clairvoyance...but we can do something else. With far greater thoughtfulness we can imagine ourselves into the star-filled sky either in thought or in real life. We can feel the depth and simultaneously see the majesty of what shines toward us. Gradually we are able to feel a sense of veneration for what is out there in the cosmos. And this very reverence, this ardent attitude of reverence, can call forth in our soul an experience when the outer sense-perceptible pictures of the stars disappear and the starlit sky becomes an Imagination. But then, if the starry sky has become an Imagination, we feel borne upward by our soul's vision.

You see, people in Plato's time still felt something very special about the physical eye while it is in the act of observing. Plato himself described the act of seeing as follows: when I look at someone I simply go out to them from my eye. In ancient times people were aware of something streaming out from their eye and embracing the person looked at. Something etheric streams out from the eye. Just as when I stretch out my hand and take hold of something, I know through my hand that I am in contact with what I am grasping, so in the time of ancient clairvoyance people knew that something etheric goes out from the eye and embraces what is being looked at. Today people believe that the eye is here and that the object seen is over there. Then the object sends out some kind of etheric movements that drum upon the eye and the drumming is then perceived by some kind of soul (even materialists speak about soul, without having any notion of what it might be). But it is not like that. Seeing is not just an effect produced by the object upon the person. Seeing is an actual outpouring of inner etheric substance *from* the person.

We perceive our etheric body and how our etheric body belongs to the universe when the starlit heavens become a great, open page of the cosmos, where the imaginative secrets of world existence are written...if we are able to see them.

Then the feeling comes over us: while you dwell here on Earth you live in a robust, sense-perceptible reality. However, you are blind; you live in darkness. When you rise up with your whole heart and mind you live within what otherwise shines down upon you from the distant universe. You live in the semblance of that distant universe. But at the same time you take your own etheric being out into the distant, flowing streams of the shining universe. You go into it with your etheric being.

Then the shining ceases to be shining. But, if we immerse ourselves in it, it cannot be nothing. We extend the reality of our inner being into this shining. And the experience I just described becomes a weaving in the cosmic shining. Before this, we lived like a blind person in the darkness of

Earth existence. Now we journey out and begin to weave with our etheric being in the shining cosmos.

But if we have the feeling that we are weaving within the shining cosmos...I will draw a picture of it [drawing on the blackboard, picture 5].

Here is our life, blinded by darkness [white arc]. Then we journey into the far distant universe [yellow rays] at whose end we can feel the cosmic Imaginations through our reverence for the shining stars [red waves].

We have traveled out of ourselves and with our etheric being are now inside this imaginative weaving of the world fabric. If we succeed at being inside this imaginative weaving of the world fabric, then we are no longer in our physical body. We have worked our way through the empty ether to the experience of cosmic Imaginations.

This is similar to when someone writes something down in the physical world and, having learned to read, they read it. The gods have written world Imaginations for us in the cosmos. By moving out into the cosmos, we perceive these world Imaginations from the other side [inward pointing arrows in the first drawing of picture 5]. First, we live here on the Earth [second drawing in picture 5: inner circle]. Then we soar upward to the world Imaginations [second drawing: outer wavy circle]. There we read these Imaginations from the other side [second drawing: inward pointing arrows].

Yes, my dear friends, my sisters and brothers, the zodiac speaks a significant language when we no longer look at it from the perspective of the Earth—ram, bull, twins, crab, lion, etc. It speaks a different language when we circle around it from the other side. This is a deed from our consciousness; we begin to read the secrets of worlds. We read the deeds of spiritual beings, just as we read about human deeds in a novel. When we look at the zodiac from the other side and read what from the Earth we only see from behind, it is comparable to what Moses was told that he might see God on Earth only from behind. For initiation is precisely this: that we are able to see from the other side of the threshold. There, seeing is not just looking but is also reading. We read the spiritual deeds of spiritual beings who have brought everything into existence.

And if we read long enough in this silence, if we put our heart and soul into this reading, we begin to hear in the spirit, and then the gods speak to us. And when the gods speak to us we are within the spiritual world.

My dear sisters and brothers, an initiate can tell you that the soul can expand into the cosmos, that we can receive world Imaginations and behold the deeds of the gods, that we can read their spiritual deeds from the other side and become capable of spiritually hearing the language of the gods. If we really enter what the initiate tells us and ponder it deeply with strong heartfelt feelings, this can happen. We shouldn't just listen greedily saying, "It would please me if I could do that. It would interest me, but as it is, I don't care." However, if we receive what is told as something that is really possible, if we begin to consider it as something that can be revered, that can be loved, that can be meditated upon repeatedly, then that way we can enter into esoteric life ourselves.

We can find this way if we meditate upon and ponder the words: [The first part of the mantra is written on the blackboard.]

1. *I live in the dark realm of the Earth,*
2. *I weave in the shining light of the stars,*
3. *I read in the deeds of the spirits,*
4. *I hear in the speech of the gods,*

Experiencing these words with the requisite feeling in meditation will work wonders in the human soul. They will transform the soul. They must flow rhythmically through the soul time and again because, in truth, they guide the human being to the cosmic being contained within his own soul.

It is necessary that such things are deeply internalized. After these words have spoken more to the head, the heart must also participate in the whole process of going out into the etheric universe, then into the spiritual universe, that is to say, into the other side of the universe. It is necessary that we take our hearts with us during this experience and call to life the feelings that, quite naturally, accompany this outward journey. But we must make these feelings truly alive. Therefore, it is good to undertake this meditative path by first completely steeping ourselves in the inner vision contained in these words:

> I live in the dark realm of the Earth,
> I weave in the shining light of the stars,
> I read in the deeds of the spirits,
> I hear in the speech of the gods,

Then try to imagine that someone else is speaking to you out the spiritual depths...not as if you are thinking it, but as if you are hearing it spoken by another being. Really try to picture that another being is speaking to you from unknown depths. Then try to generate the proper feelings for what you are hearing.

These feelings live in the second part of the mantra [the second part of the mantra is written on the blackboard.]

> 5. Earth's darkness fills me with longing,
> 6. The shining stars comfort me,

To the extent I am aware that I really live in the darkness of the Earth as if blind, to the same extent will I long to reach out, to get out, of that darkness. Once out, I am comforted by the shining stars into which my being expands:

> The shining stars comfort me,

Now from the other side:

> 7. The deeds of the spirits are teaching me,

—When I read them—

> 8. The speech of the gods works creatively in me,

Now, this mantra has to be used in the right way. While practicing this inner meditation, vividly imagine that you experience—as if from the depths of the spirit—that someone else, another being, addresses you with the first four lines of the verse. Then, generate the corresponding feeling

Tenth Lesson

for each line of the verse, so that your experience is: first you listen, then you bring the corresponding feeling to it. First listen, then meet it with feeling, and so on.

[As the following lines are spoken, connecting curves link lines 1 and 5, lines 2 and 6, lines 3 and 7, and lines 4 and 8.]

> I live in the dark realm of the Earth,
> Earth's darkness fills me with longing,
>
> I weave in the shining light of the stars,
> The shining stars comfort me,
>
> I read in the deeds of the spirits,
> The deeds of the spirits are teaching me,
>
> I hear in the speech of the gods,
> The speech of the gods works creatively in me,

This meditation is a dialogue. Always objectify the first line; then feel the second line pouring out from your heart.

Then try once more to become aware of how these lines work and weave within each other. Then try to feel what can be experienced with your will through this dialogue.

[The third part of the mantra is developed in connection with the first and second parts, while lines 9, 10, 11 and 12 are written on the blackboard.]

> From spirit depths resounds:
> I live in the dark realm of the Earth,

—The heart answers:

> Earth's darkness fills me with longing.

Then the will feels the impulse in the dialogue between lines 1 and 5:

> 9. *Earth's darkness extinguishes me.*

After this dialogue, call to mind once more the alternation of lines 2 and 6, which was:

> I weave in the shining light of the stars,
> The shining stars comfort me,
>
> 10. *The starlight's shining awakens me.*

Also, keep in mind what sounded from the spirit depths and recall the heart's response:

> I read in the deeds of the spirits,
> The deeds of the spirits are teaching me,
> Now the will feels:
>
> 11. *The deeds of the spirits call to me.*
>
> —they call me into the spiritual world.

Now comes the most sublime of all, where we feel ourselves in dialogue with the gods themselves...where the gods not only let us read, but speak:

> I hear in the speech of the gods,
> The speech of the gods works creatively in me,
>
> 12. *The speech of the gods begets me.*
>
> —It brings me forth; it creates me.

Now, imagine the entire meditation line by line. It is a dialogue with a spiritual being present in the darkened depths of spirit, who always speaks the first line of each verse, and each time our heart replies:

> I live in the dark realm of the Earth,
> Earth's darkness fills me with longing,
>
> I weave in the shining light of the stars,
> The shining stars comfort me,
>
> I read in the deeds of the spirits,
> The deeds of the spirits are teaching me,

Tenth Lesson

>   I hear in the speech of the gods,
>   The speech of the gods works creatively in me,

Now each line is recalled. I will add to it the outpouring of will, like a remembering of what has just gone on before:

>   I live in the dark realm of the Earth,
>   Earth's darkness fills me with longing,
>   Earth's darkness extinguishes me.
>
>   I weave in the shining light of the stars,
>   The shining stars comfort me,
>   The starlight's shining awakens me.
>
>   I read in the deeds of the spirits,
>   The deeds of the spirits are teaching me,
>   The deeds of the spirits call to me.
>
>   I hear in the speech of the gods,
>   The speech of the gods works creatively in me,
>   The speech of the gods begets me.

Coming to the right conviction in the dialogue results from meditating, recalling the dialogue and strengthening our recollection with our will.

If you start first with reverential feelings, and then second, if you do what I've described with inner participation, living in it and imagining it—not doing a mechanical meditation, but experiencing the meditation with your soul—this will establish a relationship to the spiritual world that will have an awakening affect upon your soul.

As I've described, the last verse must also be experienced as the remembering of a call-and-response: the call of the spirit and the response of the heart. To begin with, we must rightly feel as if the consciousness we wish to attain is extinguished by the darkness of the Earth. We have to feel as if a moment of sleep would extinguish our consciousness and how, after awakening in the second line, we hear the call of the spirits, we hear them calling us to them. Finally, we feel that spiritual beings have called us from the word of their own being, from the Cosmic Word itself, so that they may bring us forth, so that they may beget us, as beings of soul and spirit in the spiritual world.

If these nuances of inner experience pass through our soul, and if the imaginations of the spiritual being speaking to us are present, and if we bring them to life in our heart and send our devotion to that spiritual being, then our soul will be stirred by those deep feelings that, in due time, will bring our soul onto the esoteric path. For we must know that subconsciously our soul is going through mighty experiences while we make these mantras alive in our soul, as best we can. If we live sincerely in these verses in the way I've indicated, then when the first line sounds, our soul goes back unconsciously to the starting point of our life on Earth when our etheric body was first formed.

If we can, vividly imagine how this sounds to us from the spirit:

> I live in the dark realm of the Earth,

—Hearing this in the spirit, we unconsciously approach the moment when our etheric body was formed. A force works in from pre-earthly life, from the life between death and a new birth, which we honestly respond to with our heart:

> Earth's darkness fills me with longing,

—Because we bring with us the soul's yearning for the spirit as a heritage from pre-earthly existence.

Then we are again transported back to the beginning of our Earth life. What works in the warmth of our heart is what was kindled in us from pre-earthly existence:

> I weave in the shining light of the stars,

—We are transported back to the beginning of our Earth life. When thus transported, we feel the real comfort the shining stars can give us in our heart's reply:

> The shining stars comfort me,

And then:

> I read in the deeds of the spirits,

—We are transported back to the beginning of our Earth life. We recall how we were taught by spiritual beings in the life before birth:

> The deeds of the spirits are teaching me,

—Among whom I lived and weaved before I came down to Earth.

> I hear in the speech of the gods,

We have heard the gods between death and a new birth. We feel that what the gods say is not mere information, as when human beings talk. We realize that the speech of the gods is creative:

> The speech of the gods works creatively in me,

But then, if we can perceive it thus, lines 9, 10, 11, and 12 receive their proper meaning:

> I live in the dark realm of Earth,
> Earth's darkness fills me with longing,

[Line 9 is written on the blackboard again, adjacent to the curve joining lines 1 and 5.]

> *Earth's darkness extinguishes me.*

—It extinguishes my present Earth life. Then I am led back right through the region between death and a new birth and into my former incarnation. As a result, I recognize that my present consciousness is extinguished because my consciousness was, until now, the consciousness of my present incarnation.

In this moment of sleep I am carried back so that I am able to feel that I am weaving my former incarnation on Earth:

> I weave in the shining light of the stars,
> The shining stars comfort me,

[Line 10 is written on the blackboard again, adjacent to the curve joining lines 2 and 6.]

The starlight's shining awakens me.

I am carried back to what I was in my former incarnation and awakened in it. My karma, the connections of my destiny, dawn upon me from the other side:

*I read in the deeds of the spirits,
The deeds of the spirits are teaching me,*

[Line 11 is written on the blackboard again, adjacent to the curve joining lines 3 and 7.]

The deeds of the spirits call to me.

—They call me to fulfill my karma with the forces originating from my prior life on Earth.

*I hear in the speech of the gods,
The speech of the gods works creatively in me,*

[Line 12 is written on the blackboard again, adjacent to the curve joining lines 4 and 8.]

The speech of the gods begets me.

Everything I am becomes clear, now that my former Earth life permeates, radiates, weaves and pulsates through my present life. There I am. My present "I" is in the process of becoming. It is but a seed that will receive its meaning only when I have passed through the gate of death. What shines in, what works and weaves in from my previous incarnation into my present one makes me into a human being...creates me as an existing human being.

If we are truly convinced that this is the case—although we believe we are only here in the ordinary world of physical existence—our soul really makes a journey back into our former life on Earth where we become aware of the significance of what we experience here. The realization of this will flow as a flood of warming light through all our thinking, willing and feeling. Then our meditations will be filled with an inward magical feeling that is necessary for the meditation to work in the right way. We call it an "inner magical feeling" because it cannot be compared to any other feeling on Earth, because it is felt independently of the body. Even if, with our existing thinking and visualization capacities, we cannot, as yet, get out of our physical body, this magical feeling lives in the purely spiritual world. We can experience it through the gravity of our soul's activity. We experience pure soul-spirit in this magical feeling. We stand within the world of spirit and soul.

We find fulfillment in the way we experience our esoteric striving. This is what I was obliged to place before your souls today, my dear sisters and brothers.

(...)

Eleventh Lesson

Dornach, May 2, 1924

My dear friends! (...) My dear friends, in esoteric life it is essential that one should at least envision the path where real knowledge of spiritual things can be realized. How far one person or another will progress along this path depends upon their karma. It depends on what conditions they bring from their former Earth lives.

Yet, progress not only depends on such conditions, as you also know from exoteric lectures previously given here. Progress also depends upon the kind of body and on the world situation a person is destined to meet in their life on Earth. Many old karmic remnants must be worked out, and these are a hindrance for pursuing and achieving what may very well exist as potential. Many things that might well be achieved in a shorter time can only be achieved over a longer period, but for these karmic remnants.

We should never give up hope, never lose patience or energy, but we should continue on our path. When the right time has come we will surely find what is predestined for us. Notwithstanding freedom, perhaps even because of freedom, everyone's path has been predestined, to a certain extent. Every person is called to their proper task in the world, a task that will be fulfilled, if the good will exists to do so.

Here in the School for Spiritual Science everything that lived in the Mysteries, at the time when the Mysteries were truly flourishing, should really come to life again in the proper form for our time and for future times. The golden age of the Mysteries was already past when the greatest, yet most veiled of all mysteries—the Mystery of Golgotha—took place in world history. The high point of the Mysteries was already past at that point. It was followed by a period in human history and evolution when the Mysteries receded. Due to the decline in the Mysteries, people became ever more taken up into the stream of world evolution that leads to freedom. But now the time has come when the Mysteries must come to life again in a form that is right for us today in the fullest sense of the word. The historic task of the Goetheanum will be respected in the future when these things will be rightly thought about in the world. For then it will be recognized that the Goetheanum had the task of renewing the life of the Mysteries. My dear sisters and brothers, only if we are permeated with the will to regard the School in this manner—as representing a renewal of the Mysteries in the fullest sense—only then do we stand in the right relationship to these Mysteries and also to this School.

If you recall what was brought before you here in our previous lesson, then what has just been said can live in your hearts and minds. For in the previous lesson the transition was made whereby the practice of meditation enters so directly into one's immediate experience that the meditant is freed from the narrow bonds of personality.

We saw in the threefold structure of the last meditation how a person is placed in the world process in such a way that in meditation the meditant confronts not only what sounds *from* our soul, but also meets what sounds *toward* our soul, which in a certain way incorporates itself into a general cosmic language, a kind of universal Cosmic Word. Only if a gradual loosening of the individual from their personality is brought about, and only if one learns to meditate in an increasingly objective way, will the meditant be able to tread the intimate and subtle path—the true path—to human knowledge. But in order that this might be accomplished, those truths that apply to human beings must become objectively present within us in the most varied ways.

My dear sisters and brothers, you all know what has often been described as the threefold nature of the human being, where: the nerve-sense system is mainly represented by the human head; the rhythmical system is mainly represented by the chest where our respiratory and blood circulation organs are concentrated. The activity of these organs permeates the entire human organism but is more concentrated in the organs themselves than at other places. Finally, we have the metabolic–limb organization that is centered and localized downward and outward.

What can be known in this way can remain theoretical to a certain extent; but, it can also take on an objective presence in meditation. When it becomes objectively present in meditation it then passes over into the esoteric realm. Therefore, we must picture the threefold human being in our meditation in the most intense and intimate way.

In the head organization we have a true image of the whole cosmos. Then we have the breast or rhythmic organization, whose form does not reveal an image of the cosmos directly. And the metabolic-limb system reveals an image of the cosmos least of all. We must become inwardly aware of how we individually stand within the cosmos in each of these organizations. What actually lives and works in our head must become clear to us. We can immediately feel when we are thinking, because our head is active. Notice that when our head is ailing, our ability to think shuts down. In both normal and abnormal circumstances we can feel that our head is associated with the clearest and brightest of human activities. That is not to say that the head is the actual carrier of this bright and clear human activity; but what we feel makes it seem that it is.

Yet, what is the real truth? When do we see our own heads in the right way? Only when we are aware that this human head would not exist but for the vault of the starlit sky above. For the moment we shouldn't argue about what astronomy has to say about this. We will simply take into account what our eyes behold in the majestic starlit heavens.

Many things have already been said about this in previous lessons. The stars are above us and their shining rays come toward us when we look up to them. But they not only approach us, we also receive them. And we enclose what we receive from the stars within our head. From this sprouts and grows the most human activity on Earth: our thinking. Imagine it like this. Out there are the stars; our head receives the effects of their shining rays. From the outside it looks like the stars were sending their rays down

Eleventh Lesson

to us. Here our head receives the rays and what has been received from the stars is now inside our head. What is inside our head seems quite different from what is out there, and yet it is the same. The entire starlit sky, so to speak, is gathered up into a scroll in our head.

But do only the starry heavens shine down on us? No, not just the starry heavens. Then, what are the stars? What is it that shines down on us from all the individual stars? The stars are the dwelling places of the gods, the places where the gods live. That is where the gods were sought in times gone by, when instinctive clairvoyance knew where the gods lived and what dwelling places were worthy of the gods.

When such ancient clairvoyance existed, people did not look up at fiery points in the heavens, as is the case today. They looked up to the dwelling places of the gods. In doing so, they had a better idea, a truer idea, of what exists in the vast, cosmic expanse than what happens today, when astronomers look up at points of light and calculate their locations and positions.

Given that each person is a threefold being, each person speaks and acts with their "I" through what holds their three bodies together, through all the parts of their threefold being. We speak and act: through the nerve-sense system centered in the head; through the rhythmical system centered in the breast; and, through the metabolic-limb system. All of this is only held together as a unity by the physical body. But a person always sends their I through all three members. Today we will learn to distinguish the ways one sends the "I" into the individual members.

At first we speak "I" from the innermost core of our being into our head through our thoughts. It is like this [drawing begins, picture six]. What unfolds outside in the radiance of the stars [blue arc, yellow stars] also works in the human head [yellow arc and rays streaming from the stars]. It is also there inside [red dots] the head. A person speaks "I" from the central core of their being into this rolled-together cosmic space, which is the interior of our head [upward pointing arrow with the word "*I*" in yellow]. We must become aware that when we speak "I" into that part of our being that is an image of the home of the gods, the gods themselves who inhabit that dwelling are at work. We meditate correctly when we are aware that when we say "I" through the force of our head, the gods of cosmic space and time are speaking to us.

This teaching is not given to us on Earth. This teaching, my dear sisters and brothers, is given to us by the beings of the higher hierarchies themselves... first by the beings who accompany us as earthly human beings—the Angels—and in the background, by the directing Archangels. This element of human nature, this I, has a relationship to the dwellings of the gods in the radiant stars from which the divine beings speak. This "I" should let itself be taught about its own essential nature by these beings whom, in our descriptions of the hierarchies, we have always referred to as Angels.

We meditate in the right way as follows: we look up and receive the impression of the radiant stars and imagine that cosmic space itself sounds forth to us in words. These words should be:

> Cosmic starry spaces,
> Homeland of the gods!

Thus it sounds from the periphery. We imagine that we hear it from the far reaches of the cosmos.

> Cosmic starry spaces,
> Homeland of the gods!

This echoes within us. We treat it as a call, but a call that excites us because all of heaven resounds within that call. This is how to meditate. Then we become conscious of what we have to say from the depths of our soul, where in stillness we answer the cosmic trumpet call:

> From the head held on high
> Human spirit-radiance speaks
> "I am"

That is what *we* say. Now the Angel who belongs to us answers us during our meditation. When the I speaks, when the I says "I am," our Angel answers:

> Thus do you live

—You, meaning, the gods—

> Within the earthly body
> As human being.

That is the meaning of this meditation. We hear it like a worldwide trumpet call, sounding in from all sides:

> Cosmic starry spaces,
> Homeland of the gods!

We answer silently from within ourselves, in a prayerful mood:

> From the head held on high
> Human spirit-radiance speaks
> "I am"

The Angel answers, gazing upward to the source of the trumpet call:

> Thus do you (the gods) live
> Within the earthly body
> As human being.

And we take the last two lines the Angel speaks into our meditation as a teaching, as instruction.

[The first verse is written on the blackboard:]

> *Cosmic starry spaces,*
> *Homeland of the gods!*
> *From the head held <u>on high</u>*
> *Human spirit-radiance <u>speaks</u>*

—That is, the collected radiance of the stars, which becomes human radiance—

> "I <u>am</u>"

Then the Angel, the spiritual teacher, speaks:

> Thus do you (the gods) <u>live</u>

—That is, the starry worlds, the cosmos of star-filled spaces, homeland of the Gods—

> *within the <u>earthly body</u>*
> *As human being*

This is the first dialogue with the cosmos and the third hierarchy. Conceived in this way, it is a meditation that deeply penetrates the human spirit, the human soul and the human body.

Now we proceed further to the rhythmic organization. Think of the lungs and heart, their wonderful pulsation, the rhythm of breathing that in itself reveals an expression of the deepest cosmic law, whose movement we feel in us. If we enter meditatively into our head, we feel it to be at rest. But if we enter meditatively into our breast, we feel movement. This movement is an image of the movement of the planets, of the moon, the sun, Mars, Mercury, Jupiter, Venus and Saturn. The sun, which feels closest to us, represents this movement. With its apparent course around the Earth each day, the sun may stand as a representative. Just as we carry the star-filled places of the world, the homeland of the gods, rolled up inside our head, so do we carry the movement of the entire planetary system—represented by the sun—in our breathing, in our blood circulation and in all that is in movement in our organism.

Therefore, we must imagine that just as the majesty of the dwelling places of the gods was first announced like a trumpet call from all sides of the world, so now all that the movements of the planets, represented by the sun, say to us will flow through our body like a melodious sound:

> Circling cosmic sun,
> Paths of spirit action!

This is the second part, and it is quiet as compared to the great trumpet call of the world.

> Cosmic starry spaces,
> Homeland of the gods!

This sounds majestically from all directions. This is what we must meditate on. But, when meditating upon the path of the sun and planets through our breathing and blood circulation, it resounds blissfully, permeating our inner life:

> Circling cosmic sun,
> Paths of spirit action!

Now, inspired by what sounds melodiously in our body from the circling stars we speak to ourselves again, intimately:

> Human soul's weaving
> Sounds in the center of the heart
> "I live"

Now the Angel answers, addressing the gods who are active in the planets:

> Thus do you (the gods) tread the earthly path
> As human creative force.

As human beings live on the Earth through what streams into them from the dwellings of the gods, so does the human creative power live in the course of our lives on Earth through the activity of the gods in the movement of the planets. This is received into our entire rhythmic system. Again, we have here a threefold mantra: first, the objective sound as it passes through our body when we meditate upon the course of the planets; then, our own intimate response; and finally, our Angel's answer:

> Circling cosmic sun,
> Paths of spirit action!

> Human soul's weaving
> Sounds in the center of the heart
> "I live"
> Thus do you (the gods) tread the earthly path
>
> As human creative force.

[Now the second verse is written on the blackboard:]

> *Circling cosmic sun*
> *Paths of spirit action!*
> *Human soul's weaving* <u>sounds</u>
> *In the* <u>center</u> *of the heart*

—Above we have "speaks," here "sounds." Above we have "in the head held on high," here "in the center of the heart"—

> "I <u>live</u>"

—Above we have "I am"; here "I live"—

> *Thus do you (the gods) tread the* <u>earthly path</u>
> *As human creative force.*

Each mantric verse must be felt in a threefold way. Three things contribute to the creation of the verse: first, the objective sounding forth; then, our own intimate answer as an echo in us; and finally, the words of the Angel. Then the meditation will work in us in the right way.

As we proceed to the third aspect of the human being—to what lives in the arms and legs and continues inward in the metabolism—then we hear not the trumpet call from cosmic space, not the melody of the planets, but we hear the deep rumbling of the foundations of the world itself. This deep rumbling of the very foundations of the world lives in that part of us that makes us earthly human beings. Our limbs have no share in our conscious spiritual life, because they are completely formed and shaped through terrestrial forces, although our arms and hands are also formed by forces of the air. These terrestrial forces stream upward into the human being from the world's foundations. We must become conscious of this. Just as in the first verse we hear the speech of the cosmos sounding majestically from the world periphery; and as in the second verse we hear the speech of the circumference; now, in the third verse we hear the rumbling, murmuring language of the world's foundation from the depths of the Earth:

> World foundation powers,
> Radiant love of the Creator!

Eleventh Lesson

—This is not a radiance of light, but a radiance of love.—

For in those places where what otherwise lies in the periphery is gathered in the center, there lies the origin of the forces of love. Therefore, we cannot respond with an echoing answer "speak," or with "sound." Here we must answer with a deed, with something that flows from our will. Here we must not "speak," we must not "sound." We must "create." Now we answer from our inner being, pouring will into our words:

> <u>Create</u> in the body's <u>limbs</u>
> Streams of human action
>   "I will"

Now the angel answers and turns its gaze downward to what rumbles up from the world's foundation. "Rumbles" is not meant in an unsympathetic way; it is used only because of the deep dullness of the sound. The angel responds to the powers at work in the depths of the world's foundation:

> Thus do you (the gods) strive in earthly activity
> As human sense-world deeds.

Again the verse is threefold.

> World foundation powers,
> Radiant love of the Creator!
> Create in the body's limbs
> Streams of human action
>   "I will"

> Thus do you (the gods) strive in earthly activity
> As human sense-world deeds.

Now the third verse is written on the blackboard.

> *World foundation powers,*
> *Radiant love of the Creator!*
> *Create in the body's limbs*
> *Streams of human action*

—"*peaks,* "*Sounds, Create, on high, center of the heart, limbs,* which from the center strives outward—

"*I will*"

—*I am, live, will*—

Thus do you (the gods) strive in *earthly activity*

—*earthly body, earthly path, earthly activity*—

As human *sense-world deeds.*

—*human being, creative power, sense-world deeds*—that is, deeds that are visible to the outer senses.—

True meditation, the true exercise of the soul, does not live in the theoretical, intellectual content of a meditative verse; it lives in its mantric character. The mantric character of a verse is reached when the meaning of the verse is dissolved into situations, into spiritual events, so that through this we are freed from the theoretical-intellectual content and we go beyond the self, we go outside of our self. In doing so we carry something in our thoughts that is not undefined. We have a living picture of how the heavens, the encircling round and the depths of the Earth are sounding forth. And then, we ourselves respond to these sounds from the inner core of our being. Then, our Angel interprets for us and teaches us.

We should strive to attain to such an ideal setting and make the meditation into something where we not only think, feel or will but into something that is present around us, something that weaves, streams, shines and radiates around us. Then something from this weaving, streaming and shining pours back into the life of our heart, and it keeps shining and streaming in our heart, so that we feel ourselves interwoven with the weaving life of the cosmos. Now we feel that the meditation is not only alive in us but is alive in the cosmos as well. It extinguishes the cosmos and then extinguishes us, and in the extinguishing, unites us with the cosmos. We can just as easily say: "the cosmos speaks" as we can say, "we ourselves are speaking." This gradually expands the character of the meditation.

If the meditation is practiced in this way—experiencing the dissolution of what had appeared to be one's ordinary self—it will gradually be possible to perceive one's self as real spirit

Insofar as we enter onto such a path of knowledge and honestly approach such paths, we learn to know that in meditating we are not alone in the world. We are in a dialogue with the spiritual world and are coming increasingly closer to a true renewal of the Holy Mysteries. Certainly there once were outer temples; they were perhaps in places on Earth that we today would call uncivilized areas. Outer temples were there and people needed these outer temples in the past. But these outer temples were not the only ones; they were not the most important ones. The most important, the most significant, temples have neither place nor time. One reaches them only by traveling "60 miles," so to speak. We reach them when we exercise our soul in the manner described here and in the way it was in the Mysteries throughout all time.

Let us be very clear about this, my dear sisters and brothers. Living in this way in such a mantric formula things are like this. Here I stand—each of us may rightly say this—and all around me is the everyday, ordinary world. Ordinary walls and chairs or maybe a natural forest, visible trees or houses… all these surround me. All of this is here. I am fully conscious that this is my environment; it is there. I can see it and touch it. And now the meditation arises in my soul while I am in this external, dull, sense world. The meditation arises in me:

> Cosmic starry spaces,
> Homeland of the gods!
>
> From the head held on high
> Human spirit-radiance speaks
> "I am"
>
> Thus do you (the gods) live within the earthly body
> As human being.

What do I feel weaving around me? What do I feel forming above me? It is something; it is nothing. I can sense the presence of walls, but I don't see them.

> The meditation continues:
>
> Circling cosmic sun,
> Paths of spirit action!
>
> Human soul's weaving sounds
> In the center of the heart
> "I live"
>
> Thus do you (the gods) tread the earthly path
> As human creative force.

What I felt weaving and forming above me—a temple vault, a temple roof, temple walls—begins to be visible to the eye of the soul. It hovers around me. Now all that was previously visible around me, the ordinary, visible world of trees, clouds and so on, becomes invisible. Something new stands there and becomes visible. The temple, which I had only sensed at first, becomes real in the second verse.

> And now I hear the murmuring, rushing and growling from below:
>
> World foundation powers,
> Radiant love of the Creator!
>
> Create in the body's limbs
> Streams of human action
> "I will"
>
> Thus do you (the gods) strive in earthly activity
> As human sense-world deeds.

The temple is complete. It has secured its foundation. And in the temple are those spiritual beings with whom we want to make a connection. The temple is there. It is visible to the eye of the soul. The temple has been found.

Meditation does not exist so that we may have visions. Meditation leads us into the spiritual world. The spiritual world arises. My dear sisters and brothers, I am describing how this meditation can take its course. After the first verse we feel the temple vault weaving above us and with the eye of the soul we see the temple around us. The temple is completed. In the temple are the beings we want to connect with, the gods, the teachers of humanity. We are inside the temple. This is brought about by the first, second and third verses of a true mantric meditation. It is the path to the temple. It is a true spiritual path.

If we become aware of the fact that we can find the temple, then we rightly understand what the content of this esoteric School is meant to be.

(...)

Twelfth Lesson

Dornach, May 11, 1924

My dear friends! To begin with, we will speak the verse that make us aware of what comes from the cosmos itself as a call to acquire self-knowledge:

O Man, Know Thy Self!
Thus sounds the Cosmic Word.
You hear it with strength of soul,
You feel it with might of spirit.

Who speaks so powerfully through the world?
Who speaks so tenderly within your heart?

Does it work through the far-spread rays of space
Into your senses' experience of life?
Does it sound through the weaving waves of time
Into the evolving stream of your life?

Is it you, yourself, who,
By sensing space,
By experiencing time,
Begets this word,
Feeling yourself estranged in the psychic void of space,
Because you lose the force of thought
In the annihilating stream of time?

My dear sisters and brothers, self-knowledge is what can lead us in a spiritual sense to knowledge of the cosmos. It has often been said that there has to be understanding for the way spiritual knowledge flows from the spiritual world itself. People must understand how all who are able to communicate knowledge of the spiritual world have to approach the threshold. The Guardian of the Threshold stands at the threshold and protects human beings in their ordinary consciousness from entering into the spiritual world unprepared.

But, just when we get to know the Guardian, at first through healthy human understanding, then later—after being prepared through such healthy human understanding we come to know him in his true form, in his real being—then, if we want to enter the spiritual world in the right way the Guardian presents us with his counsel, his guidance. And then we stand within the experiences of the spiritual world in the right way.

Now, it is often said that living within the spiritual world is pictured incorrectly because people want something other than what it is actually like to be in the spiritual world. They want it to be something similar to the sense world. But that is not how it is in the spiritual world. It is, after all, suprasensory and can never lead to a vision that is comparable to sense-perceptible vision. Imaginative suprasensory vision is, in fact, only a picture and the picture must lead to a real experience of the spiritual world. My dear sisters and brothers, many of you have far more experience in the spiritual world than you think. You are merely not attentive enough. You do not pay attention to how the spiritual works and weaves in your soul's experience. The spiritual works and weaves within you. The real need is to bring intimate attention to this working and weaving and to perceive it.

My dear sisters and brothers, knowledge flows in these Class Lessons directly to you from the spiritual world. Real indications will repeatedly be given so that you can feel how the human soul stands in the spiritual world. The following is such an indication.

Take one of the mantras, or some other verse, and speak what lies in it. It doesn't matter which one, although it should be one you know well. Take any mantra for your meditation and speak it in the most beautiful way you can. Speak it to yourself. Speak any one of the mantras to yourself, not loudly, but in a gentle, quiet voice. For example:

O Man, Know Thy Self!
Thus sounds the Cosmic Word.
You hear it with strength of soul,
You feel it with might of spirit.

After you have spoken such a mantra to yourself try to sense how its speaking works in you. Try to discover what you feel when you speak it. Feel the difference in your body between the state of silence and the state you are in when you are speaking. Try to sense the speaking in your organs and how it takes its course. You will feel it through the various pressures and vibrations in your organs of speech.

And if you have felt this, then ask yourself: when I think something in the present that has been prompted by what someone has told me, or by a thought caused by an impression of an outer event in the present, I ask myself: can I sense and feel this, too?

If you have learned to feel the speaking, it is also easy to sense that the thinking called forth in the immediate present is finer and more delicate in feeling than is the speaking, but it can be felt. And from feeling speaking, we can learn to feel thinking, to sense thinking.

Then, just as you can sense your speaking, you will be able to sense your thinking, to touch it inwardly, to perceive it. It is like this [drawing begins: a profile in white, picture 7]. When speech is sensed in this way, then we will feel it about here [red]. You will feel thinking above this [green], up here, rather toward the back of the head. This is where you will feel your thinking.

It is good to practice such an exercise because it will surely help you make intimate self-observations. When you have done this, my dear sisters and brothers, proceed now to make a thought active, a memory-thought, something you have thought of days, weeks or months ago. Try to make it as alive as possible. Now, when you try to feel this memory-thought, you will have the sense that you feel it *under* the region of speech [yellow]. You will say to yourself: when I speak it I experience it in the region of my speech organs. When I think it, I experience it

Twelfth Lesson

above in my head. And when I remember it, I experience it *below* the area of speech.

When this becomes an intimate experience for you, if you really feel it, then you have taken hold of something spiritual, which can be the beginning of an increasingly wider grasp of spiritual matters. However, to feel things in this way it is absolutely necessary to be closed off from other, ordinary, daily experiences. It is not good to say that to achieve this seclusion I have to withdraw from people for a few weeks to be where nothing disturbs me, for example, to be in a cabin on Mount Blanc where I can have absolute peace. It is not good to think like this because progress will never be made if you think this way. The best thing is to be in the very midst of the turmoil of life, exposed to all that life brings you from morning until night. Then, despite this, reserve a time through your own initiative, however brief it may be, when you are outside of the world's turmoil and yet in the middle of it. You are outside of it purely by your own inner power. That will be best. To withdraw in solitude in order to have some quiet is not as effective as to create solitude through your own, inner power. That is what can lead you definitely and with certainty to the goal. This will provide a good foundation for being able to meditate in the way necessary.

My dear sisters and brothers, you have learned to know mantras that are spoken quietly within the soul. Such were the first mantras given during these Class Lessons. Then we advanced further to mantras that partly sound forth from the soul and partly have to be thought of as sounding toward us, coming to us from the cosmos. Indeed, we do not meditate by speaking inwardly, instead we meditate by hearing inwardly. We imagine ourselves in the situation where we hear what is spoken to us, be it from a vast distance or spoken by a spiritual being. It is of particular importance that we imagine ourselves in situations where other beings speak to us. This condition, where other beings speak to us, will enable us to bring about the inner mood of soul that feels itself within the spiritual world.

You see, today's mantra will be given for this purpose. The soul should imagine that it is completely silent, entirely silent. Then the soul should imagine that it is already on the other side of the threshold within the spiritual world and standing before the Guardian. The soul itself, entirely silent, perceives three different sounds. The first sound comes from the vast universe; the second is from the Guardian; the third comes from those beings named later in the mantra. The mantra placed before your souls today should be understood in this way. From the vast expanse of the universe, pouring in from all sides, there sounds:

> Listen to the realm of thinking:

What happens is that the true essence of thinking is revealed by a cosmic experience of spirit and soul.

Then the Guardian speaks. After all that sounded from the universe has died away—for this is a situation we must live in spiritually—then the Guardian speaks the next three lines:

> He speaks who wants to show you
> Your paths in spirit light
> From Earth life to Earth life:

These are the Guardian's words.

Then the angel, who guides our path from Earth life to Earth life, speaks:

> Behold your senses' luminous nature.

The angel who guides us from incarnation to incarnation speaks these lines that we hear in our contemplative life.

> The Guardian speaks again:
>
> He speaks who wants to bear you
> In realms of being, set free from matter,
> To other souls on wings of soul:

Now the being who watches over us from the hierarchy of the Archangeloi speaks:

> Behold the forces working in your thinking.

Twelfth Lesson

This goes upward to where the Archangeloi are.

First it was "look upon your senses' luminous nature." The fact is that in ordinary life we think that the sun shines and our senses don't shine. In fact, our senses do shine. Our senses shine in the act of perception, although we don't perceive their radiance. Therefore, the being who belongs to us from the hierarchy of the Angels admonishes us to "look upon your senses' luminous nature."

Generally, we think with our ordinary consciousness; but we don't take hold of our thinking. We do not sense it; we do not feel it. The being that belongs to us from the realm of the Archangels admonishes us: "Look upon the forces working in your thinking."

Now we go up to the realm of the Archai. The Guardian advises us in three lines that we should listen to the being from the realm of the Archai, who instructs us. The next three lines come from the Guardian:

> He speaks who wants to give you
> A firm ground for existence
> Among the spirits in the creative realm
> Far from Earth:

I could also say the "throne of existence," but it is better to say "a firm ground for existence." That is, the one who speaks wants to establish you upon the firm ground of spirit in the spirit realm, in the same way that you stand on physical ground in the realm of the senses.

After the Guardian of Threshold has said this, the being from the realm of the Archai speaks:

> Behold your memory's image-forming.

That is the third thing. First, we have to see the radiance of our senses; then, we look at the forces working in our thinking; and then, we look at what lies deep down in our memory pictures. What lies deep down below the realm of speech lies in our memory pictures: "Look upon your memory's image-forming."

We ourselves have listened with silent souls to the threefold speech given to us. In the first line, the voice came from the cosmos: "Listen to the realm of thinking." Then we heard the Guardian speak the three lines that lie between the actual hierarchical instructions. Then we heard the actual beings who belong to us from the realm of the hierarchies speak the lines that are always characteristic and that should speak most deeply to our inner being. Such is the entire structure of the mantra, which I will write down. Here it is:

> Listen to the realm of thinking:
>
> He speaks who wants to show you
> Your paths in spirit light
> From Earth life to Earth life:
> Behold your senses' luminous nature.
>
> He speaks who wants to bear you
> In realms of being, set free from matter,
> To other souls on wings of soul:
> Behold the forces working in your thinking.
>
> He speaks who wants to give you
> A firm ground for existence
> Among the spirits in the creative realm
> Far from Earth:
> Behold your memory's image-forming.

[Mantra I is now written on the blackboard.

> I. *Listen to the realm of <u>thinking</u>:*
>
> 1. *He speaks who wants to show you*
>   *Your paths in spirit light*
>   *From Earth life to Earth life:*
>   <u>*Behold your senses' luminous nature.*</u>
>
> 2. *He speaks who wants to bear you*
>   *In realms of being, set free from matter,*
>   *To other souls on wings of soul:*
>   <u>*Behold the forces working in your thinking.*</u>

> 3. He speaks who wants to give you
>   A firm ground for existence
>   Among the spirits in the creative realm
>   Far from Earth:
>   <u>Behold your memory's image-forming.</u>

With this our soul has experienced the guidance for self-knowledge resounding from the three lower hierarchies:

The first from the hierarchy of the	*Angeloi*
The second from the hierarchy of the	*Archangeloi*
The third from the hierarchy of the	*Archai*

Before undertaking this exercise, concentration of the soul can be brought about by placing a quite distinct image before us [drawing begins, upper part left]: an eye looking upward [eye], beholding the circle of the higher hierarchies [arc above the eye], from whom the forces of the universe stream down upon the eye [upper rays], which then perceives the circle of the lower hierarchies [wavy line between the eye and the arc], who reach up to the higher hierarchies and send the rays on to human beings [lower rays].

Call up this image in your soul and keep it there, so that it remains present: the eye looking up, both lines—the curved one and the wavy one—the rays streaming downward. And while doing the exercise, without thinking about it further, the image of the eye looking upward should remain before for your soul.

Again we hear resounding from all sides of the cosmos:

> Listen to the realm of feeling.

The Guardian speaks the next three lines:

> He speaks who as a thought
> Calls you to cosmic existence
> From the sun rays of the spirit:

The voice that sounds forth from a higher hierarchy already speaks a more lofty language. Whereas in the first mantra we are made aware of what is already there within us, here in this mantra we are addressed by the Guardian not only to look at our senses, our thoughts and our memories, but we are also called to learn how we ourselves are called into the world, called into cosmic existence. This resounds from the hierarchy of the Exusiai.

Then the being that belongs to us from the hierarchy of the Exusiai speaks:

> Feel the stirring of life in your breath.

The next three lines are again spoken by the Guardian:

> He speaks who gives you
> Cosmic existence in spirit realms
> From the life forces of the stars.

Then a being from the hierarchy of the Dynamis speaks:

> Feel the surging weaving in your blood.

Here we must imagine, or rather feel, the universal movement of the world in the surging weaving of our blood.

Again the Guardian speaks to counsel us that we should listen to what is spoken by a being from the ranks of the Kyriotetes:

> He speaks who wants to create for you
> Spirit sense from earthly will
> In the light of lofty realms divine:

And then the being from the Kyriotetes speaks:

> Feel the powerful resistance of the Earth.

Only when we feel the powerful resistance of the terrestrial forces can we properly penetrate into the world of pure spirit.

Here is how the inner experience of this mantra must sound:

Twelfth Lesson

Listen to the realm of feeling:

He speaks who as a thought
Calls you to cosmic existence
From the sun rays of the spirit:
    Feel the stirring of life in your breath.

He speaks who gives you
Cosmic existence in spirit realms
From the life forces of the stars:
    Feel the surging weaving in your blood.

He speaks who wants to create for you
Spirit sense from earthly will
In the light of lofty realms divine:
    Feel the powerful resistance of the Earth.

Self-knowledge is stimulated in us by ascending into the realm of the second hierarchy through the instruction given by a being that belongs to us from the ranks of the Exusiai, following the counsel first given by the Guardian that such a being will speak to us.

My dear sisters and brothers, in earthly life we think that our thoughts are mere empty nothings. But when a being of the rank of the Exusiai thinks, he thinks in us. *Our I* is being thought. *Our I* exists as the thought of a being from the realm of the Exusiai. If on Earth we say I to ourselves, what are we beholding? This I, when we speak "I" [a circle with the word "I" is drawn; yellow in picture 7], we look back to this "I" [red arrows] and speak the word I. But for a being from the rank of the Exusiai [green line], the "I" is a thought, a real thought. We *exist* inasmuch as we are *thought* by beings of the rank of the Exusiai. And when we speak "I" to ourselves, we are actually recognizing that we are thought by divine beings. Our higher self exists because we are being thought by divine beings.

After this, a being from the rank of Dynamis instructs us how we have received our spiritual existence as a gift from him from the life forces gathered from the stars.

And a being from the rank of the Kyriotetes instructs us that what lives in us on Earth as will is lifted up into the heights of heaven and, through the transformation it undergoes there, our earthly will is given back to us so that we can make use of it in spiritual willing. Earthly will is just a transformation of spiritual will. Will is continually carried up and down again. Above, it is heavenly will; below, it is earthly will. In the end, the Guardian counsels us that that the being from the ranks of Kyriotetes says: "Feel the powerful resistance of the Earth." When we feel the Earth's resistance, we sense the blessing bestowed on us, through grace, by the forces from the heavenly heights.

[Mantra II is written on the blackboard. In the first line "feeling" is underlined and the last lines of Parts 1, 2, and 3 are underlined:]

> II. Listen to the realm of <u>feeling</u>:
>
> 1. He speaks who as a thought
>   Calls you to cosmic existence
>   From the sun rays of the spirit:
>   <u>Feel the stirring of life in your breath.</u>
>
> 2. He speaks who gives you
>   Cosmic existence in spirit realms
>   From the life forces of the stars:
>   <u>Feel the surging weaving in your blood.</u>
>
> 3. He speaks who wants to create for you
>   Spirit sense from earthly will
>   In the light of lofty realms divine:
>   <u>Feel the powerful resistance of the Earth.</u>

Such is the course of the second mantra:

> Listen to the realm of feeling:
>
> He speaks who as a thought
> Calls you to cosmic existence
> From the sun rays of the spirit:
> Feel the stirring of life in your breath.

Twelfth Lesson

He speaks who gives you
Cosmic existence in spirit realms
From the life forces of the stars:
Feel the surging weaving in your blood.

He speaks who wants to create for you
Spirit sense from earthly will
In the light of lofty realms divine:
Feel the powerful resistance of the Earth.

The first sounds from the hierarchy of the	*Exusiai*
The second from the hierarchy of the	*Dynamis*
The third from the hierarchy of the	*Kyriotetes*

In conclusion, now that all this has taken place in us, and so that we may remember what kind of image stood before us, we place the image once again before our souls...remembering that it was there all along during the entire exercise.

[The image developed after the mantric words "Listen to the realm of thinking"—left upper part of the drawing—is now drawn once more: eye, arc, upper rays, wavy line, and lower rays.]

Further ascent into the ranks of Seraphim, Cherubim, and Thrones will be given in the next Class Lesson. At this moment, however, the meaning of all this must be made even clearer.

My dear sisters and brothers, at the beginning of today's Class Lesson there came to us the formulaic words from cosmic existence, from the Cosmic Being, that summon us to self-knowledge. Self-knowledge, as has been said, leads to world knowledge...but only if we can bring the self into connection with the world.

But the self and its true essence is not related to any natural being or process. It is related only to what is in the spiritual world, where the beings of the higher hierarchies are. If we truly want to enter into our true self—the "I"—then we must experience life together with the beings of the hierarchies and not with external nature. From the aspect of external nature what we may call our I is only the outer reflection of our true I. The true I lives in the same realm where the beings of the hierarchies live. As soon as we achieve self-knowledge, we must enter the realm of the higher hierarchies. Then we must become aware of and understand the language of the higher hierarchies.

The admonitions of the Guardian of the Threshold are always present in mediation so that we may undertake it with all of our inner strength. They are there so that we don't make this into an anemic theory, but that we do it with all our strength. In order that the whole may stand before us in meditation with due majesty, there are two—next time you will hear the third—mighty admonitions coming from the cosmos: "Listen to the realm of thinking;" and "Listen to the realm of feeling."

Only if we can feel ourselves actively engaged in this threefold way of speaking, only if we experience ourselves in the spiritual world in this mantric manner, can these things really bring us forward. Only then do we bring the right mood to them. We have to seek this mood above all else. For real, inner devotion must be present if meditation is to contribute to initiation. This inner devotion comes only from the mood through which we are removed for a while from the outer world and live solely in the content and substance of the meditation. If we can enter into this in a fully living way, so that self-knowledge is not just an introspective brooding but an intensive conversation with the world, with the Guardian, and with the hierarchies, then we will find our way to true self-knowledge.

Basically, we should avoid thinking of such things at all if we cannot summon up the right mood. We should think about such things as were given today only when we can really create this inner mood in our soul. This mood consists purely of feeling how the majesty of distant spaces and cosmic worlds comes to us as with the voice of cosmic thunder. And then, what comes from the Guardian of the Threshold sounds with a gentle, authoritative voice. Following that, one of the hierarchies speaks to us, deeply penetrating our soul. We should always remember this mood. We should really only think of these mantras when we can generate feelings connected with this mood. We do this so that we don't inwardly desecrate the mantras or deprive them of their power by thinking of them with the usual, dry, common way of thinking. We first must put ourselves into the proper mood of soul.

Because this is the case, we should bring about an inner mood of soul that feels human self-knowledge to be something festive, earnest and sacred. These things should only be spoken of inwardly in the soul, let alone outwardly, in such a way that they are experienced as something earnest, festive and sacred.

It is a great hindrance to progress on an esoteric path that so many of these things are often talked about in a cliquish kind of way, even with a touch of vanity, without having also developed this mood of earnestness, festiveness and sacredness. We forget that in esoteric life everything depends on the truth, the complete truth. One can accomplish nothing in esoteric life if one does not know that truth, absolute truth, must prevail. One cannot merely speak of truth and at the same time take things as one does in ordinary life. This is precisely what we do when we make these things the subject of everyday, idle talk.

Common, idle chatter about these things often throws hindrances and obstacles onto the esoteric path. It is essential that everything to do with self-knowledge is brought into connection with this solemn, festive and sacred mood in our soul. Then, to show that we allow the words to work in our soul in the right way, now at the end we must speak them again as they were spoken at the beginning of today's Class Lesson:

> O Man, Know Thy Self!

Yes, this is guidance in self-knowledge:

> O Man, Know Thy Self!
> Thus sounds the Cosmic Word.
> You hear it with strength of soul,
> You feel it with might of spirit.

Who speaks so powerfully through the world?
Who speaks so tenderly within your heart?

Does it work through the far-spread rays of space
Into your senses' experience of life?
Does it sound through the weaving waves of time
Into the evolving stream of your life?

Is it you, yourself, who,
By sensing space,
By experiencing time,
Begets this word,
Feeling yourself estranged in the psychic void of space,
Because you lose the force of thought
In the annihilating stream of time?

It is real question. The answer lies in the words given here today.

Twelfth Lesson

11. Mai 1924

II.) Vernimm des Fühlens Feld:

1.) Es spricht, der als Gedanke
   Aus Geistessonnenstrahlen   Exusiai
   Dich zum Weltendasein ruft:

   Fühl' in deines Atems Lebensregung.

2.) Es spricht, der Weltendasein
   Aus Sternen-Lebenskräften   Dynamis
   Dir in Geisteszeichen schenket:

   Fühl' in deines Blutes Wellenweben.

3.) Es spricht, der dir den Geistes=Sinn
   Im lichten Götter-Höhenreiche   Kyriotetes
   Aus Erdenwollen schaffen will:

   Fühl' der Erde mächtig Widerstreben.

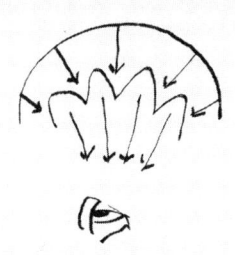

Rudolf Steiner's handwriting

Thirteenth Lesson

Dornach, May 17, 1924

My dear friends! First, the words will be spoken once more that sound into our souls from the spiritual cosmos, words that counsel us to true observation and true knowledge of our being:

> O Man, Know Thy Self!
> Thus sounds the Cosmic Word.
> You hear it with strength of soul,
> You feel it with might of spirit.
>
> Who speaks so powerfully through the world?
> Who speaks so tenderly within your heart?
>
> Does it work through the far-spread rays of space
> Into your senses' experience of life?
> Does it sound through the weaving waves of time
> Into the evolving stream of your life?
>
> Is it you, yourself, who,
> By sensing space,
> By experiencing time,
> Begets this word,
> Feeling yourself estranged in the psychic void of space,
> Because you lose the force of thought
> In the annihilating stream of time?

My dear sisters and brothers, in the previous lesson we tried to find the inner words of soul that can connect human beings with what is revealed from the hierarchies, with whom our soul and spirit are connected. By entering deeply into what can come about through a specific deepening of our thinking, we have put before our souls how we can reach up into the realm of the third hierarchy where the Angels, Archangels and Archai reside.

By this we do not mean the ordinary thinking of everyday life, but the thinking that lives behind everyday thinking, the kind of thinking that, in fact, can only be created from our whole organization when we ponder in meditation such words as have been presented to us, beginning with "Behold the realm of thinking."

I indicated last time how this kind of thinking can be felt in the human organism itself above the region of speech, whereas the field of memory-thoughts can be felt below the region of speech. The region of speech itself can be felt when we say something inwardly and fully alive, be it spoken in a low voice or loudly. We feel it speaking in us and we can indicate the place where we feel it. There we have a starting point for speech, which is perhaps the easiest to experience.

Above the region of speech and toward the back of the head we can find the inner thinking through which we can discern the Angeloi. Through speech itself we can feel the Archangeloi; and, the Archai can be felt in the memories lying below the region of speech.

The mantric verse leading to this experience takes its course in the way described in the last Class Lesson.

Through this verse we first imagine how the vast expanse of the cosmos speaks to us; how, in a way, the universe itself resounds to us. Then, in the midst of this universe, there sounds what the Guardian of the Threshold tells us we ought to consider—that we should to listen to what the specific Angeloi, who belongs to us from the rank of the third hierarchy, has to say to us.

Then, the Guardian of the Threshold counsels us a second time to listen to the being that belongs to us from the ranks of the Archangeloi. And the Guardian calls to us a third time, telling us to listen to the being belonging to us from the ranks of the Archai. We should imagine this mantric verse in such a way that we hear the universe itself sounding to us from afar. We hear the Guardian speak and then we hear the hierarchies speak:

> Listen to the realm of thinking:
>
> He speaks who wants to show you
> Your paths in spirit light
> From Earth life to Earth life:
> > Behold your senses' luminous nature.
>
> He speaks who wants to bear you
> In realms of being, set free from matter,
> To other souls on wings of soul:
> > Behold the forces working in your thinking.
>
> He speaks who wants to give you
> A firm ground for existence
> Among the spirits in the creative realm
> Far from Earth:
> > Behold your memory's image-forming.

If we can repeatedly feel ourselves in this situation where the cosmic expanse speaks to us, where the Guardian of the Threshold speaks and the hierarchies speak, if we can imagine it vividly surrounding us, as it were—using the picture I wrote on the blackboard last time [picture 7]—then we can gradually come to feel the thinking that is situated above the region of speech in the back of the head, through which we approach the weaving light of the third hierarchy.

Thus, my dear sisters and brothers, one can say that we connect ourselves with the beings of the third hierarchy through this mantric verse.

Similarly, we make a connection with the second hierarchy through the second verse that was recently given and is to be felt, or spiritually perceived, in the way described. We should completely forget that we ourselves are speaking and should immerse ourselves in the situation as I've described.

Thirteenth Lesson

Listen to the realm of feeling:

He speaks who as a thought
Calls you to cosmic existence
From the sun rays of the spirit:
    Feel the stirring of life in your breath.

He speaks who gives you
Cosmic existence in spirit realms
From the life forces of the stars:
    Feel the surging weaving in your blood.

He speaks who wants to create for you
Spirit sense from earthly will
In the light of lofty realms divine:
    Feel the powerful resistance of the Earth.

Next, we endeavor to make a connection with the Exusiai, Dynamis and Kyriotetes. An interconnection is brought about between the realm of feeling—which involves our breathing and blood circulation—and the region where the will enters, which is still only felt as will. The connection is thereby brought about between our full humanity and the beings of the second hierarchy.

My dear sisters and brothers, today it remains for us to consider the realm of the will. The realm of will most dominates and controls human beings. It is the realm that works most powerfully in us. And yet, at the same time, it is the one we live in with the least amount of awareness, the region where we are the least conscious. We know extremely little about how our will works, how it takes its course in daily life.

At first, the will finds expression in our organism when it is set in motion, when it is brought into movement.

My dear sisters and brothers, you must be prepared to make these intimate ideas your own if you want to find your way to the spirit who speaks through this esoteric school, who wants to guide you on your path.

Imagine yourself walking and, perhaps, moving your arms. Usually we think that we move our legs and our legs carry us forward. This is the easiest picture we can make. We think that an unknown force—of course, it is unknown because nobody can know anything about this force with their ordinary consciousness—is somehow made to stream into our legs. One leg is put before the other and so we carry ourselves through the world.

But it is not like that. In the first place, our legs do not have the task to carry us through the world. That is simply not true. We come here to the point where our normal consciousness suddenly reveals itself as Maya. For it is Maya if we believe that we walk with our legs and that our physical legs are there for us to walk with.

My dear sisters and brothers, obviously this does not mean that you must now go out into the Philistine world and proclaim: "It is not true that human beings have legs in order to walk." Naturally, no one would understand what you mean because no one realizes in what a profound sense it is true, that everything presented to our ordinary consciousness is Maya...the Great Illusion. This Great Illusion extends not only to what we see in our surroundings, but also includes how we experience ourselves in relation to the world.

The situation is as follows. Picture it schematically at first like this [drawing on the blackboard, picture 8]. Suppose these are human legs, one stepping in front of the other [white legs]. The human ether body [red] contained within these legs is that part of the ether body that corresponds to the legs. Here is the astral body that corresponds to the legs [yellow] and here also is the organization of the "I" [violet]. The fact is, we don't walk with our physical legs, we don't walk with our etheric legs, and we don't even walk with our astral legs. Rather, we walk with the forces that correspond to the "I"-organization. We live with the forces that belong to the "I"-organization in the gravitational forces of the Earth, forces that are invisible [new drawing: arc with arrow going outward]. We experience the forces of gravity with the forces of our "I"-organization [short strokes beside the arrows]. What corresponds to will and movement takes place between the invisible "I"-organization and the invisible gravitational forces of the Earth.

The "I"-organization depends upon encountering some resistance when it connects with the force of gravity. The astral and ether bodies of the legs, and especially the physical legs themselves, are there so that the "I"-organization can feel itself, can perceive itself, can become aware of itself. Without this perception it cannot connect with the organization of the Earth because it must connect consciously with the Earth organization. In order for the "I"-organization to become conscious of itself while walking and to connect with the Earth organization, the physical body and other organizations have to be present.

Therefore, walking is an entirely suprasensory process. The sense perceptible organization is only there so that human beings can perceive the act of walking, because walking can only be accomplished when it is perceived. My dear sisters and brothers, you no more walk with your physical legs than you walk with your socks. You walk with what belongs to your "I"-organization in your legs. Just as you have socks to keep your legs warm, so you have physical legs to give you consciousness of walking.

What I have just said has to be felt. We have to learn to feel that walking is a suprasensory process, and everything that is sense perceptible about it is only there to make us conscious of it. In our waking life on Earth, such consciousness does not fully come about, or comes about incompletely, because our legs are heavy. Because of this we not only connect with the gravitational forces of the Earth, but we also connect with the gravitational forces working in our physical legs. Consequently, when we are without our physical legs, as when we are asleep, then we speed through the universe with our I and astral body in a much livelier manner than when we walk in physical existence. We surely do move about during sleep, but we are unaware of it in ordinary consciousness because our physical legs are what make us aware of it.

Who is it, then, that provides us with the ability to move during sleep or during periods of clairvoyant consciousness? As I said, we are able to move in physical life because we have consciousness of our movement by means of our physical legs. Who is it, my dear friends, that replaces this function when we are asleep? The Thrones, the beings of the first hierarchy, are the spiritual beings who connect with us during sleep to replace this function for movement. We cannot perceive the Thrones in our ordinary waking consciousness or in our ordinary sleep consciousness; therefore, they cannot help us. Nevertheless, when one becomes capable of perceiving through intuition what happens in sleep, then it will be noticed that during sleep one is connected via the Thrones with the world of higher consciousness, just as in physical life we are connected with our ordinary Earth life through our physical legs.

All of this must pass over into our feelings. We must learn to sense this inwardly. Then we also begin to feel the weaving, flowing world of spirit—a world that we are actually always in the midst of.

Once again, we can lift ourselves up to such inner feelings and experiences if we let them work upon us in this situation, as we did with the other mantras previously given for the realms of thinking and willing. We feel ourselves in a situation where something comes toward us from the far reaches of the universe like a voice of thunder. And the Guardian of the Threshold makes us aware that we ought to listen to the Thrones and hear what they have to say. The Thrones speak to us about our instinctual urges, as we call them. They speak about the driving forces in our soul and how they pass over into our will whenever we perform an act of will in the world.

Therefore, we will let the third part of this mantra work upon us, as it resounds again from the far reaches of the cosmos:

> Behold the realm of will:
>
> Then, the Guardian of the Threshold:
>
> He speaks who guides the dull cosmic forces
> From their dark subterranean depths
> Into your limbs to quicken you:
>
> Behold the fiery nature of your instincts.

This is the first thing. The second thing will lead us deeper into the realm of the soul. If we continue in pursuit of understanding the quickening impulses of our will through inner meditative practice, we will make a great discovery. Ultimately, humanity must make this great discovery if it is to progress in its evolution.

My dear sisters and brothers, I must now speak of something you all know about because it is already part of ordinary consciousness...something we call the "voice of conscience." The Voice of Conscience! But this "voice of conscience" speaks into our consciousness in an undefined way. As a rule, we don't quite know what it is that speaks to us from the mysterious depths of our soul concerning our moral bearing...what we call the "voice of conscience." We do not reach down with our ordinary consciousness so deeply into our being that we can reach the "voice of conscience." The "voice of conscience" rises up, but we are incapable of reaching down to it. Therefore, we never have the opportunity to look at it face-to-face.

If one progresses further into world of the Cherubim, those wisdom-filled beings that live and weave throughout the world, we then make the great discovery that the "voice of conscience" enters us via the cosmic forces stemming from the world of the Cherubim.

The "voice of conscience" is of exalted origin, of exalted being. It actually lives in the world of the Cherubim. It weaves its way into human nature and sounds from the depths of the human being from the world of the Cherubim...at first in an indefinite manner. But it is a great and awe-inspiring encounter when in the intuitive life—where we can connect with the realm of the Cherubim—we encounter the world where conscience lives and has its origin. It is the greatest personal discovery a human being can make.

To this end the Guardian of the Threshold instructs us with the words:

> He speaks who lets the clear rays of spirit
> Filled with grace from God's fields of action
> Circulate through your blood:
>
> See how conscience guides your soul.

In truth, it is the spirit that originates from the realm of the Cherubim and circulates in our blood that constitutes the "voice of conscience." Blood is physically present everywhere in human beings. Since it is physically present throughout us, blood carries the "voice of conscience" throughout our physical nature, along with other things. Waves of Cherubic life weave in the soul life of our blood.

> We will get a better grasp of this meditation if we imagine the situation like this:
>
> First there speaks what comes from the far distances of the cosmos:
>
> Behold the realm of will.
>
> The Guardian of the Threshold counsels us:
>
> He speaks who guides the dull cosmic forces
> From their dark subterranean depths
> Into your limbs to quicken you:

Now let us visualize [drawing begins, picture 8] weaving clouds [blue] symbolizing the Thrones. With the picture of these weaving clouds in mind let us listen to the Thrones—voices from the first hierarchy:

> Behold the fiery nature of your instincts.
>
> Then the Guardian of the Threshold continues:
>
> He speaks, who lets the clear rays of spirit
> Filled with grace from God's fields of action
> Circulate through your blood:

Now let us imagine lightning [red] flashing through the clouds. Lightning bolts—these are the tools of the Cherubim, the fiery swords of the Cherubim. When lightning flashes through the clouds we feel it in the words:

> See how conscience guides your soul.

Thirteenth Lesson

Then the Guardian of the Threshold speaks:

He speaks who brings what has been accomplished in human nature—that is, what has been accomplished in our previous lives on Earth –

Through deaths and births with balanced karma
To breath of life in present time on Earth:

Here we should imagine that the entire sky above the lightning is ablaze, weaving with warmth [yellow], throbbing with heat, sending down the lightning. In the heat pulsating in from the vast distances of the cosmos we feel the speech of the Seraphim:

Behold your destiny's spiritual trials.

—As your destiny reaches from Earth life to Earth life into your present life—
This mantra is especially effective if it is felt together with the above image. Because the will is the most mysterious of all, we can prepare ourselves for this mantra by putting aside all the ordinary meaning of these words and feel the cautioning, guiding, and world-directing, bestowing power in this picture. Instead of the word *Thrones* we will use the word *Seats*, which is a good word from our language. But *Seats* could easily be taken for its trivial meaning. That must be put aside when we use it here.

Now, my dear sisters and brothers, imagine that you feel the word "Seats." [Writing on the blackboard:]

Seats

—Seats of clouds. Form a picture of clouds in your mind and let this picture stand before you. Then form the word *Lightning*. [Above *Seats* is written:]

Lightning Streak

– Again, picture the shooting lightning; picture lightning flashing through the clouds. Then form the word *Heat*. [Above *Lightning Streak* is written:]

Heat

—Cosmic heat. Feel in the threefold "eē" sound the ascent from the cloud seats to the lightning bolts to the cosmic heat whence the lightning originates. Now you feel prepared for the mantra.

    Seats—Lightning Streak—Heat

After all of this stands before you, combined with the picture, then you feel the power of the mantra.

[Mantra III is now written on the blackboard:]

III. Behold the realm of <u>will</u>:

1.   *He speaks who guides the dull cosmic forces*
   From dark subterranean depths
   Into your limbs to quicken you:
       <u>*Behold the fiery nature of your instincts.*</u>

2.   *He speaks who lets the clear rays of spirit*
   Filled with grace from God's fields of action
   Circulate through your blood:
       <u>*See how conscience guides your soul.*</u>

3.   *He speaks who brings the fruit of former lives*
   Through deaths and births with balanced karma
   To breath of life in present time on Earth:
       <u>*Behold your destiny's spiritual trials.*</u>

There are no mere empty phrases in such verses. Here, in the first verse, we have "into your limbs to quicken you." As I described, this is the working together of the "I"-organization with the forces of the Earth—a completely suprasensory process. We must be conscious of this in the first part of the mantra.

In the second part of the mantra we must be aware of the blood coursing through our whole organism—the blood, which carries the "voice of conscience" in its circulation.

Destiny, however, really lives in our breathing, in the upper part of the rhythmic system. Our breathing is suffused not only with what gives us

Thirteenth Lesson

life today, but also by what has been formed from earlier stages of Earth existence.

Here [in part 1] the Guardian of the Threshold draws our attention to the:

                                  Thrones
Here [in part 2] to the: *Cherubim*
Here [in part 3] to the: *Seraphim*

["Thrones" is written beside part 1, "Cherubim" beside part 2, "Seraphim" beside part 3.]

The symbol chosen to give this mantra the necessary inner strength and to consolidate it spiritually, the symbol that beautifully conveys the manifestation of the first hierarchy, is "clouds." At the same time we look at what is spiritual in the clouds, from which the Thrones derive their substance, their very being, their essence.

[The following is written on the blackboard with "being" underlined.]

   Clouds—Thrones—Being

We look up at the lightning. The Cherubim are already more hidden than the Thrones. With the Thrones we can sense how they weave themselves in the clouds. The towering clouds provide the Thrones with substance. The Cherubim do not make it so easy for us to see them; they are more concealed than the Thrones. They do not show themselves to us in forms but appear to us in lightning—which they use as their instruments, their tools. The Cherubim stand behind their tools. Through lightning they show us only their tools, not their very being.

[The following is written on the blackboard:]

   Lightning—Cherubim—Tools

We now ascend to cosmic heat where the Seraphim are deeply hidden. They are more deeply veiled than the Cherubim, who are behind their tools—lightning. Cosmic heat is merely the radiance of the Seraphim. The Thrones reveal themselves through their being. The Cherubim reveal themselves through their instrumentalities, their tools. The Seraphim reveal themselves through the radiance that streams out from them.

[The following is written on the blackboard:]

Cosmic Heat—Seraphim—<u>Radiance</u>

In this way we establish a connection between human beings and the first hierarchy in the realm of the will:

Behold the realm of will.

He speaks who guides the dull cosmic forces
From dark subterranean depths
Into your limbs to quicken you:
   Behold the fiery nature of your instincts.

He speaks who lets the clear rays of spirit
Filled with grace from God's fields of action
Circulate through your blood:
   See how conscience guides your soul.

He speaks who brings the fruit of former lives
Through deaths and births with balanced karma
To breath of life in present time on Earth:
   Behold your destiny's spiritual trials.

But in these situations, everything depends on whether we feel that *we ourselves are not speaking,* that we ourselves are not doing the thinking, feeling or the willing. Rather everything depends upon the fact that we should forget ourselves entirely and that we only sense, feel and are spoken to in the threefold manner described above.

Yes, my dear sisters and brothers, it is necessary that we really take such inner mantric exercises seriously. Then they will have the effect they should have. They will carry us forward to the threefold realms of the spiritual world: the realm of thought, the realm of feeling, the realm of will. It all depends on how seriously we are able to live into these things.

Thirteenth Lesson

For this to take place it is also necessary to bear something else in mind. The meditant will, of course, fall back again into the routine of ordinary life. The meditant has to do this because between birth and death one is an earthly human being. One must return again and again to the consciousness of ordinary life. But we can exist in ordinary life in such a way that, for example—to take a negative example that does happen—imagine that you have a pain that persists and becomes chronic. If you have such pain, you always feel it. Sometimes you may forget about it, but you will still feel it. We should feel a similar experience if the power of meditation has finally taken hold of us. We should actually always feel that we can say to ourselves: this ordinary consciousness of mine has begun to meditate; it has been taken hold of by the penetrating power of meditation. We should be able to feel that meditation was present in this consciousness and that we were present in it. We must thereby feel that we have become a different person, that meditation has changed us. Therefore, having once begun to meditate, we can never again in our life forget—not for a single moment, my dear sisters and brothers—that we are people who meditate. Such is the proper inner mood of one who meditates.

We should live a life permeated by meditation—even if we only meditate for brief periods so that we don't disturb the rest of our life. We should always feel that we are a person who meditates. And should we once forget that we are meditants and later realize that there were moments in life when we forgot that we are meditants, we should feel as ashamed as we would feel if we were to find ourselves walking naked down a crowded street without any clothes on. We ought to acquire this feeling. We should experience the transition from *not being* a meditant to *being* a meditant in such a way that there would never be moment when we would have to be ashamed of ourselves for forgetting that we are meditants. A great deal depends on this.

Then we will really make progress in what is said to us through the cosmic words we began this lesson with:

O Man, Know Thyself!
Thus sounds the Cosmic Word.
You hear it with strength of soul,
You feel it with might of spirit.

Who speaks so powerfully through the world?
Who speaks so tenderly within your heart?

Does it work through the far-spread rays of space
Into your senses' experience of life?
Does it sound through the weaving waves of time
Into the evolving stream of your life?

Is it you, yourself, who,
By sensing space,
By experiencing time,
Begets this word,
Feeling yourself estranged in the psychic void of space,
Because you lose the force of thought
In the annihilating stream of time?

But we must bring before our souls again and again the idea that knowledge is a serious thing, that the world of the Great Illusion, the world of Maya, does not give us knowledge. First we must come to the threshold where the Guardian stands. All the deceptive forms that fill the reality of the sense world, that fill our ordinary thinking, disappear at the threshold.

We are able to feel this when, from the same cosmic depths that we heard the Cosmic Word just spoken, there now sounds toward us:

Thirteenth Lesson

> First know the earnest Guardian,
> Who stands before the gate of spirit land,
> Denying entry to your senses' power
> And to the strength of your intellect,
> Because in the weaving of your senses
> And in the forming of your thoughts
> First you must find—
> From the nothingness of space,
> From time's delusive powers—
> The strength to conquer
> The truth of your own being.

When we have heard these words we are able to speak our response reverently from the depths of our soul:

> I came into this sense world
> Bearing thought's heritage within me,
> Led by a divine power.
> Death stands at journey's end.
> I want to feel the Being of Christ.
> He awakens spiritual birth in matter's death.
> In spirit, thus, I find the world
> And know *myself* amid the world's evolving.
>
> (...)

Fourteenth Lesson

Dornach, May 31, 1924

My dear friends! We have looked at the position of the human being in relation to the Guardian of the Threshold. As we tread the path of knowledge we have gradually brought before our souls what this relationship to the Guardian of the Threshold is like. Today, we want to place vividly before our souls the situation when we stand in front of the Guardian of the Threshold so we can take a step forward in our esoteric study.

I will repeat from prior lessons the circumstances we are in when one leaves the physical world where ordinary consciousness is developed. There, where we stand, the realization arises that the physical sense world can be majestic and full of joy, but also can be painful and full of suffering and that we have many reasons to belong to it with our consciousness. At the same time, we realize that we can never have self-knowledge if we only turn our gaze and our feelings toward the physical world. We must say to ourselves: however great and sublime all this may be that assembles color on color and form on form, I shall never find what I myself am in my origin and in my own being in all the space around me.

Yet, at this moment, the most important task in human life speaks to us. The words of self-knowledge ring forth from all sides of the universe and we hear: O Man, Know Thy Self!

In addition to this it becomes clear that we are protected our ordinary life from entering the spiritual world—the world of our true being—unprepared. The Guardian of the Threshold shows himself as the being who protects us every night when we enter the spiritual world when we are asleep. He is the being who protects us from having conscious awareness of what surrounds us in sleep. For if a person were to perceive where they are in sleep unprepared, they would undergo an experience so shattering that they would be unable to live their waking life in a proper, human fashion.

The Guardian also makes it clear to us that the Guardian himself is the only gate to true knowledge.

We then become aware of approaching an abyss before entering the realm of knowledge. At first it appears as a bottomless abyss; the support we stand on in the physical world is no longer there. We cannot step across. We can only cross the abyss if we are able to free ourselves from all that is physical. We can only cross the abyss when, symbolically, we can "grow wings" to cross the abyss as a being of soul and spirit.

But before this happens, the Guardian of the Threshold calls out to us to be aware of the abyss and, above all, to be aware of the beasts who rise up from the abyss as spirit forms. People must realize that these beasts are the outward reflection of their own unpurified willing, feeling and thinking. These beasts must first be overcome. We are shown in a vivid picture how one's own willing, feeling and thinking manifest in these three beasts: one spectral; one hideous to look at; and so on.

Then the Guardian shows us how thinking, feeling and will become strong in themselves after having resolved in full consciousness to overcome the beasts. Until the human being has entered into the spiritual world it is necessary to develop situational meditations of the spiritual world. It is necessary to learn to live into situations where the cosmos speaks to human beings, how the hierarchies speak to human beings and, indeed, how all things speak about what awaits human beings on the other side of the threshold in the spiritual world.

Through what rises up in our soul in the mantra we will increasingly perceive how we, as human beings, must become altogether different if we wish to cross the abyss and seek what lives on the other side. We become progressively aware that we live here on Earth with the beings of the three kingdoms of nature and with human beings. On the other side of the threshold we live with discarnate souls and with the beings of the higher hierarchies. A different way of relating is required there and an entirely different attitude of soul is demanded for this other way of relating.

Once again, it is the task of the Guardian of the Threshold to point out to human beings how one has to conduct oneself and has to come to terms with the fact that when one crosses the abyss, or gets to know anything about the spiritual world, one has to bring oneself into an entirely different attitude of soul.

People will become aware of how two attitudes of soul can become realities within oneself: the attitude of soul on this side of the abyss with ordinary consciousness and the attitude of soul on the other side of the abyss outside of the physical and etheric bodies—the attitude of soul in the pure spiritual world.

There, human beings should anticipate great dangers where this difference appears between the attitudes of soul. The dangers that initially appear as small deviations from the normal condition of the soul can, in their extreme, cause morbid malformations of the soul. Of course, it must be emphasized that when the journey into higher worlds is undertaken in the way carefully described in *How to Know Higher Worlds* and in the second part of my *Occult Science*, and in some of the smaller anthroposophic writings, then aberrations from the normal condition of the soul cannot take place, not even in the slightest degree. Human beings will go consciously into the spiritual world, not only through knowledge and a sound common sense, but also through initiation. Human beings must know—if not paying attention to the proper guidance when entering the spiritual world—that a twofold divergence will occur from what gives one a firm stand in everyday life and attitude of soul.

Here on this side of the threshold we stand on the solid element of Earth. The ground beneath our feet supports us. All around us we have the element of water, which also plays a part in our body's formation. In ordinary life this watery element cannot be our support, although it permeates us and forms itself into our blood. It is part of our processes of growth and the forces of nutrition. We breathe in the air. Air, or the gaseous element, is all around us. And lastly, warmth surround us, the

Fourteenth Lesson

warmth ether, the fourth of the elements. In ordinary life these elements are separate from each other. Where there is solid earth there is no water. Where there is water there is no air. Where there is air there is no water. Only fire—warmth—permeates everything. It is the only one that permeates them all.

My dear friends, the very moment we leave our physical body, this differentiation, this separation of elements, ceases to exist. We expand; we spread out and are simultaneously in earth, water, air and fire. We can no longer distinguish one from the other since the properties of the four elements no longer exist. Earth no longer supports us because its firmness is gone. Water no longer forms us because its formative forces cease to be. Once in the spiritual world, it is as though we are dissolving, as ice melts in warm water, for we have become one with the water. We cannot float in it because that would mean we are still separate from it. Similarly, blood is no longer a separate element in our blood vessels. Our blood becomes one with the all-pervading watery element of the universe. Equally, air ceases to be the formative breathing force in us. Warmth ceases to enkindle us into an "I"; we stop feeling ourselves as a self within the warmth. All this ceases to exist. We must meet the ending of the differentiation of earth, water, air and fire with the right mood.

So now let us imagine that we have already flown across the abyss. My dear sisters and brothers, we have arrived on the other side and now the Guardian of the Threshold calls us to turn around and face him.

My dear sisters and brothers, let us imagine as vividly as we can that a person has arrived on the other side of the threshold where truths and knowledge about the spiritual world are revealed. This person is standing on the other side. The Guardian makes this person turn around to receive the warnings that are necessary, now that the person has been touched by the condition of soul present in the spiritual world where the person now stands within the elements of earth, water, air and fire.

Here one of the dangers approaches…that one may fall prey to the illusion of being in love. Forgive the trivial expression, my dear sisters and brothers. The danger is falling in love with the state of being released from the solid earth, from water's forming force, from the creative powers of the air and from the force of warmth that awakens the self. One feels enraptured with a sense of spiritual bliss. One feels given over to spiritual ecstasy and wants to remain in this blissful spiritual state.

This feeling overcomes the person because the luciferic temptation approaches them. Depending upon a person's karma, one can be open to this luciferic temptation to a greater or lesser extent. If a person is accessible and falls completely in love with dissolving into the elements of earth, water, air and fire, the luciferic power will take hold of them and they will never want to leave this mood of soul. The person is in danger of prolonging this soul mood after returning to daily life. Therefore, the Guardian of the Threshold has to call to the person, saying: you may not do so, you must not fall prey to Lucifer. You must not be content to feel only rapturous bliss when dissolving into earth, water, fire and air. Now that you have returned to the physical world, you must make a firm resolve to resume the mood of soul appropriate to ordinary consciousness. Otherwise, you will be confused in the future and lost in dreams in the physical world.

This is the luciferic danger that after returning from the spiritual world, from the other side of the threshold, we become confused and no longer know our way around in the world...like a visionary who incorrectly takes dreaming for idealism and lives in contempt for ordinary consciousness. This we may not do. The Guardian of the Threshold urgently warns us to make the resolve to live appropriately in either world, be it the earthly or the suprasensory world.

The Guardian now adds a second warning to this admonition. The second warning is to be aware of how many earthly inclinations, earthly habits, are still present in our thinking, feeling and willing after we have arrived on the other side of the threshold where our thinking, feeling and willing are separate from each other.

Then again, a person may have the tendency to take the experience on this side of the threshold, where the Earth provides firm support, make it doubly hard and firm and then cross over the threshold with this materialistic attitude, bringing along the hardened and solidified formative forces of water. There a person can be plagued by earthly pride and say: in my earthly life I breathed in the breath from which the Father God once created human souls and human lives. I can do this, too,... if only I am freed from the limitations of earthly life.

But, if by virtue of breathing, a person wants to carry the creative power of the gods across to the spiritual world, they will fall prey to the enticements of Ahriman and cannot return to this side before being overtaken by faintness and feebleness. One becomes more or less unconscious; one's consciousness is paralyzed. Through this diminished consciousness one becomes more or less a tool of the ahrimanic powers in the spiritual world.

Today, since the dawn of the new Michael Age, spiritual life virtually draws human beings across to the spiritual world in a crude state hardened by materialism. My dear friends, the significance of the ahrimanic power when human consciousness is subdued in the waking state was potently revealed when the great World War broke out.

When the World War broke out, I said to many people that it is not possible to write the history of this war from only the physical plane. Documents alone will not tell the truth. Of the thirty to forty people in Europe who played a part in the outbreak of the war, quite a number of them had their consciousness clouded at the decisive moment and they became unwitting tools for ahrimanic powers. Many things that happened in the World War were instigated by ahrimanic powers. This World War can only be written about in an occult way. We could see the same thing happening to many leading personalities on this side of the threshold at the outbreak of war, the same thing that is perceptible in those who carry the soul's habits across to the other side of the threshold. There they are paralyzed, are in a state of diminished consciousness; and so, they become the tools of ahrimanic powers.

One must be clear and fully conscious and must not bring over to one side of the threshold the state of soul that belongs on the other side of the threshold. One must cultivate a strong, inner consciousness for either realm and beyond.

This now emerges for each of the four elements in the admonitions of the Guardian. Once again, we should take these warnings and work with them in meditation.

My dear sisters and brothers, imagine now that you already stand on the far side of the threshold. The Guardian has beckoned you. You turn and look him in the face. He calls to you with earnest warning: where is the solidity of the Earth that sustained you?

Although we do not have it any longer, the heart stirs within and wants to answer. Even so, the heart can be prompted from the cosmos to answer in three different ways.

The heart can be inspired by Christ's power. Then the heart will answer:

> I forsake its solid ground,
> —That is, the solid ground of the Earth—
> > as long as the spirit supports me.

This is the right mood: I leave the firm support of Earth as long as the spirit supports me in the spirit realm, outside of my body.

But the heart can also be inspired by Lucifer. Then the heart will answer:

> I feel rapturous joy that I no longer need its support.

The human being speaks in arrogance and pride, as though this firm support is not needed, not even after returning again to the physical world.

Or the heart can be inspired by Ahriman. Then the heart will answer:

> I will hammer it even firmer with the power of the spirit.
> —It is the firm support that is carried over, hammered firmer—

No one must shrink from bringing all three answers before the soul again and again in meditation. Only then can the first answer be chosen in freedom. We must truly feel how our inner life is prone to vacillate between Lucifer and Ahriman. We must face this in meditation.

Therefore, the meditation must contain this for the Earth element:

Fourteenth Lesson

[The first part of the mantra is written on the blackboard:]

I) *The Guardian*—he speaks: *Where is the solidity of the Earth that sustained you?*

The human heart must answer. If inspired by Christ it answers:

Christ: I forsake its solid ground <u>as long as</u> the spirit supports me.

But if the soul is inspired by Lucifer it answers:

Lucifer: I feel rapturous joy that I no longer need its support.

The heart omits the words *as long as* and wants to replace the period of time by eternity and changes the sentence.

If the heart is inspired by Ahriman it answers:

Ahriman: I will hammer it even firmer with the power of the spirit.
—That is the firm support—

So that the soul may give itself fully to what it is facing, a second warning comes from the Guardian of the Threshold that is related to water's forming forces. This formative forces in water form our solid organs. All that we take in as nutrition must first become liquid and then our organs are formed from it. All of the distinctly contoured organs we possess come forth from the fluid element. These formative forces cease as soon as we cross over to the realm beyond the threshold. The Guardian warns us that this will happen. Therefore, he calls to us again as we stand on the other side of the threshold facing his stern countenance once more.

[The second part of the mantra is written on the blackboard.]

II) *The Guardian: Where is water's formative force that pervaded you?*

If the heart is inspired by Christ, the human being answers:

My life extinguishes it as long as the spirit forms me.

> *Now, while we are outside of our body, the spirit begins to form us.*
>
> *Christ: My life extinguishes it,*
>
> *—"It" is the waters forming force—*
>
> > *as long as the spirit forms me.*

Again, with inner humility, the words "as long as" are present.

> *But the soul prompted by Lucifer omits the words "as long as" and changes the sentence proudly and arrogantly:*
>
> *Lucifer: My life melts it away*
>
> *—What can be quenched can be rekindled; but what is melted away remains melted away; my life melts it away—*
>
> > *that I may be free of it.*
>
> *If inspired by Ahriman, the soul answers:*
>
> *Ahriman: My life solidifies it that I may transport it to spiritual realms.*

My dear sisters and brothers, observe how everything is carefully and meaningfully formed in mantric verses. Here [in the first verse] we have the words: "I forsake," "I feel," "I will"; thus, in answer the ego replies. In the second verse, the ego no longer responds so egocentrically but says "my life," "my life extinguishes," "my life melts," "my life solidifies." This is properly spoken on entering this reality when it corresponds to the spiritual. Carelessness in formulation, which is so common in the physical realm, must not be carried over into the spiritual realm. Everything spoken in the spiritual realm must be exact and precise.

My dear friends, you must also bear in mind the reality that this esoteric School, as noted earlier, has been established not by human will but by the spiritual world. Everything given in this esoteric school at the Goetheanum emerges in speech through my lips, but is dictated by the spiritual world. This must be so in every duly constituted esoteric school, in the present and in the future, as was the case in the Holy Mysteries of ancient times. This esoteric School is the real School of Michael, instituted by those spiritual beings who receive the direct inspiration of Michael.

Once again, with regard to the realm of air, the Guardian speaks with earnest counsel: where is the quickening power of the air that awakened you?

—Awakened you into existence—

As Yahweh transformed the human being from a living being into a sentient being by blowing the breath of life, so the human being is made a sentient being by the stimulus of the outer world on the senses. But what are the senses?

My dear sisters and brothers, the senses are nothing other than differentiated breathing organs. The eyes, ears, and the like are all refined breathing organs. The breath extends into all the senses. Just as the breath lives in the lungs, so does it live in the eyes; except in the lungs it unites with carbon, where in the eyes it unites with highly rarefied silica. Carbon dioxide is generated in the body [drawing red; "carbon dioxide" is written, picture 9]. Silicic acid is generated in the senses in a very rarefied state [yellow; "silicic acid" is written]. The human being lives downward when the body converts oxygen into carbon dioxide. The human being lives upward in the region of the nerve sense system where oxygen combines with silica and generates a highly rarified silicic acid [green]. When the breath enters the blood it forms carbon dioxide. When the breath enters into the senses it generates a highly rarified silicic acid [yellow arrows]. Downward and outward through the breath: carbon dioxide. Toward the senses and then returning from the senses into the breathing process: a highly rarified silicic acid.

The Guardian of the Threshold calls out to us in connection with all that is in the air: Where is the quickening power of the air that awakened you?

A person with a Christ-inspired heart replies:

My soul breathes heaven's air,

—No longer Earth's air but heavens air—

> as long as the spirit is about me.

The Lucifer-inspired heart answers:

My soul, wrapped in spirit bliss, couldn't care less.

The Ahriman-inspired heart answers:

My soul sucks it up that I may learn how the gods create.

As Jehovah long ago created with air, so does the ahrimanically inclined human being absorb air in order to carry it across into the spiritual world.

The Guardian speaks to the human being:

[The third part of the mantra is written on the blackboard.]

> *III) The Guardian: where is the quickening power of the air that awakened you?*
>
> *The Christ-inspired heart speaks:*
>
> Christ: *My soul breathes heaven's air <u>as long as</u> the spirit surrounds me.*

The Lucifer-inspired heart speaks:

> *Lucifer: My soul, wrapped in spirit bliss, couldn't care less.*
> —My soul does not care about the quickening power of air—

The Ahriman-inspired heart speaks:

> *Ahriman: My soul sucks it up that I may learn how the gods create.*

As for fire, or the warmth element, the Guardian speaks what for the moment is the last of his elemental words, warning the human being not to lose one's self in the element of warmth and also not to carry over the warmth element into the spiritual world in the way it works in physical existence on Earth.

But before giving it, my dear sisters and brothers, I just want to point out the ascending mood:

> First the human being speaks "I."
>
> The human being speaks "My life."
>
> The human being speaks "My soul."
>
> Now the Guardian warns about the element of fire.

[The fourth part of the mantra is written on the blackboard:]

> IV) *The Guardian: Where is the purifying*—or cleansing—
> *fire that set your I aflame?*

Our "I" lives in all that permeates us as warmth, or fire. Once before, my dear sisters and brothers, I pointed out in these esoteric lessons that the solid element remains unconscious in human beings. The fluid element also remains unconscious, although we feel a sense of wellbeing in the fluid element. A person who is hungry or satisfied has some experience of the quality of the fluid element. We already experience the element of air in our soul. When we become short of breath, when the composition of air is not right, fear arises with shortness of breath. Here we are already in the life of soul; warmth is something we feel entirely within. A person's total self, a person's "I," participates in the sensation of warmth and cold. Warmth sets the "I" aflame.

> The heart, inspired by Christ, answers:
>
> *Christ: My I burns in the fire of God <u>as long as the spirit</u>*
> <u>*ignites me.*</u>

Human beings do not need earthly, material warmth when the spirit sets the "I" aflame, for then one's "I" is aflame in the fire of God, not in earthly warmth, not in earthly fire.

But if inspired by Lucifer, the heart answers:

My I has the force of flame through the spirit's solar power.

In greatest pride the "I," seduced by Lucifer, now wants to claim for itself what issues spiritually from the sun as fire and then holds it, not for the time when the spirit sets it aflame, but wants to keep it for eternity and never give it back.

> *Lucifer: My I has the force of flame through the spirit's solar power.*

The Ahriman-inspired heart answers as if to possess for itself the fire it received on Earth and then carried across to the spiritual world, there to master the spiritual world with the ego fire of the physical world.

> *Ahriman: My I has fire of its own that burns pure through unfolding self-development.*

The "I" wants to be aflame not through the spirit; it wants to unfold a fire of its own.

Once again there has been an ascent in the formulation:

At first the human being speaks "I":

I leave
I feel
I will

Then the human being becomes more objective. What is attached to the person is described as "mine:"

My life quenches
My life melts away
My life makes firm

Then the human being goes further into the inner life and becomes objective:

> My soul breathes
> My soul could care less
> My soul sucks it up

Now one descends still deeper into one's self. Note well the difference, my dear sisters and brothers. In the first verse the word was simply "I"; now the "I" becomes objective: "my I" as though it were another thing, speaking about it as a possession. We are indeed far more outside; we are outside the body, which makes us speak so egotistically about the "I."

> Now say: My I

—as if it is an object. That is the proper form of speech at this point.

We learn this way of speaking, my dear sisters and brothers, with all depth and intensity when we converse with souls who have gone through the gate of death and have already been in the spiritual world for some time. They never say "I"; they always say "my I": I have never heard a soul speak after death and say "I" unless it was very shortly after death. A certain time after death the dead always say "my I" because they behold the "I" with the eyes of the gods. It becomes objective to them. This is characteristic. Therefore, a communication from a deceased who died some time ago can never be genuine if the deceased says "I" and doesn't say "my I." So here, in the fourth part, the soul facing the Guardian says "my I."

That, my dear friends, is the wonderful dialogue that takes place at the threshold between the Guardian and the human being. It has its own characteristic, and this characteristic comes about when we stand before the Guardian of the Threshold in the situation described. We must sense this characteristic and feel it when we meditate and unfold the dialogue in the right way. Therefore, my dear sisters and brothers, you will meditate the words offered today as mantric words in the right way when you hear these words as if spoken by yourself after first hearing the Guardian in your soul. We meditate and at first hear the Guardian four times at I,

II, III and IV regarding earth, water, air and fire. Then we let our own soul answer: the first answer is inwardly ensouled by Christ. The second answer sounds like the voice of the tempter. The third answer sounds like the voice of the puffed-up, materialistic ahrimanic spirit that approaches us with the wish to take our mineralized being across into the spiritual world.

Therefore, as a conclusion to this esoteric lesson, let us speak the words today in the way they should be meditated:

> Where is the solidity of the Earth that sustained you?
> I forsake its solid ground as long as the spirit supports me.
> I feel rapturous joy that from now on I no longer need its support.
> I will hammer it even firmer with the power of the spirit.
>
> Where is water's formative force that pervaded you?
> My life extinguishes it as long as the spirit forms me.
> My life melts it away that I may be free of it.
> My life solidifies it that I may transport it to spiritual realms.
>
> Where is the quickening power of air that awakened you?
> My soul breathes heaven's air as long as the spirit surrounds me.
> My soul, wrapped in spirit bliss, couldn't care less.
> My soul sucks it up that I may learn how the gods create.
>
> Where is the purifying fire that set your I aflame?
> My I burns in the fire of God as long as the spirit ignites me.
> My I has the force of flame through the spirit's solar power.
> My I has fire of its own that burns pure through unfolding self-development.
>
> (…)

Fifteenth Lesson

Dornach, June 21, 1924

My dear friends! Today, we will again begin with the mantric words that sound toward us from all events and beings of the world, if only we are able with true heart and soul to grasp what the many different beings and processes of the cosmos can tell us:

O Man, Know Thy Self!
Thus sounds the Cosmic Word.
You hear it with strength of soul,
You feel it with might of spirit.

Who speaks so powerfully through the world?
Who speaks so tenderly within your heart?

Does it work through the far-spread rays of space
Into your senses' experience of life?
Does it sound through the weaving waves of time
Into the evolving stream of your life?

Is it you, yourself, who,
By sensing space,
By experiencing time,
Begets this word,
Feeling yourself estranged in the psychic void of space,
Because you lose the force of thought
In the annihilating stream of time?

My dear sisters and brothers, my dear friends, because a considerable number of members are here today who have not been part of these

Class Lessons, it will be necessary to say a few words of what must be known to put the content of today's lesson in context so it can be received with understanding.

My dear sisters and brothers, on our way to real knowledge we have experienced how the great pictures of life appear before our soul as we approach the abyss. This abyss opens up between the surrounding world where we live and the world we want to know and where we live with our true being, where our real human nature exists.

When we perceive the world around us in the right way, we become aware of how this world demands our closest attention as we turn our gaze from the lowliest creatures up to the shining stars sparkling in the sky. We look around at all the kingdoms of nature from which we derive so much of what we bear within ourselves. We have every reason to look at all that is around us in the radiant, bright sunlight. We deeply feel its greatness, significance and majesty in our soul and heart. We must not be misled or turned aside from any type of esotericism or Spiritual Science by participating in it with an ascetic frame of mind. For it would only be a false asceticism to turn away from the lowliest creatures or the lofty, starry sky because we must not fail to feel their greatness, majesty and sublimity or the significance they have for us as a member of this visible world.

We must feel all of this. As true adherents to Spiritual Science, we should above all feel that we belong to the world around us. But we must also become aware of beings and processes of the world and we can become aware of them if we relate ourselves to all things in our heart and soul. We should become aware of the fact that our higher, true human existence is nowhere to be found in any of the realms of nature. However great and sublime is this sun-illumined world, our highest self is not found there. We must seek it in a world that, to our perception, is separated from us by an abyss. What lies beyond the abyss—in the world of our true origin—first presents itself to us as the blackest darkness. It faces us like a wall, a black wall, and the abyss lies in front of it.

The first being we meet is standing at the abyss. We must emphasize repeatedly that every night when we go to sleep we would find ourselves actually within that realm where we belong with our innermost, true being. Then again, we are only allowed to enter this realm at full maturity. The Guardian of the Threshold saves us from prematurely entering this realm. He is the first spiritual being we meet when we develop the earnest and sincere will to enter the world of our true origin.

The Guardian of the Threshold speaks the first words to us when we want to set out on the path to cross the abyss into the spiritual realm from which we originate. The Guardian of the Threshold himself now calls us to turn around and look back at ourselves so that we may seek in self-knowledge the true foundation for knowledge of the world.

At the entrance to the spiritual world the Guardian of the Threshold himself shows us how our soul life—our will, feeling and thinking—assumes a form that can appear before us in imaginative knowledge. He shows us how in our present time on Earth, our feeling, thinking and will appear in the shape of three beasts who rise from the abyss. Then the instructions of the Guardian of the Threshold follow, to behave in a certain way toward these three beasts—meaning toward ourselves—so that we may really find the way to understand the world from which we originate. All this was placed before the souls of those who participated in these lessons in mantric verses. This led us to what was put before us in the previous lesson.

We came to the actual threshold situation in meditation. We were led to see ourselves already on the other side of the abyss, yet still subject to the cautions of the Guardian of the Threshold. Now he addresses us with words that should lead us to understand the situation we are in, now that we have flown over the abyss into the realm that is, to begin with, dark for us.

As long as we remain in the terrestrial realm, whence we do not originate, we have the firmness of the Earth beneath us; the solid ground supports us. As we have seen, we touch it with our entire body as we stand upon it. This is the first thing: the Earth element.

Then we carry in us what in Spiritual Science is called "water," which means everything that is fluid, or liquid. We feel the fluid element in us as what forms us, which makes us grow and from which all our organs are brought forth. This is the second thing: the water element. The Guardian of the Threshold warns us about the water element, which is also the element of our blood.

The Guardian of the Threshold addresses us with significant words concerning air, what we take in through our breath, and likewise about everything we take in through warmth, the element of fire.

Cosmic powers work within us so that we seek in our soul for a response to the Guardian's warning question. If this response, which cosmic powers help us formulate, comes from Christ, it will be the right answer. Or it can come from Lucifer; then it will be the wrong answer. Or it can come from Ahriman; and then again, it will be the wrong answer.

Christ's teachings will always be in such a form—this will be the case for each of the four elements—that Christ will speak within us. On the other side, in the spiritual world, we feel ourselves to be truly spiritual and in harmony with the spirit; but, we must know that as long as we are earthly human beings we always need to go back across the abyss to Earth existence. We must not want to carry the characteristics of the spiritual world within us for any longer than we are there. Christ will always speak to us in a way that instructs us. As long as we are in the spiritual world we should unite with the spiritual world. When we return to the Earth, we should live on the Earth as true earthly human beings. For we should desire to be in the spiritual world only with our spirit.

Lucifer will always try to inflame and tempt us and make us want to remain in the spiritual world, to merge with it and dissolve into the blissful rapture of being in the spiritual world.

Ahriman will always inspire us to enter *his* service and to carry the spiritual world back across the threshold with us, down into the physical world.

All of this must be allowed to work on our soul so that we feel ourselves completely in the situation in which one finds oneself when confronting the spiritual world.

Fifteenth Lesson

We now feel ourselves in complete darkness, standing in the spiritual world beyond the abyss. At the abyss the Guardian of the Threshold admonishes us with his right hand to stay, questioning us in a way that cuts deeply through our soul. Let us feel how in response to each question a threefold answer comes from us: Christ's answer, Lucifer's answer and the answer of Ahriman.

The Guardian speaks:
What becomes of the solidity of the Earth that sustained you?

—There is no solid ground on the other side of the threshold; we are in the spiritual world.

The Guardian asks:
What becomes of the solidity of the Earth that sustained you?

Christ within us answers:
I forsake its solid ground as long as the spirit supports me.

Lucifer within us answers:
I feel rapturous joy that I no longer need its support.

Ahriman answers:
I will hammer it even firmer with the power of the spirit.

The Guardian speaks:
What becomes of water's formative force that pervaded you?

Christ within us speaks:
My life extinguishes it as long as the spirit forms me.

Lucifer within us:
My life melts it away that I may be free of it.

Ahriman within us speaks:
My life solidifies it that I may transport it to the realm of spirit.

The Guardian speaks:
Where is the quickening power of the air that awakened you?

Christ within us:
My soul breathes heaven's air as long as the spirit surrounds me.

Lucifer within us:
My soul, wrapped in spirit bliss, couldn't care less.

Ahriman within us:
My soul sucks it up that I may learn how the gods create.

The Guardian speaks:
Where is the purifying fire that set your "I" aflame?

Christ within us:
My I burns in the fire of God as long as the spirit ignites me.

Lucifer within us:
My "I" has the force of flame through the spirit's solar power.

Ahriman within us:
My "I" has fire of its own that burns through self-development.

Thus we are tried and tested by the Guardian's warning questions. Tried as to what our attitude will be toward the firm support of Earth, toward the forming force of water, toward the astral quickening power of air, and toward the "I"-bearing power of fire. Christ answers within us, calling forth our true humanity. Lucifer answers within us, tempting us to forever seize for ourselves the spiritual bliss that we should only kindle in ourselves in the moments when we dedicate ourselves to the spirit. Ahriman answers within us, as if we would carry back to the realms on Earth what we shared in the land of spirit.

We must allow all that is possible in the soul to work within our souls. Not only must we expose ourselves to the voice of Christ, but also to the voices of Lucifer and Ahriman. We must put ourselves into this situation through meditation. Then, my dear sisters and brothers, we shall be so far liberated through being challenged in our innermost being that in this liberating experience of the spirit we shall truly be capable of making the spiritual element our own.

Fifteenth Lesson

Today, we must start again from this situation. We must clearly feel ourselves to be standing on the far side of the threshold of the abyss with the cautioning Guardian at our side. We must feel the voices of Lucifer and Ahriman within us, voices that pull us in different directions,. We must also feel the voice of Christ showing us the true way, while Lucifer on one side and Ahriman on the other seek to mislead us. So shall we achieve the inner mood that makes it possible for us to begin to feel the spiritual world.

My dear sisters and brothers, we can only do this if we gradually acquire the ability to feel toward the higher spiritual beings the way we feel toward the beings of the three kingdoms of nature.

When we are in the sense world, we feel the nature of stone, the mineral nature, outside of us and we say: this mineral nature also lives within us. We have salt inside us. Salt lives in our mineral nature, which alone makes it possible for us to be human beings on Earth.

We look at the world of plants. We know that we take plants into ourselves. We have plants within the boundaries of our skin. We carry plant life in us as we grow along with all the organs that form in us. We have the plant world within us and in all that we develop while we are asleep. We feel that we carry the being of plants in us when we look out at the plants around us.

We look at the animals and know that we carry the essence of animal nature in our astrality, in our breathing processes. We look at the variety of animals and say: we feel part of this animality because we carry it within us, except that we organize it upward to a human level.

Thus we feel ourselves as human beings standing here in the sense perceptible world among the beings of the three kingdoms of nature. When we are in the spiritual world, we must learn to feel ourselves among those beings with whom we exist with our spirit and soul just as much as we exist among the beings of the three kingdoms of nature with our etheric and physical being here on Earth. Just as we learn to be aware of ourselves as physical beings among other physical beings, so must we also learn to be aware of ourselves as human beings of spirit and soul among beings of spirit and soul.

We have come to know the world of soul and spirit that touches our humanity in the form of the three hierarchies. In this same way, we have come to know everything that approaches us from the outside—the beings of the sense world in the three kingdoms of nature. With our etheric and physical sheaths we belong to the three kingdoms of nature. With our soul and spirit we belong to the three kingdoms of the hierarchies. It is natural for us to belong to the three kingdoms of nature when standing in the world of the senses, letting them flow through us and standing within them. It is natural for our soul and spirit to belong to the beings of the higher hierarchies when in the world of spirit and soul. We must know ourselves to be among these hierarchies while we feel ourselves to be in the spiritual world, which is similar to how we know we are facing the beings of the three kingdoms of nature. The Guardian of the Threshold draws our attention to this once more. The mantric words that now come down from the spiritual world by the magic power of the Guardian's voice must resound again and again in our souls when we meditate. Then by the simple way they are formed, through their specific structure, and through repetition, they will have the power to call to life the feeling of being within the spiritual world among the hierarchies.

That's why we must imagine the next mantra spoken by the Guardian as follows. We are standing in darkness on the far side of the threshold. In the spiritual world we learn to feel before we learn to see. The Guardian speaks again of the elements of earth, water and air. (The element of fire will be the subject of the next Class Lesson.) The Guardian speaks about the elements of earth, water and air: everything solid in us; everything fluid in us, especially our blood the fluids in our tissues; and everything that is air within us, the air we take in from outside and is in us as breathing. The Guardian speaks about all of this. He calls forth what resounds from the world of the hierarchies.

After the Guardian has spoken, one hierarchy after the other speaks. In the first mantra the third hierarchy speaks: first the Angeloi, then the Archangeloi and thirdly the Archai. This is the situation we find ourselves in. The Guardian speaks to us. Then it sounds forth from the darkness, as if it sounds forth from deeply hidden depths while, at the same time, it earnestly speaks to our souls.

> The Guardian speaks:
> What becomes of the solidity of the Earth that sustained you?
>
> From the third hierarchy, the Angeloi:
> Sense how we are sensing in your thinking.
>
> From the third hierarchy, the Archangeloi:
> Experience how we have experience in your feeling.
>
> From the third hierarchy, the Archai:
> Perceive how we perceive in your willing.

We receive a significant threefold teaching from the cosmos in answer to the Guardian's question. With magic power his words call forth the responses of the Angeloi, Archangeloi and Archai.

What do the Angeloi teach? They teach that we human beings think. At first we believe that only we experience our thoughts. Yet, all the time that our thoughts pass through our souls the Angeloi are in reality living in them. Just as we sense things with our senses, just as we touch an object and take hold of it, so do the Angeloi live in our thinking. Our thinking is their sensing. They make us aware of this. Just as the Angeloi are sensing in our thinking, so the Archangeloi are experiencing in our feeling, and the Archai are beholding in our willing.

My dear sisters and brothers, when any thought passes through your soul, feel that a being of the hierarchy of Angeloi is sensing something in this thought. Human thinking, human feeling and human willing are not merely processes inside the human being. While we think, the Angeloi are sensing; when we feel, the Archangeloi are experiencing; and, when we will, the Archai are beholding.

[The first part of the mantra is written on the blackboard:]

> *The Guardian speaks:*
> *What becomes of the solidity of the Earth that sustained you?*

From the third hierarchy comes the response of the Angeloi:

["Third hierarchy" is written vertically down the left side of the blackboard and underlined:]

> Angeloi: Sense how we are sensing in your thinking.

From the hierarchy of the Archangeloi resounds:

> Archangeloi: Experience how we have experience in your feeling.

From the hierarchy of the Archai resounds:

> Archai: Perceive how we perceive in your willing.

This is what takes the place of the element of Earth in the spiritual world. For the supportive power of the Earth is not there. The solid ground is no more; everything firm has gone away. The third hierarchy—Angeloi, Archangeloi and Archai—do not build firmness the way minerals build something solid. We would not only sink down in our thinking, but sink down in all directions were it not for the Angeloi working and sensing within us. Our feelings would scatter in all directions, into formlessness, were it not for the Archangeloi living in our feelings. Our will would disappear into nothingness if not for the Archai's strength of beholding in our will.

Second, water, the fluid element, gives us formative force. Imagine once more that we are standing in the spiritual world on the far side of the abyss, where it is still dark. A first we learn to feel in the spiritual world. The Guardian speaks again, warning and questioning, but this time with regard to the force of the fluid element. The beings of the second hierarchy respond: the Exusiai, the Dynamis, the Kyriotetes.

> The Guardian speaks:
> What becomes of water's formative force that pervaded you?
>
> From the second hierarchy the Exusiai reply:

>   Recognize the spirit's cosmic creating in the human body's creating.
>
> The Dynamis in the second hierarchy:
> Feel the spirit's cosmic life in the human body's life.
>
> The Kyriotetes in the second hierarchy:
> Will the spirit's cosmic process in the human body's being.

We are made conscious that with regard to all that now surrounds us, we do not stand as separate beings. We must learn to feel how even in our bodily existence, with all that we carry within the boundary of our skin, part of cosmic existence lives there. The second hierarchy lives and works in us as if we were cosmic beings who belong to and are part of the entire cosmos.

Through these mantras we must become deeply aware that we continually stand in the midst of great cosmic processes. From the tiniest vibration of a cell to the majestic wave movements in our blood, the rhythm of our breathing, right up to the rhythms of day and night, these processes are not only going on inside of us...they are all part of the universal cosmic process.

[The second part of the mantra is written on the blackboard.]

> *The Guardian speaks:*
>
> *What becomes of water's formative force that pervaded you?*
>
> *From the second hierarchy the Exusiai answer:*

["second hierarchy" is written vertically on the blackboard and underlined].

> *Exusiai:*   *Recognize the spirit's cosmic creating in the human body's creating.*
>
> *From the second hierarchy the Dynamis answer:*
>
> *Dynamis:*   *Feel the spirit's cosmic life in the human body's life.*

> *From the second hierarchy the Kyriotetes answer:*
>
> Kyriotetes: *Will the spirit's cosmic process in the human body's being.*

As I have so often said, every detail in these mantric verses needs to be taken exactly. Therefore, the question may arise: why does "cosmic process" stand next to "body's being" in the last line? We must take every word exactly if a mantric verse is to work properly in our soul. Outside of us, the spirit's cosmic process surges on and we feel it as a process. The spirit's cosmic process fills the universe, worldwide. Inasmuch as it goes on inside us, we feel it is a self-contained existence because we are contained within our skin and feel ourselves to be complete and separate beings. We do not feel everything weaving and surging within us as we do with things outside us. Therefore, in this line of the mantra, "process" must stand in contrast to "being," whereas in the other lines, they are quite rightly the repetitions of cosmic "creating" and body "creating"; cosmic "life" embodies "life."

The Guardian of the Threshold raises his warning question with respect to the element of air. The beings of the first hierarchy—the Thrones, Cherubim and Seraphim—provide the answer. They counsel that we must become conscious of how the cosmos works within us. The beings of the first hierarchy lead us from mere consciousness to self-consciousness.

> The Guardian speaks:
>
> What becomes of the quickening power of the air that awakened you?
>
> From the first hierarchy the Thrones answer:
>
> With wisdom grasp your inner being within your divine cosmic being.
>
> From the first hierarchy the Cherubim respond:
>
> Enkindle warmth of inner life within your divine cosmic life.

Fifteenth Lesson

From the first hierarchy the Seraphim speak:

Awaken your inner light within your divine cosmic light.

Now, where at first we felt impelled to merge with the cosmos, to give ourselves up to it through the magic words of the second hierarchy, we are now taught that we must reawaken our self-consciousness on a higher level.

[The third part of the mantra is written on the blackboard.]

The Guardian—speaks:

What becomes of the quickening power of the air that awakened you?

From the first hierarchy [first hierarchy is written vertically on the blackboard and underlined] the cosmic response sounds:

Thrones:	*With wisdom grasp your inner being within your divine cosmic being.*
Cherubim:	*Enkindle warmth of inner life within your divine cosmic life.*
Seraphim:	*Awaken your inner light within your divine cosmic light.*

Truly, my dear sisters and brothers, until we have felt the influence of this last mantra as it sounds forth from the fiery, lightning power of the Seraphim—"Awaken your inner light within your divine cosmic light"—until this fiery word has sounded forth from the flaming seraphic lightning, we shall not begin to feel how a force must be awakened from our own soul so that we—standing there in the darkness on the far side of the abyss, only groping about—may feel the world slowly coming nearer to us. Gradually, then, we may have the first glimmering, then a lightening up, and then an increase of the glimmering going away from us further into space. We advance farther and farther until the glimmering becomes lighter, more luminous and more shining, until at length the night-enveloped darkness in the spiritual world grows light through our own power.

So it must come to pass. So must we try to achieve a kindling power of our own self, the power that kindles itself in the fire of our innermost being. This, then, lights up the spiritual world where, at first, it was dark.

So do we feel our way into a threefold world of spirits—the world of the Angeloi, Exusiai, Thrones and so on, in the same way that we feel our way here in the sense world to the sense perceptible beings of the kingdoms of nature. We learn to feel ourselves as essential and true human beings in spiritual surroundings, just as we feel ourselves as sense perceptible human beings on Earth. We learn this as we ascend from the third hierarchy that unfolds the spirit in us, our own spirit where the third hierarchy is living. We ascend from them to the second hierarchy that unfolds the cosmic spirit in us, creating, living and forming. And finally we come to the first hierarchy where we find support once again, but spiritual support that, in essence, comes from above, not from below. This is where we have the wielding wisdom of the Cherubim who bring us self-consciousness, where we once again can warm our inner life in true self-knowledge, and where we can experience and warm the self until this warm self finally becomes a living light element, enlightening what until now was dark before us.

Feeling such things as these we stand at the side of the Guardian of the Threshold. We feel deeply the counsel that resounds to us from all the beings and processes of the universe so that from self-knowledge we may gain world knowledge and from world knowledge we can gain knowledge of the human being. So we stand, both in nature's being and in the spirit's being, taking hold of ourselves on both sides of reality—on the side of nature and on the side of the spirit.

The Cosmic Word rings forth now in a new form, not with different wording, but we feel it differently, strengthened by the guidance of all the hierarchies of the spiritual world from which we originate.

Fifteenth Lesson

O Man, Know Thy Self!
Thus sounds the Cosmic Word.
You hear it with strength of soul,
You feel it with might of spirit.

Who speaks so powerfully through the world?
Who speaks so tenderly within your heart?

Does it work through the far-spread rays of space
Into your senses' experience of life?
Does it sound through the weaving waves of time
Into the evolving stream of your life?

Is it you, yourself, who,
By sensing space,
By experiencing time,
Begets this word,
Feeling yourself estranged in the psychic void of space,
Because you lose the force of thought
In the annihilating stream of time?

(…)

Sixteenth Lesson

Dornach, June 28, 1924

My dear friends! We begin again with the words that sound to us, that sound to every human soul that understands the world rightly. They sound to us from both near and far in the cosmos.

(...)

Now the mantric words are spoken that are always spoken at the beginning of our esoteric discussions. They make us mindful of instructions to the heart that sound forth to human beings from all the processes, things and beings of the world. It is the call to self-knowledge, which is the true foundation for world-knowledge:

> O Man, Know Thy Self!
> Thus sounds the Cosmic Word.
> You hear it with strength of soul,
> You feel it with might of spirit.
>
> Who speaks so powerfully through the world?
> Who speaks so tenderly within your heart?
>
> Does it work through the far-spread rays of space
> Into your senses' experience of life?
> Does it sound through the weaving waves of time
> Into the evolving stream of your life?
>
> Is it you, yourself, who,
> By sensing space,
> By experiencing time,
> Begets this word,
> Feeling yourself estranged in the psychic void of space,

Sixteenth Lesson

Because you lose the force of thought
In the annihilating stream of time?

My dear friends, we progressed from the mantric verses that come from the spiritual world to those mantric verses that make us feel within esoteric situations. The esoteric situation consists first of all by imagining in meditation how that spiritual being speaks to us who stands there at the abyss of existence.

Let us picture this once more because we cannot recall it often enough in our souls. The human being looks around at all that surrounds them in the three kingdoms of nature on Earth. The person looks upward to the majestic stars, looks at the drifting clouds, and wind and waves; looks at lightning and thunder; looks at everything one sees from the lowliest creature up to the lofty revelation of the sparkling stars. Only a false asceticism, which we should not look for in genuine esoteric life, would despise this world that speaks to our senses. Anyone who wants to be a true human being cannot do otherwise but feel most intimately this reality of the senses and the intellect, from the lowliest creature to the majestic and divine sparkling stars.

But then the moment comes that can take hold of us in the depths of our soul, the moment where we must say to ourselves: great and mighty, beautiful and majestic is all that we see around us. We must not disguise it; we must acknowledge this as a fact. We must gradually penetrate more of what our eyes can see, what our ears can hear, what our other senses can perceive and what can be grasped with our intellect. Yet, when we look around us into the far distances of space and into the weaving waves of time in this way, in spite of all the greatness and beauty in our surroundings, we will never perceive the innermost core of our being in these realms. You must say to yourself: the innermost core of my being must be sought somewhere else. This is the moment where the power of such a thought can take hold of us.

What then follows for the soul can only be expressed in Imaginations. These imaginative pictures lead us at first to a wide open field where all that is earthly and perceptible to the senses is spread out before us. We find everything illumined by the sun, glistening in the light and yet, looking around, our inner being is nowhere to be found. We look ahead and find that the sun-illumined field, all that is so great and beautiful for our senses—where we ourselves are not—is closed in by a dark, night-enveloped wall. We now feel our way deep into the darkness. We feel our way into the darkness to perhaps find there the light, to find the source of our being. Yet, we are unable to see in this darkness.

As we now follow the path ahead, the abyss of existence opens up before us, the abyss that is the threshold to the spiritual world. First we must cross this abyss. There stands the Guardian who warns us to be mature enough to cross the abyss. For with our ordinary habits of thinking, feeling and willing as they exist in the physical world, we cannot cross the abyss of existence into the true spiritual world where our own true being has its origin.

The first spirit figure we encounter is the Guardian of the Threshold. Every night when we sleep we are in that spiritual world. Yet, our "I" and astral body are surrounded by darkness because we may only enter the spiritual world when we are mature enough to do so. The Guardian of the Threshold protects us from entering prematurely. But now that we come before him, he gives us his great counsel. And this counsel is presented to us in the mantric verses that have thus far formed the content of these esoteric lessons.

(...)

These mantras have not only shown us how we must carry our heart if we want to reach the other side of the abyss of existence, they have also shown us how we find ourselves in our soul condition when we have flown across the abyss. Gradually we will feel—not yet see, but only sense—how the darkness, which at first is as dark as the night, gradually becomes lighter. First, we feel that the darkness grows lighter, and then we sense the elements—the earthly, watery, airy and fiery elements—how they become quite different on the other side, where we now live in another world. And this world where we seek to know our own existence and the true nature of the elements...this is truly another world.

Last time there came before our soul the meditation where we imagined the Guardian standing at the abyss of existence. We are already on the other side of the abyss and there, at first, we feel—we do not see yet —how the darkness becomes lighter. The Guardian speaks to us. He has already made clear how we should behave regarding the four elements. The Guardian speaks about how these elements are now different for us. He poses questions to us.

Who is it that answers? The hierarchies themselves answer the questions. From one direction the third hierarchy, the Angeloi, Archangeloi and Archai reply; then from another direction the second hierarchy responds; and from a third direction, the first hierarchy.

The third hierarchy—Angeloi, Archangeloi, Archai—answer when the Guardian of the Threshold asks what becomes of the firmness of the Earth. The second hierarchy—Exusiai, Dynamis, Kyriotetes—answer when the Guardian of the Threshold asks what becomes of water's formative forces that work in us and give us our inner form. And the first hierarchy— Thrones, Cherubim, Seraphim—answer when the Guardian asks us what becomes of the quickening power of the air that awakens us from a dull, plantlike existence into a sentient-feeling existence.

Such mantric verses must penetrate our heart and soul so that we feel ourselves entirely within the spiritual situation. The Guardian of the Threshold poses searching, testing questions to us. The hierarchies answer.

The Guardian:	What becomes of the solidity of the Earth that sustained you?
Angeloi:	Sense how we are sensing in your thinking.
Archangeloi:	Experience how we have experience in your feeling.
Archai:	Perceive how we perceive in your willing.
The Guardian:	What becomes of water's formative force that pervaded you?
Exusiai:	Recognize the spirit's cosmic creating in the human body's creating.

Dynamis:	Feel the spirit's cosmic life in the human body's life.
Kyriotetes:	Will the spirit's cosmic process in the human body's being.
The Guardian:	What becomes of the quickening power of air that awakened you?
Thrones:	With wisdom grasp your inner being within your divine cosmic being.
Cherubim:	Enkindle warmth of inner life within your divine cosmic life.
Seraphim:	Awake in you the inner light within your divine cosmic light.

My dear sisters and brothers, these words of admonition come from the communion of the Guardian of the Threshold with the hierarchies. In the course of time these words will help our soul to increasingly make progress if we repeatedly experience them in the right way.

In the way that is right for a person of today and in the future, we will undergo what in the ancient Holy Mysteries was described as the moment when the pupil recognized being led into the being of the elements of earth, water and air.

But warmth is also an element and warmth permeates everything. The earth element, which supports us with firmness, contains warmth. In the watery element that forms us as human beings, that gives our organs definite contours and brings about life and growth, here the element of warmth is living. Warmth also lives in the air element through which the Yahweh spirit once breathed soul into human beings. Even today, the soul rises through the air above the dull, plant existence. Warmth lives everywhere; it lives in everything. We must come to know it as the element that permeates everything. We must dive into this all-permeating element; we are also close to it in our feeling.

We feel remote from the earth element even though we feel its firm support. We even feel remote from the element of water. The air element already comes closer to us and has a more intimate connection with us.

For when the air element does not fill us quite regularly—when we have either too much or too little breath—our inner life shows how air is connected with us. Too much breath makes the soul fearful and anxious; too little breath brings about faintness. Our soul life is definitely influenced by the element of air.

We are most intimately connected with the warmth element. What is warm or cold in us is we, ourselves. We can only stay alive by generating a certain degree of warmth within us. We are most akin to warmth. And when we want to draw near to it, then not just one hierarchy can speak by itself, but the council of several hierarchies must sound together.

This is why the Guardian of the Threshold addresses his cautionary words to us, the warning question about the element of warmth. But the answer from the universe, sounding from the cosmos, is now different.

> The Guardian speaks:
> Where is the purifying fire that set your I aflame?

We already know the question—and now the question leads us into the element of warmth, or fire.

Then, not only does one hierarchy, or one rank from the hierarchies, answer, but a chorus made up of the Angeloi, Exusiai and Thrones provides the answer. Next, the Archangeloi, Dynamis and Cherubim answer the Guardian's question; and third, the Archai, Kyriotetes and Seraphim give answer. Three answers regarding the all-permeating element of warmth resound in a choir spoken by the three hierarchies. We must, therefore, imagine that when we advance to the Guardian's question that warns us about warmth, the moment the answers sound from our "I"—inspired by the hierarchies—there first resounds from all directions the speech of the Angeloi, Exusiai and Thrones. Second comes the speaking of the Archangeloi, Dynamis and Cherubim. And third, the Archai, Kyriotetes and Seraphim follow. All three hierarchies always speak. One rank from each of the three hierarchies always speaks. In this way the cosmic answer connected with this question comes to us.

> The Guardian speaks:
> Where is the purifying fire that set your I aflame?
>
> Angeloi, Exusiai, Thrones:
> Awaken for yourself in the expanse of cosmic ether the
> > flaming script of life.

All three hierarchies advise us to consider that everything that happens to us in our life on Earth is recorded in the cosmic ether and that we behold it inscribed in the cosmic ether when we have passed through the gate of death. There, after passing through the gate of death and looking back upon our earthly life—and also looking forward into the etheric realm of the cosmos—is inscribed what we have accomplished by way of thoughts, feelings and deeds during our life on Earth. It is a flaming script...the flaming script of our life.

> Archangeloi, Dynamis and Cherubim answer in us:
> Create for yourself in cyclic waves of time your soul's
> > atonement forces.

We are made mindful of the second stage we must undergo after death. There we experience in reverse order and in mirror images—that is to say, with just atonement—everything we've accomplished in life. Did we act some way or other toward someone? We then experience during the retrospect what the other person experienced because of us, as we go backward through the stream of time. In the way I have expressed it, the Archangeloi, Dynamis and Cherubim remind us about the nature of this second stage that is experienced between death and rebirth. In the third stage we work out our karma when we, as human souls, collaborate with other human souls and with the beings of the hierarchies, when the Archai (primeval powers), Kyriotetes and Seraphim counsel us.

> Archai, Kyriotetes, Seraphim:
> Ask for yourself from eternal deeds of being the spirit's
> > redemptive powers.

We must feel ourselves living fully in this situation where the Guardian of the Threshold instructs us, speaks to us and reaches out to us with his earnest gesture. And then, from the vast reaches of the cosmos, there sounds toward us, moving our hearts, what connects us with the riddles of life.

[The fourth part of the mantra is written on the blackboard.]

> *The Guardian speaks:*
> *Where is the purifying fire that set your I aflame?*
>
> *Angeloi, Exusiai, Thrones:*
> *Awaken for yourself in the expanse of cosmic ether the*
> *   flaming script of life.*
>
> *Archangeloi, Dynamis, Cherubim:*
> *Create for yourself in cyclic waves of time your soul's*
> *   atonement forces.*
>
> *Archai, Kyriotetes, Seraphim:*
> *Ask for yourself from eternal deeds of being the spirit's*
> *   redemptive powers.*

What stood before us like black, night-enveloped darkness is not yet glowing with light to our soul's vision. Yet, we have the feeling, as we stand in this night-enveloped darkness, that we sense a glimmering light in all directions. And we find ourselves in this situation, aware that we are within this glimmering light, which we can only feel. We feel our way to the Guardian of the Threshold. We really only saw him when we were still on the other side in the sense world. Then we stepped across into the darkness where we only heard his admonishing and questioning words. But now, these stern, questioning words have led us to where we feel something like a weaving, moving light, a gentle light. Looking for help amidst this weaving, active light, we turn toward the Guardian of the Threshold. It is a strange experience: it is not yet light, but we feel the presence of light. We feel in the presence of this light how the Guardian reveals himself, as if he were now growing more intimate with us, as if he were leaning toward us and we were also coming closer to him.

What he now says works as it does in life when someone says something very quietly and confidential into our ear. What first sounded forth as warning words from the Guardian of the Threshold, what sounded like a trumpet call—powerful and majestic, sounding from all directions of the cosmos into our heart—now continues as an intimate conversation with the Guardian of the Threshold in the weaving, active light. Now it is as though he is no longer speaking to us, but is whispering in our ear:

Has your Spirit understood?

Our inner being becomes warm on hearing these confidential words when the Guardian says: "Has your Spirit understood?" Our inner being becomes warm, experiences itself in the warmth and feels compelled to answer. Our inner self answers with reverence—so we imagine it in meditation. It answers in reverence, quietly and with humility:

> The cosmic spirit in me
> Has held its breath
> And may its presence
> Illuminate my "I."

Without any pride or arrogance our "I" answers the question "Has your Spirit understood?" by saying "I have understood." But the "I" feels that divine being is streaming through its innermost being. It is the breath of God in you that stops quietly for a moment and prepares your understanding.

[The first verse of the new mantra is now written on the blackboard:]

> *The Guardian:*
> *Has your Spirit understood?*
>
> *The "I":*
> *The cosmic spirit in me*
> *Has held its breath*
> *And may its presence*
> *Illuminate my "I."*

> And second, the Guardian asks us confidentially:
>
> Has your soul comprehended?
>
> Our "I" answers:
>
> The cosmic souls within me
> Lived in the council of stars
> And may their harmonies,
> Resounding, fashion my "I."

Once again, when the Guardian asks: "Has your soul comprehended?" the "I" is not tempted to answer in an arrogant fashion. The soul becomes conscious that cosmic souls speak within it; the souls of the beings of the higher hierarchies speak within your soul. In their speaking, an individual being is not present but a group of beings holding council together is speaking. As when the stars of a planetary system are orbiting and send their forces of light to one another, so do cosmic souls hold council and send their advice to one another. This is what the soul perceives. The soul hopes that that sounding will so fashion its "I" that the "I" existing in the human being becomes an echo of the cosmic harmonies. These harmonies arise when cosmic souls take counsel among themselves. Their advice and harmonies resound in the human soul—like the wandering stars (planets) in the planetary system.

[The second part of the mantra is written on the blackboard.]

> The Guardian:
> Has your soul comprehended?
>
> The "I":
> The cosmic souls within me
> Lived in the council of stars
> And may their harmonies,
> Resounding, fashion my "I."

The third confidential question the Guardian poses to human beings in this situation is this:

Has your body experienced?

The soul feels that the great forces of the cosmos—which are everywhere—are concentrated in its body at one point in space. But these cosmic forces do not appear now as physical forces. The soul has long since become aware of how these forces, which appear in the outer world as active, physical forces—as gravitational, electrical and magnetic forces, as forces of warmth and light—how these forces, when active in the human body, are moral forces and are transformed into will forces. The soul feels these cosmic forces as constituting that eternal cosmic justice that works throughout successive Earth lives. The soul feels them to be like forces of judgment woven into the verdicts of karma, and thereby, woven into the true "I." When the Guardian intimately asks:

Has your body experienced?

—The human being feels compelled to answer humbly, devoted to cosmic justice:

> The cosmic forces in me
> Judge the deeds of men
> And may their verdicts
> Guide the "I" in me.

[The third verse is written on the blackboard:]

> *The Guardian:*
> *Has your Body experienced?*
>
> *The "I":*
> *The cosmic forces in me*
> *Judge the deeds of men*
> *And may their verdicts*
> *Guide the "I" in me.*

Thus, having experienced the transformation, the metamorphosis, of the cosmic elements in this way together with the Guardian of the

Threshold and the hierarchies, the soul answers these three questions with inner devotion. It weaves into its own being what has been poured into it. Once again the soul has progressed a little further in answering the riddle posed by the words "O Man, Know Thy Self!"

We now want to compare the opening mantric words with what came to us in a devotional mood, feeling ourselves into this warmth element with regard to the spiritual content of the cosmos. Then we feel once more how we have made progress in complying with the great admonition: O Man, Know Thy Self! We will see how we, as human beings, stand in the middle between the call to self-knowledge sounding from all the events and beings of the cosmos and the mantric dialogue in our soul that we received in today's lesson:

> O Man, Know Thy Self!
> Thus sounds the Cosmic Word.
> You hear it with strength of soul,
> You feel it with might of spirit;
>
> Who speaks so powerfully through the world?
> Who speaks so tenderly within your heart?
>
> Does it work through the far-spread rays of space
> Into your senses' experience of life?
> Does it sound through the weaving waves of time
> Into the evolving stream of your life?
>
> Is it you, yourself, who,
> By sensing space,
> By experiencing time,
> Begets this word,
> Feeling yourself estranged in the psychic void of space,
> Because you lose the force of thought
> In the annihilating stream of time?
>
> Where is the purifying fire that set your I aflame?
>
> > Awaken for yourself in the expanse of cosmic ether the flaming script of life.

Create for yourself in cyclic waves of time your soul's atonement forces.

Ask for yourself from eternal deeds of being the spirit's redemptive power.

Has your Spirit understood?

The cosmic spirit in me
Has held its breath
And may its presence
Illuminate my "I."

Has your soul comprehended?

The cosmic souls within me
Lived in the council of stars
And may their harmonies,
Resounding, fashion my "I."

Has your Body experienced?

The cosmic forces in me
Judge the deeds of men
And may their verdicts
Guide the "I" in me.

The Guardian speaks:
  Where is the purifying fire that set
  your "I" aflame?

Angeloi, Exusiai, Thrones:
  Awaken for yourself in the expanse of
  cosmic ether the flaming script of life.

Archangeloi, Dynamis, Cherubim:
  Create for yourself in cyclic waves of time
  your soul's atonement forces.

Archai, Kyriotetes, Seraphim:
>Ask for yourself from eternal deeds of being
>the spirit's redemptive powers.

The Guardian:
>Has your Spirit understood?

The "I":
>The cosmic spirit in me
>Has held its breath
>And may its presence
>Illuminate my "I."

The Guardian:
>Has your soul comprehended?

The "I":
>The cosmic souls within me
>Lived in the council of stars
>And may their harmonies,
>Sounding, fashion my "I."

The Guardian:
>Has your Body experienced?

The "I":
>The cosmic forces in me
>Judge the deeds of men
>And may their verdicts
>Guide the "I" in me.

Seventeenth Lesson

Dornach, July 5, 1924

My dear friends! Today we will again begin with the verse that, through a correct understanding of the universe, resounds in human hearts from all that is and all that is becoming as the ever-present call to self-knowledge. Only by this means can one attain true knowledge of the cosmos.

> O Man, Know Thy Self!
> Thus sounds the Cosmic Word.
> You hear it with strength of soul,
> You feel it with might of spirit.
>
> Who speaks so powerfully through the world?
> Who speaks so tenderly within your heart?
>
> Does it work through the far-spread rays of space
> Into your senses' experience of life?
> Does it sound through the weaving waves of time
> Into the evolving stream of your life?
>
> Is it you, yourself, who,
> By sensing space,
> By experiencing time,
> Begets this word,
> Feeling yourself estranged in the psychic void of space,
> Because you lose the force of thought
> In the annihilating stream of time?

Seventeenth Lesson

Once more let the content of the previous Class Lesson pass before our souls. It was a meditation born from what human beings can experience when they feel themselves completely immersed in the cosmos, above all when they feel themselves connected with the spiritual world.

The path a person takes to the abyss of being—where the Guardian of the Threshold stands—appeared before our souls. We listened to the teachings the Guardian gives to those who cross the threshold. We heard how when a person first arrives on the other side of the threshold they feel themselves to be within light. They also experience the world in a new way because they hear what the Guardian says and also hear what the beings of the higher hierarchies are saying. In the previous dialogue, the Guardian asks a question and the Angeloi, Exusiai, Thrones, Archangeloi, Dynamis, Cherubim, Archai, Kyriotetes and Seraphim reply, one after the other. They speak about the element of warmth that penetrates everything and reveals itself to be a moral element on the other side of the abyss. We saw how again the Guardian then speaks to the "I," asking three questions that penetrate deeply into human beings. As was explained last time, these are questions the "I" answers with humility in a deep, intimate conversation with the Guardian.

> The Guardian speaks:
> Where is the purifying fire that set your I aflame?
>
> Angeloi, Exusiai, Thrones:
> Awaken for yourself in the expanse of cosmic ether
> the flaming script of life.
>
> Archangeloi, Dynamis, Cherubim:
> Create for yourself in cyclic waves of time your
> soul's atonement forces.
>
> Archai, Kyriotetes, Seraphim:
> Ask for yourself from eternal deeds of being the
> spirit's redemptive powers.

> The Guardian: Has your Spirit understood?
>
> The "I": The cosmic spirit in me
> Has held its breath
> And may its presence
> Illuminate my "I."
>
> The Guardian: Has your Soul comprehended?
>
> The "I": The cosmic souls within me,
> Lived in the council of stars
> And may their harmonies,
> Resounding, fashion my "I."
>
> The Guardian: Has your Body experienced?
>
> The "I": The cosmic forces in me,
> Judge the deeds of men
> And may their verdicts
> Rightly guide the "I" in me.

The human being, now beyond the threshold of existence where the Guardian stands, feels it is within the weaving, living light. Gradually it becomes not only a light we can *feel*, but a kind of light we can *see*.

From the feeling of light that weaves and waves, that has, so to speak, been grasped spiritually only in thought, a light gradually dawns that is seen with the eye of the spirit.

Nevertheless, one is unable see this light without hearing another deeply founded admonition from the Guardian. This admonition refers to a powerful cosmic Imagination that points to something one can receive as a sense impression here in the sense world. This is a tremendously majestic Imagination for one with the heart to receive it. Rainbows appear in the sense world when the right cloud formations and a magical kind of illumination are present. Then one can feel that the spirits beyond the physical, sense perceptible glow of the rainbow shine in through its colors. A rainbow appears; it stands there built-up from the universe and then... it

Seventeenth Lesson

disappears back into the universe. All this is placed in the universe like a mighty Imagination.

The moment we are about to see this dawning light with spiritual sight, the Guardian reminds us of the impression of the rainbow. [A rainbow is drawn on the blackboard; picture 10].

The Guardian reminds the person who has come across to the spiritual world to inwardly activate this picture of the rainbow that spans the universe from their memory of the sense world. It is remarkable, my dear sisters and brothers, that when we cross over from the physical sense world to the spiritual world, the image of the rainbow is the easiest to remember. The image of the rainbow allows us most easily to recall the relationship between the spiritual world, where it is becoming light, and the physical sense-world we left behind, along with our capacities for knowledge.

Not the sight of the rainbow, but the *memory* of the rainbow, is called forth by the Guardian of the Threshold. The Guardian now instructs us...we will hear his words in a moment. With the force you normally use to see with your eyes, try to prepare for yourself the substance you will penetrate this rainbow with, and then pass beneath the rainbow and beyond to its other side.

If we can imagine [a second drawing is made on the blackboard] that here in the cloud formation [white in the upper right-hand corner]—looking up from the Earth [small arrow]—the rainbow would be here [red in the cloud formation]. We imagine this and then the Guardian instructs us to penetrate through the rainbow. From this new vantage point, [a line is drawn to the small circle on which the words vantage point is written] on the other side of the rainbow, he instructs us to look back at the rainbow from that cosmic distance. The Guardian instructs us to make our imagination more profound, to deepen our meditations, if we wish to advance beyond the point we reached during our previous lesson.

Imagine, my sisters and brothers, that when we go behind the blackboard [white arrow pointing up and left in the first drawing] and look at the rainbow from behind [red arrow pointing down and left] as it appears in memory, when looking at it from behind the rainbow becomes a mighty bowl, a cosmic chalice. The rainbow inverts, becoming a chalice. We no longer see an arc, we see an immense chalice the size of half the sky, where colors flow into each other.

This is the Imagination the Guardian first calls up in us:

See the ether-colored rainbow
Powerful orb of light.
Let light's creative force
Pass through your eyes
And your I penetrate its circle.
Then behold from yonder vantage point
Colors flowing in the cosmic chalice.

[The first verse of the mantra is written on the blackboard]

The Guardian: See the ether-colored rainbow
Powerful orb of light.
Let light's creative force
Pass through your eyes
And your "I" penetrate its circle.
Then behold from yonder vantage point
Colors flowing in the cosmic chalice.

The Guardian speaks powerful words. My dear sisters and brothers, put yourselves into the living image that pupils of the Guardian of the Threshold find themselves in when called upon to observe the cosmic chalice filled with color-flooding light:

See the ether-colored rainbow
Powerful orb of light.
Let light's creative force
Pass through your eyes
And your I penetrate its circle.
Then behold from yonder vantage point
Colors flowing in the cosmic chalice.

We must penetrate such images. If such images work deeply and intimately into the "I," we then see how the beings of the third hierarchy—Angeloi,

Archangeloi and Archai—appear in the flood of colors that fill the chalice. They breathe the colors into their own angelic being.

Thus, we gain an idea about the cosmic creativity that lies behind the sense world, which is the product of the deeds of the higher hierarchies. We have a conception of how spiritual beings act beyond the rainbow, first by breathing in the colors of the cosmic chalice, taking them into their own being.

We observed how what flows from the cosmos to the rainbow penetrates it, and then appears behind the rainbow as thoughts. We observed how it is absorbed and breathed in by the angelic beings. We now learn the true nature of the rainbow. All the thoughts thought by people in a particular place are gathered up from time to time through the rainbow bridge and sent farther out into the spiritual world where they are breathed in by the beings of the third hierarchy.

What so magically appears in the vastness of the universe—the rainbow—has not only a physical meaning; it also has an inner, spiritual significance. A phenomenon like the magical etheric rainbow cannot be known from within the physical sense world. It can only first be known when one stands beyond the threshold of existence, after we have heard, as we have thus far heard, the many admonitions of the Guardian of the Threshold.

It is precisely through the impression we receive from the perspective of viewing the rainbow as a cosmic chalice that we become clear how light gradually spreads out before us, a light that at first stood before us as a dark and night-enclosed sphere. We are now within that light; it grows brighter. The cosmic chalice with its flooding colors, seen from the other side of the rainbow, is the sun.

Then the Angeloi, Archangeloi and Archai begin to reflect, or mirror, their consciousness within human souls of how they breathed in the flooding colors so that what exists here on the Earth as sensory illusion may be carried into the spiritual realm, insofar as it is of use in that realm.

And then, when one has perceived how the beings of the third hierarchy have breathed in what they took from the sense world, when one has become aware of what penetrated into them through the rainbow, and has understood what they have transformed so that it can be taken into the spiritual world, then—with what they have absorbed within themselves—they now turn in service to higher spirits, to the spirits of the second hierarchy. For the spirits of the third hierarchy—the Angeloi, Archangeloi and Archai—stand in service to the spiritual world. We now hear from them about what we see when we behold the color-flooded cosmic chalice... the world beyond the rainbow.

> Angeloi, Archangeloi and Archai:
>
>> Feel how our thoughts
>> Have color-breathing life
>> In the chalice's flowing light.
>> We carry sense-illusion
>> To realms of spirit-being.
>> Imbued by the world we turn
>> Ourselves to serve the higher spirits.

[The second verse is written on the blackboard]

> *Angeloi, Archangeloi, and Archai:*
>
>> *Feel how our thoughts*
>> *Have color-breathing life*
>> *In the chalice's flowing light.*
>> *We carry sense-illusion*
>> *To realms of spirit-being.*
>> *Imbued by the world we turn*
>> *Ourselves to serve the higher spirits.*

My dear sisters and brothers, let us place this image before our souls once again. We see the cosmic chalice spanning half the sky with colors flooding it within. We normally see such colors interweaving and living in one another only on the surface of the rainbow, but here they approach us as beings from the third hierarchy: Angeloi, Archangeloi and Archai. The thoughts of the beings of the third hierarchy become visible for our soul in this breathing of color.

We observe how the beings of the third hierarchy, permeated with these cosmic thoughts, turn to the beings of the second hierarchy whom they serve: the Exusiai, Dynamis and Kyriotetes. This powerful image stands before us: pure spiritual beings appear, residents of the sun, who only appear when the physical image cast by the sun disappears. Despite the magnitude of the sun in comparison with the Earth, it is a small image, only an image. The infinitely larger sun majestically fills the entire universe when this great cosmic image disappears. Then the beings of the second hierarchy appear, weaving and living in the realm of pure spirit, receiving what the Angeloi, Archangeloi and Archai bring them. These are not dead thoughts such as we have. Dead thoughts are taken from the mirage of the senses and become living thoughts through the breathing of the Angeloi, Archangeloi and Archai. In a mighty offering the Angeloi, Archangeloi and Archai place these living thoughts before the second hierarchy. Thoughts that were only illusions, only semblances in earthly life, are awakened into being by the second hierarchy.

We see how the beings of the second hierarchy receive the thoughts that have been brought to life by the third hierarchy. And now, like a mighty resurrection, a new world comes into being. The Angeloi, Archangeloi and Archai receive and take up what was dead substance from the world of sense-illusion. Then through the activity of the Exusiai, Dynamis and Kyriotetes a new world comes into being, a world arising from what was dead.

Then we see how the mysterious secret of the world, the secret of the cosmos, works. We see how the Exusiai, Dynamis and Kyriotetes give over what they received from the third hierarchy to what we call "rays" in earthly life—the rays of the sun and the rays of the stars. The awakened, now living world-thoughts are surrendered, are given over, to all that rays from the sun and stars.

The truth is, such rays are not physical. In truth, spirit streams in all that rays forth from the sun and stars. When we look at the rays as they reach us we fail to see what they have previously been given from the realm of the second hierarchy. With these streaming rays—the rays from the stars and the sun—are given what the beings of the second hierarchy weave into world thoughts, and also what they allow to be resurrected from the dead thoughts, from our earthly thoughts, which were made alive by the beings of the third hierarchy. And now we hear how the second hierarchy gives these radiating spiritual forces what works as creative love in the cosmos. These solar and stellar rays, through which love weaves and floods the entire cosmos, are actually the creative force for the entire cosmos. We see now how the second hierarchy entrusts this love to the rays of the stars and the sun. We now see with spiritual eyes how the beings of the second hierarchy—radiating spirit, awakening love, bearing love—incorporate these forces into the world.

So now we hear them speak... but not to us. We become witnesses to a dialogue between the beings of the second hierarchy and the beings of the third hierarchy. Their voices sound across to each other: we only listen. This is the first time in the course of our meditations that we hear the beings of the hierarchies speak to each other.

> What we received from you,
> From the dead world of sense-illusion, is enlivened.
> We waken it to existence.
> We bestow upon it the rays of light
> That reveal the nothingness of matter,
> Weaving love into spiritual existence.

By witnessing this heavenly dialogue, what was previously night-enveloped darkness gradually grows lighter to the eye of the spirit. It becomes filled with a soft, gentle light. [The third verse is written on the blackboard:]

> *Exusiai, Dynamis and Kyriotetes:*
>> *What we received from you,*
>> *From the dead world of sense-illusion, is enlivened.*
>> *We waken it to existence.*
>> *We bestow upon it the rays of light*
>> *That reveal the nothingness of matter,*
>> *Weaving love into spiritual existence.*

Seventeenth Lesson

Now, if we have heard and absorbed the meaning of these words, we will see something more taking place with the eye of the spirit. We have already seen how earthly thoughts are made into living thoughts by the third hierarchy. We have seen that what was breathed in and made alive is received by the second hierarchy, is then imparted to the rays of the stars and the sun, and is then transformed into love. Now we see it taken over by the beings of the first hierarchy and made into the elements from which they create new worlds. What the Angeloi, Archangeloi and Archai breathe in from the world, what the Exusiai, Dynamis and Kyriotetes receive from them and transform into creative forces, from this the Thrones, Cherubim and Seraphim shape new worlds.

This is something remarkable. First we witnessed a conversation in heaven between the third and second hierarchies. Now our spiritual ears hear something more. The beings of the first hierarchy begin to speak their cosmic language. At first it seems as though we were only going to be listeners to a heavenly conversation, but it soon becomes clear that this is not so.

First the Angeloi, Archangeloi and Archai let their voices be heard; then a dialogue developed between the Exusiai, Dynamis and Kyriotetes and the Angeloi, Archangeloi and Archai; after that the Thrones, Cherubim and Seraphim joined in the conversation. A whole choir resounds in the spiritual spheres. We now become aware that the voices of all nine choirs of angels sound together... and what resounds from them is directed to us human beings. And so in the end the entire spiritual world speaks to us. But only when what has been spoken in the spiritual world is included in the cosmic speech of the Seraphim, Cherubim and Thrones, only at that point does it sound to us human beings. This is what resounds:

> Within your worlds of will
> Feel our cosmic working.
> Spirit shines in matter
> When we create thinking.
> Spirit creates in matter

When we live in willing.
The world *is* the "I"-willed Spirit-Word.

The world is the Spirit-Word that wills the I. And in the creative activity of the Seraphim, Cherubim and Thrones *is* the world.

[The fourth verse is written on the blackboard]

Thrones, Cherubim, Seraphim:

> *Within your worlds of will*
> *Feel our cosmic working.*
> *Spirit shines in matter*
> *When we create thinking.*
> *Spirit creates in matter*
> *When we live in willing.*
> *The world is the "I"-willed Spirit-Word.*

The Spirit-Word that wills the "I" *is* the world. And insofar as we, with our spiritual ears, hear these words directed at our humanity, the spiritual world becomes bright. The gentle light that was previously there now changes into spiritual brightness.

This is the experience we have with the Guardian of the Threshold while the spiritual sphere grows brighter:

> See the ether-colored rainbow,
> Powerful orb of light.
> Let light's creative force
> Pass through your eyes
> And your I penetrate its circle.
> Then behold from yonder vantage point
> Colors flowing in the cosmic chalice.
>
> Feel how our thoughts
> Have color-breathing life
> In the chalice's flowing light.
> We carry sense-illusion
> To realms of spirit-being.

Seventeenth Lesson

> Imbued by the world we turn
> Ourselves to serve the higher spirits.
>
> What we received from you,
> From the dead world of sense–illusion, is enlivened;
> We waken it to existence.
> We bestow it upon the rays of light
> Which reveal the nothingness of matter,
> Weaving love into spiritual existence.
>
> Within your worlds of will
> Feel our cosmic working.
> Spirit shines in matter
> When we create thinking.
> Spirit creates in matter
> When we live in willing.
> The world is the "I"-willed Spirit-Word.

And then it is as though the Guardian of the Threshold touches us gently with his spiritual hands. We feel his presence as if he closed our spiritual eyes and for a moment we saw nothing, despite having been in a bright, spiritual space the moment before. Words arise from the depths of our own inner being, words we shall not yet include among the mantras we have given. We will, however, put them at the end of this lesson to be saved for next time.

When—if we may express it with a sense-perceptible picture that takes place in a purely spiritual way—the Guardian of the Threshold places his hands softly over our eyes so that we do not see the spiritual brightness around us, words rise up from the depths of our being that seem like a memory of the world of the senses...a world we left behind in order to acquire knowledge in the spiritual world. These words rise up:

> I came into this sense world
> Bearing thought's heritage within me,
> Led by a divine power.
> Death stands at journey's end.
> I want to feel the Being of Christ.

He awakens spiritual birth in matter's death.
In spirit, thus, I find the world
And know *myself* amid the world's evolving.

(…)

Eighteenth Lesson

Dornach, July 12, 1924

My dear friends! At the beginning of these reflections we will once again pass before our souls the call to self-knowledge that the human soul can hear when listening with an open mind to all the beings and events in nature and in the life of the spirit:

> O Man, Know Thy Self!
> Thus sounds the Cosmic Word.
> You hear it with strength of soul,
> You feel it with might of spirit.
>
> Who speaks so powerfully through the world?
> Who speaks so tenderly within your heart?
>
> Does it work through the far-spread rays of space
> Into your senses' experience of life?
> Does it sound through the weaving waves of time
> Into the evolving stream of your life?
>
> Is it you, yourself, who,
> By sensing space,
> By experiencing time,
> Begets this word,
> Feeling yourself estranged in the psychic void of space,
> Because you lose the force of thought
> In the annihilating stream of time?

My dear sisters and brothers, we have traversed the path that leads to the abyss of being and to the Guardian of the Threshold, where the soul can find the answer to this question. Following the instructions of the Guardian of the Threshold, we have pressed forward to the point where what previously stood before us as something dark and gloomy—although we already knew that it contains our real being, the very source of our existence—we pressed forward to the point where what spread around us as darkness began to grow light. There, amidst the growing light, we heard the Guardian's call:

> See the ether-colored rainbow,
> Powerful orb of light.
> Let light's creative force
> Pass through your eyes
> And your I penetrate its circle.
> Then behold from yonder vantage point
> Colors flowing in the cosmic chalice.

In response to these words of the Guardian the Angeloi, Archangeloi and Archai raise their voices to address the souls of human beings:

> Feel how our thoughts
> Have color-breathing life
> In the chalice's flowing light.
> We carry sense-illusion
> To realms of spirit-being.
> Imbued by the world we turn
> Ourselves to serve the higher spirits.

So we behold how, through this light flooding the cosmic chalice, which we learned about in the last lesson, the beings of the third hierarchy illuminate and are themselves illuminated. We see the multitudes of beings—Angeloi, Archangeloi, Archai—turn themselves to the higher spirits they serve: the Exusiai, Dynamis and Kyriotetes. And we witness how the Exusiai, Dynamis and Kyriotetes tell their serving spirits to fulfill the needs of human beings.

> The Exusiai, Dynamis and Kyriotetes speak thus:
> What we received from you,

Eighteenth Lesson

> From the dead world of sense-illusion, is enlivened.
> We waken it to existence.
> We bestow upon it the rays of light
> That reveal the nothingness of matter,
> Weaving love into spiritual existence.

Then, impelled by our own inner life, we must turn our gaze upward to the highest spirits—to the first hierarchy—who now address human beings with blessings. From them we hear:

> Within your worlds of will
> Feel our cosmic working.
> Spirit shines in matter
> When we create thinking.
> Spirit creates in matter
> When we live in willing.
> The world *is* the "I"-willed Spirit-Word.

Thus, witnessing what the beings of the higher worlds say to each other, and thus permeated by what the highest beings pour forth as Cosmic Word into human souls so that human hearts may beat in response to it, we must now feel ourselves to be within the all-prevailing, all-creative cosmic light, where we ourselves live and have our being.

There now dawns in us a truth that is perceived in that region where beings live who are not incarnated, where spiritual beings live *their* life, where spiritual beings think *their* truth, where they radiate *their* beauty and accomplish *their* spiritual deeds. An awareness now rises in us of the great, all-encompassing truth that weaves throughout the spiritual world: *spirit is*. For we stand in spirit; we move and live in spirit; we grasp spiritual being.

Now we realize that spirit, which we live in the midst of, alone *is*. We also know that even here, where we otherwise live in the world of sense-illusion, *spirit alone exists. There is only spirit.* This now stands before our soul as an unshakable, all-pervading truth: *spirit exists; spirit is*. We will do well to place this truth before ourselves in picture form.

[Drawing: red; picture 11.]

What is expressed in the drawing is spirit. It is only spirit. What appears here *is*, it exists, it has being. It is spirit. And what lies outside the red is not, does not, exist: it is *nothing*.

[While the speaking continues, the word *is* is written in several places within the red shading.]

The spiritual world tells us: here *is*, here *is*, here *is*, here *is*. Wherever there is spirit, there is something. And wherever spirit is not, there is nothing.

We are deeply impressed by this truth: wherever there is spirit, there is something; and wherever there is no spirit, there is nothing. Now we ask ourselves: how did all this appear to us over there in the world of sense-illusion whence we came, now that we have crossed the threshold of the spiritual world where our soul comes face-to-face with true spiritual being? Over there we did not see what is here drawn in red. Over there we are too weak to see what is drawn in the red.

[While the lecture continues, the word *nothing* is written in several places between the red shadings, along with the words *minerals, plants,* and *animals*.]

What remains, then, on the other side? *Nothing.* Over there we see *nothing*: and we call it *minerals*, one kind of *nothing*; we call it *plants*, a second kind of *nothing*; and we call it *animals*, a third kind of *nothing*, and so on.

We perceive nothing because we are too weak to see something. We call these nothings the kingdoms of nature. That is the great deception; that is the Great Illusion. Only different kinds of nothing are before our eyes when we see over there while in our body. Deep down in our feelings we have the impression that, while we live over there and give names to what, fundamentally, is really nothing, we feel: This is the Great Illusion. What lives on the other side as nothing, what we give names to, appears to us as the sum total of all the names we have given to this nothingness. For now, when we have entered the spiritual world, all beings exists for us in reality, in their true nature. Names dedicated to the nothing have been wasted upon the void of non-being. Moreover, beings—who are not from the divine realms that we belong to and should belong to—such beings are able to usurp the names that we waste on the nothingness. They bear these names from now on.

We fall into the greatest illusions with these names as long as we do not realize that here on Earth we are giving names to the nothingness. We must know that we are giving names to nothingness. This now stands before our soul, in that we live and move in the light, so that the spiritual strength of our heart, which has stayed with us on our way, can now feel it deeply and deeper still. Now we know that we have moved from the realm of illusion into the realm of truth. Earnestness, sacred earnestness in the face of truth, begins to rule our soul.

We now look back toward the faithful Guardian of the Threshold who stands at the abyss of being. He does not talk at this moment. Previously he spoke from the darkness. He spoke when we first felt the presence of the light. He spoke while the light was growing brighter. Now that we stand in the full brightness of the light, shocked by the great truth that *"only spirit exists,"* at this moment he does not speak, although he silently points on high where the beings of the higher hierarchies speak to one another. Then, with presence of mind, we think for a moment: down there in earthly life we perceived the impressions made upon us by the minerals, plants, animals and physical human beings. Down there we heard what the clouds were saying, what the mountains were saying. We heard springs bubbling, lightning striking, thunder rolling and stars whispering cosmic secrets. These were our experiences down below. Now all of that is silenced beyond the abyss of being. Now we are witnesses to how the gods speak to one another. The entire choir of Angeloi begins to speak.

We look up and see them turning to higher spirits, to the spirits of the second hierarchy whom they wish to serve. We behold the gestures of loving service of the Angeloi, Archangeloi, and Archai as they turn toward the Exusiai, Dynamis and Kyriotetes. We behold the hosts of the third hierarchy acting in loving service.

We have a vision of the hosts from the second hierarchy performing their world-creating, world-ruling, world-enlightening activity. And we hear what these spiritually enlightened, divine-willed spirits, willing the divine will, say to one another.

We hear the Angeloi's words ring forth. From their concern for the guidance of human souls their words resound:

Human beings are thinking! Human beings can think!

This weighs upon the Angeloi. They are concerned as to how they should guide human souls when human beings are thinking. They turn with this concern in supplication to the Dynamis so that they may receive the forces to properly guide human beings in their thinking.

Angeloi:
> Human beings are thinking!
> We need the light from the heights
> That we may illuminate their thinking.

From the realm of ruling, dynamic light the Dynamis reply lovingly and benevolently:

> Receive the light from the heights
> That you can illuminate thinking
> When human beings are thinking.

The surging tide of light, the power that gives light to thinking, flows from the Dynamis to the Angeloi. What the Angeloi receive gives light to human thinking without their ever knowing it. Now we perceive what works and lives in human thinking: the light of the Angeloi. But they receive the illuminating power of this light from the Dynamis.

[The first part of the mantra is written on the blackboard:]

I. *Angeloi:*

"Human beings are thinking!"

Eighteenth Lesson

– This is their worry; these are their words of concern.

Human beings are thinking!

– Now they turn to the Dynamis with their concern:

*We need the light from the heights
That we can illuminate thinking.*

The Dynamis answer:

Dynamis:
Receive the light from the heights
That you can illuminate thinking
When human beings are thinking.

Now our spiritual vision expands. We behold the hosts of the Archangeloi turning in service to the second hierarchy. They look to the Exusiai and Kyriotetes, two ranks of the second hierarchy. The Angeloi turn to the Dynamis; the Archangeloi turn to the Exusiai and Kyriotetes. And their concern is for the feeling life of human beings. They pray to the Exusiai and Kyriotetes for what they need for the feeling life of human beings, which is their responsibility to guide.

Archangeloi:

Human beings are feeling!
We need the warmth of soul
That we may live in feeling.

The Archangeloi must breathe the breath of life into feeling. With mighty voices—because two choirs are answering—there rings forth in the spiritual universe from the Kyriotetes and Exusiai:

Receive the warmth of soul
That you can live in feeling
When human beings are feeling.

[The second part of the mantra is written on the blackboard:]

II. Archangeloi:

> *Human beings are feeling!*
> *We need the warmth of soul*
> *That we can live in feeling.*
> *The answer is given by:*

Kyriotetes and Exusiai:

> *Receive the warmth of soul*
> *That you can live in feeling*
> *When human beings are feeling.*

Now we turn to the third rank of the third hierarchy, the Archai. Their concern is to care for the will of human beings. This is the third concern of the third hierarchy.

We feel it when the Angeloi turn to the Dynamis and the Dynamis in the heights become active, producing the light of the heights so they can give it to the Angeloi and meet their concerns for the thinking life of human beings. We feel it when everything generated by the Exusiai and Kyriotetes as cosmic warmth in the encircling sphere is then given to the Archangeloi so they may guide the feeling life of human beings. And deep down, where the spirits and gods of the depths prevail, where from the depths much evil prevails, the good forces of the depths have to be drawn up by all the gods of the second hierarchy, working together. In their concern for the will-life of human beings, the Archai need the forces of the depths. And they speak:

> Human beings are willing!
> We need the forces of the depths
> That we can work in willing.

With one mighty, cosmic voice, the voices of the powerful spirits of the second hierarchy—Kyriotetes, Dynamis and Exusiai—reply. All three ranks speak together; the three choirs of Angels speak in unison:

> Receive the forces of the depths
> That you can work in willing
> When human beings are willing.

Eighteenth Lesson

[The third part of the mantra is written on the blackboard.]

> III. *Archai:*
>
> *Human beings are willing!*
> *We need the forces of the depths*
> *That we can work in willing.*

Kyriotetes, Dynamis, and Exusiai answer together:

> *Kyriotetes, Dynamis, and Exusiai:*
>
> *Receive the forces of the depths*
> *That you can work in willing*
> *When human beings are willing.*

This is the world as it exists in the sacred words of creation, sounding to us as we are witnesses in the spiritual world, in the same way we witness what goes on in the mineral, plant and animal kingdoms here on Earth.

This is what we hear, and this hearing becomes our experience:

> Human beings are feeling!
> We need the warmth of soul
> That we can live in feeling.

> Receive the light from the heights
> That you can illuminate thinking
> When human beings are thinking.

> Human beings are feeling!
> We need the warmth of soul
> That we can live in feeling.

> Receive the warmth of soul
> That you can live in feeling
> When human beings are feeling.

> Human beings are willing!
> We need the forces of the depths
> That we can work in willing.

> Receive the forces of the depths
> That you can work in willing
> When human beings are willing.

We grow into the spiritual world. Instead of what surrounds us in the sense world, we are surrounded by the choirs of the spiritual world. We become witnesses to what the gods say when they speak about their concerns for the world of human beings. We witness what they create from their concern for humanity.

Only then do we experience true reality—when our meditation transitions from the complete elimination of what we are here on Earth to a feeling of awareness of what the gods on the other side, through their divine speech, make into a world. Only when we've experienced this reality do we also have the truth about what actually surrounds us between birth and death. Because behind the world of appearance that surround us between birth and death lies the true reality that we live in between death and a new birth.

People of earlier times lived on Earth in a dull, dreamlike clairvoyance. Their souls were filled with dreamlike pictures that spoke of the spiritual world. Let us imagine a person of olden times. When they had stopped working—even when the sun was in the sky—they laid their work aside in order to rest and to ponder. Pictures would then arise in their soul reminding them of experiences in pre-earthly life in the spiritual world. People did not understand the connection between their earthly life and that other form of existence that shone into their clairvoyant dreams. But the teachings of the initiates were present and available. And the initiates explained, first to their pupils, and then through their pupils to all humankind, what the connection was. People lived in the earthly world experiencing memories of their pre-earthly existence.

In today's earthly life, all memories of pre-earthly existence have been extinguished. Initiates can no longer explain the connection between earthly life and pre-earthly existence because people have forgotten what they experienced before they came down to Earth. No explanation is called for. Today there's no need to explain cosmic memory because cosmic memory no longer exists.

Nevertheless, what the gods are saying behind the veil of our senses must be heard by means of initiation science. People must come to learn it. Increasingly the time will come when people who have passed through the gate of death will only understand the world they have entered—the spiritual world—if they can say what follows.

When a person has passed through the gate of death into suprasensory existence he finds himself within the reality of the spiritual world—in the world of the Angeloi, Archangeloi, Archai, Exusiai, Dynamis, Kyriotetes, Thrones, Cherubim and Seraphim. If he experiences all this he has to be able to remember his experiences while on Earth through initiation science; otherwise, his post-mortem experiences will remain dark and incomprehensible

It is of the utmost importance for understanding the life between death and rebirth that, during this time, human beings hear what otherwise cannot be understood by recalling what they previously heard on Earth, resounding in these words:

> Human beings are thinking!
> Receive the light from the heights.
>
> Human beings are feeling!
> Receive the warmth of soul.
>
> Human beings are willing!
> Receive the strength of the depths.

My dear sisters and brothers, these words need to be heard in esoteric schools today. They should ring forth in the teachings of those who guide the esoteric schools with the power of the Age of Michael. Then it can be thus: In esoteric schools the Angels' voices are the first ones heard within Earth existence:

> Human beings are thinking!

The Dynamis answer:

> Receive the light from the heights.

Then the voices of the Archangeloi are heard:
Human beings are feeling!

The Kyriotetes and Exusiai answer:
Receive the warmth of soul.

The voices of the Archai are heard:
Human beings are willing!

The response comes from all three ranks of the second hierarchy: the Exusiai, Dynamis and Kyriotetes:

> Receive the strength of the depths.

People who have heard this in esoteric schools on Earth will go through the gate of death and will hear these words again sounding in harmony together—in the esoteric schools here and during the life between death and a new birth there. They will understand what rings forth. Or, people will be dull and unwilling to respond to what the esoteric schools, prepared by general Anthroposophy, have to say. They'll fail to perceive what can be heard through initiation science from the realms of the heights. They pass through the gate of death. There they hear what they should have already heard while here on Earth...but they do not understand it. These words of power—when the gods speak to one another—sound to them like an unintelligible clanging, mere cosmic noise.

The Gospel—Saint Paul—tells us that through the teachings of Christ human beings should protect themselves against "death in the spirit land." Because death soon comes in the spirit land if we pass through the gate of death and do not understand what resounds there, if we hear only unintelligible noise instead of the intelligible words of the gods. Because, instead of the life of the soul, the death of the soul overcomes us. Initiation science exists so that souls may live. Esoteric schools exist so that souls may remain alive when they pass through the gate of death. We should permeate ourselves with these ideas.

Let us now recall the path we have traversed in spirit. Let us remember how we first approached the Guardian in order to learn how to get across the abyss of existence. Now that the impressions from the other side have worked upon our soul, let us receive into our soul what stands before us as the inner drama of self-knowledge.

We have traveled along the path. Three tablets, so to speak, stood there. We now stand before the third one, having taken into our soul, in all of its profundity, our witnessing a conversation among the gods. On the first tablet, long before we came to the abyss of existence, there resounds:

> O Man, Know Thy Self!
> Thus sounds the Cosmic Word.
> You hear it with strength of soul,
> You feel it with might of spirit.
>
> Who speaks so powerfully through the world?
> Who speaks so tenderly within your heart?
>
> Does it work through the far-spread rays of space
> Into your senses' experience of life?
> Does it sound through the weaving waves of time
> Into the evolving stream of your life?
>
> Is it you, yourself, who,
> By sensing space,
> By experiencing time,
> Begets this word,
> Feeling yourself estranged in the psychic void of space,
> Because you lose the force of thought
> In the annihilating stream of time?

Then we approached closer to the Guardian. There stands the second tablet. On it is written:

> Know first the earnest Guardian,
> Who stands before the gate of spirit land,
> Denying entry to your senses' power
> And to the strength of your intellect,
> Because in the weaving of your senses
> And in the forming of your thoughts
> First you must find—
> From the nothingness of space,
> From time's delusive powers—
> The strength to conquer
> The truth of your own being.

Thereafter, we cross the threshold, going past the Guardian. Then we listen to a conversation among the gods that sounds like this:

> Human beings are thinking!
> Receive the light from the heights.
>
> Human beings are feeling!
> Receive the warmth of soul.
>
> Human beings are willing!
> Receive the strength of the depths.

Then we look back into the world of the senses and feel, with regard to the sense world, these words:

> I came into this sense world
> Bearing thought's heritage within me,
> Led by a divine power.
> Death stands at journey's end.
> I want to feel the Being of Christ.
> He awakens spiritual birth in matter's death.
> In spirit, thus, I find the world
> And know *myself* amid the world's evolving.

> (...)

Nineteenth Lesson

Dornach, August 2, 1924

My dear friends! Once again we will begin by bringing before our souls the verse that can remind us of everything in the world that was, is and will become: what was past, what is in the present and what will be in the future. From all this there sounds the call forever summoning us to seek self-knowledge, which is the foundation of all real, true knowledge:

> O Man, Know Thy Self!
> Thus sounds the Cosmic Word.
> You hear it with strength of soul,
> You feel it with might of spirit.
>
> Who speaks so powerfully through the world?
> Who speaks so tenderly within your heart?
>
> Does it work through the far-spread rays of space
> Into your senses' experience of life?
> Does it sound through the weaving waves of time
> Into the evolving stream of your life?
> Is it you, yourself, who,
>
> By sensing space,
> By experiencing time,
> Begets this word,
> Feeling yourself estranged in the psychic void of space,
> Because you lose the force of thought
> In the annihilating stream of time?

My dear sisters and brothers, we have let mantric verses pass before our souls that, in their power, contain the path into the spiritual world, past the Guardian of the Threshold, into what is at first dark, gloomy and enveloped by night, where at first we feel the light, and where later on the spiritual world becomes brighter to our soul's perception. We have seen in the spiritual world how the human being takes part—as a rule unconsciously, but one can become conscious of it—in the conversation the higher hierarchies have with one another. In this conversation it is as though the universe itself, the universal Cosmic Word, is speaking, weaving and working together with the higher hierarchies. Finally, we are able to move ourselves to that cosmic realm where the choirs of the different hierarchies resound together. Let us once more bring before our souls how the choirs of the various hierarchies sound together. Having passed through what the beings of the second hierarchy speak and through what the beings of the first hierarchy speak, let us again hear them speak together in the unison of a great choir.

As we know from earlier lessons, the Guardian makes us aware of this.

> See the ether-colored rainbow,
> Powerful orb of light.
> Let light's creative force
> Pass through your eyes
> And your I penetrate its circle.
> Then behold from yonder vantage point
> Colors flowing in the cosmic chalice.

After the Guardian has pointed out this secret—the spiritual mystery of the rainbow—the choirs of the Angeloi, Archangeloi and Archai sound forth:

> Feel how our thoughts
> Have color-breathing life
> In the chalice's flowing light.
> We carry sense illusion
> To realms of spirit-being.
> Imbued by the world we turn
> Ourselves to serve the higher spirits.

The spirits of the third hierarchy explain how in the service of humanity they want to serve the spirits of the second hierarchy, the Exusiai, Dynamis and Kyriotetes. From their realm we hear again in chorus:

> What we received from you,
> From the dead world of sense-illusion, is enlivened.
> We waken it to existence.
> We bestow upon it the rays of light
> That reveal the nothingness of matter,
> Weaving love into spiritual existence.

And if we have heard how the beings of the second hierarchy, in world-creating, approach our "I," then the choir of the first hierarchy—the Thrones, Cherubim and Seraphim—resounds:

> Within your worlds of will
> Feel our cosmic working.
> Spirit shines in matter
> When we create thinking.
> Spirit creates in matter
> When we live in willing.
> The world *is* the I-willed Spirit Word.

Now we stand within the Spirit-Word that underlies the foundation of the world's creating. We feel the Spirit-Word around us. We feel the entire world permeated by the Spirit-Word. We feel ourselves woven within and by this Spirit-Word. We feel the Spirit-Word penetrating the core of our human essence. Finally, we feel this worldwide Spirit-Word pouring into our heart. We feel our whole humanity immersed in the waves of this Spirit-Word. We feel ourselves as spirit within the World-Spirit, woven by the Word.

The Guardian lies in the far distance; we have passed him by. He is now far away. Only faintly do we hear him with our spiritual ears, speaking his last words of warning from afar.

The Guardian speaks from afar. The human I knows itself to be within the realm of the Spirit-Word sustained by the Seraphim, Cherubim and Thrones. The Guardian speaks:

> Who speaks in the Spirit-Word
> With a voice
> That burns in the cosmic fire?

From the realm of the first hierarchy the answer resounds:

> The flames of the stars are speaking.
> Seraphic powers of fire flame forth;

—Thus do we feel the speech of the cosmos—the language of the Cosmic Word—in our innermost being:

> They also burn in my heart.
> In primal being's fount of love
> The human heart finds
> The creative language of spiritual fire.
>   *It is I.*

My dear sisters and brothers, whoever wishes to enter the realm of esoteric life should begin by feeling that the sacred, ancient words "Ejeh Asher Ejeh"—"I am I," "I am"—are indeed the holy words that sound across to us from a reality found on the other side of the threshold. What we take hold of in our fleeting thoughts as "I am" is merely a reflection of the true "I am."

Actually, we must be aware that the true "I am" does not, at first, speak from us within this earthly realm. If we wish to say "I am" truly and worthily, we must first enter the realm of the Seraphim, Cherubim and Thrones, for only there does the "I am" ring true. Here in the earthly realm it is an illusion.

To experience the true "I am" within us we must hear the Cosmic Word. We must listen to the question the Guardian of the Threshold asks: who really is speaking in the Cosmic Word? The Seraphim who weave their way through the cosmos with spirit-lightning flames, they speak the fire language of the Cosmic Word, where we now stand. The Word is fire, it is a flaming voice. And to the degree that we experience this burning,

Nineteenth Lesson

cosmic fire that speaks the language of fire with a flaming voice, to that degree do we experience the true "I am."

This is contained in the words that now come to us from afar as a question from the Guardian of the Threshold, for we have long since passed him by. And the answer comes from the first hierarchy:

> Who speaks in the Spirit-Word
> With a voice
> That burns in the cosmic fire?

> The flames of the stars are speaking.
> Seraphic powers of fire flame forth;
> They also burn in my heart.
> In primal being's fount of love
> The human heart finds
> The creative language of spiritual fire:
>   It is I.

[The first part of the mantra is written on the blackboard.]

The Guardian speaks from afar:

(The human "I" knows itself to be within the realm of the Spirit-Word, sustained by the Seraphim Cherubim and Thrones.)

> *Who speaks in the Spirit-Word*
> *With a voice*
> *That burns in the cosmic fire?*

From the realm of the first hierarchy:

> *The flames of the stars are speaking.*
> *Seraphic powers of fire flame forth;*
> *They also burn in my heart.*
> *In primal being's fount of love*
> *The human heart finds*
> *The creative language of spiritual fire:*
>   *It is I.*

When human words are spoken, then human thinking speaks from human words. And when a cosmic Spirit-Word sounds, then cosmic thinking speaks from the cosmic Spirit-Word. This is contained in the second question the Guardian poses from afar:

The human "I" knows itself to be within the realm of the Spirit-Word sustained by the Seraphim, Cherubim and Thrones.

> What thinks in the Spirit-Word
> With thoughts that are
> Fashioning cosmic souls?

They are thoughts that issue from all of the cosmic souls belonging to the beings of the various hierarchies. These thoughts build, shape and mold everything that exists in the kingdoms of the world. Therefore, the Guardian asks: who thinks the thoughts that fashion all things?

> What thinks in the Spirit-Word
> With thoughts that are
> Fashioned from cosmic souls?

Once more, the answer comes to us from the realm of the first hierarchy:

> The radiance of the stars is thinking.

First, it was flames—the flames of the stars—that speak the words. Now it is the radiance of the stars, from which the flames proceed, that thinks.

> The radiance of the stars is thinking.
> Cherubic formative forces shine forth;
> They also shine within my head.

—The human being, who stands within it all, says:

> In primal being's fount of light
> The human head finds
> Thinking that works formatively in the soul.
>   It is I.

This is the second dialogue. It is as though the beings of the first hierarchy inside us were giving us cosmic consent, allowing us to experience the "I am":

> What thinks in the Spirit-Word
> With thoughts that are
> Fashioning cosmic souls?
>
> The radiance of the stars is thinking.
> Cherubic formative forces shine forth;
> They also shine within my head.
> In primal being's fount of light
> The human head finds
> Thinking that works formatively in the soul.
>   It is I.

[The second part of the mantra is written on the blackboard.]

> *The Guardian speaks from afar:*
>
> *What thinks in the Spirit-Word*
> *With thoughts that are*
> *Fashioning cosmic souls?*
>
> *From the realm of the first hierarchy:*
>
> *The radiance of the stars is thinking.*
> *Cherubic formative forces shine forth;*
> *They also shine within my head.*
> *In primal being's fount of light*
> *The human head finds*
> *Thinking that works formatively in the soul.*
>   *It is I.*

The Cosmic Spirit-Word speaks. Thoughts stream out from it. But these thoughts are creative; they are permeated with power. These thoughts pour forth cosmic beings, cosmic events. Everything that exists originates from them. The thought-bearing Cosmic Words live in the world-fashioning cosmic thoughts. This is not mere thinking, or mere speaking. This is creativity—a powerful force. Power streams through these words. These forces inscribe thoughts into cosmic beings; they inscribe thoughts into cosmic events.

All this is indicated by the third question the Guardian asks from afar:

> What wields strength in the Spirit-Word
> With forces
> That live in the cosmic body?

Just as what thinks and speaks in a human being is carried by the human body, so what sounds through the Cosmic Word throughout the universe is illumined by cosmic thinking and is carried by the cosmic body—the body of the cosmos. The Thrones carry it, or to say it more accurately, the Thrones carry the thought-illumined, cosmic Spirit-Word that is within the cosmic body.

Therefore, the answer to the Guardian's question comes from the realm of the first hierarchy:

> The star-world-body wields strength.
> The Thrones' sustaining powers body forth.

Here we have to coin an unaccustomed word. Just as we may make from the noun "light" the verb "to enlighten," and from the noun "life," the verb "to live," so from the power that the "body" must bring forth to bear it we can form the verb "to body" or "to embody" or "to body forth." "Embody" is not something dead or finished. "Embody" is something that is active every minute, something mobile and alert. The "body" "embodies" or "bodies forth."

> The Thrones' sustaining powers body forth;
> They also embody my limbs.
> In primal being's fount of life
> The human limbs find
> Ruling strength of world-bearing powers.
> It is I.

Nineteenth Lesson

Cosmic Word, cosmic thoughts, cosmic body—this is the speaking and thinking of the cosmic body. The Guardian's third question relates to this:

> What wields strength in the Spirit-Word
> With forces
> That live in the cosmic body?
>
> The star-world-body wields strength.
> The Thrones' sustaining powers body forth;
> They also embody my limbs.
> In primal being's fount of life
> The human limbs find
> Ruling strength of world-bearing powers.
>   It is I.

[The third verse of the mantra is written on the blackboard.]

The Guardian speaks from afar:

—The human "I" knows itself to be within the realm of the spirit words sustained by the Seraphim, Cherubim and Thrones.

> *What wields strength in the Spirit-Word*
> *With forces*
> *That live in the cosmic body?*
>
> *From the realm of the first hierarchy:*
>
> *The star-world-body wields strength.*
> *The Thrones' sustaining powers body forth;*
> *They also embody my limbs.*
> *In primal being's fount of life*
> *The human limbs find*
> *Ruling strength of world-bearing powers.*
>   *It is I.*

In a certain sense, my dear sisters and brothers, this forms a kind of end point to the path that began in the realm of illusion, the realm of Maya.

This path led us to the Guardian of the Threshold and to self-knowledge, and self-knowledge led us into spiritual realms where we heard the choirs of the hierarchies. It is, in a way, a kind of conclusion that we now stand in a place where we may experience within ourselves the true "I am"—"Ejeh Asher Ejeh."

We can experience in this dialogue how the words "It is I" rise up from our hearts three times. May they truly rise up from our hearts so that they become an echo of what the Seraphim, Cherubim and Thrones resound in our hearts.

> Who speaks in the Spirit-Word
> With a voice
> That burns in the cosmic fire?
>
> The flames of the stars are speaking.
> Seraphic powers of fire flame forth;
> They also burn in my heart.
> In primal being's fount of love
> The human heart finds the
> Creative language of spiritual fire:
>   It is I.
>
> What thinks in the Spirit-Word
> With thoughts that are
> Fashioning cosmic souls?
>
> The radiance of the stars is thinking.
> Cherubic formative forces shine forth;
> They also shine within my head.
> In primal being's fount of light
> The human head finds
> Thinking that works formatively in the soul.
>   It is I.
>
> What wields strength in the Spirit-Word
> With forces
> That live in the cosmic body?

Nineteenth Lesson

> The star-world-body wields strength.
> The Thrones' sustaining powers body forth;
> They also embody my limbs.
> In primal being's fount of life
> The human limbs find
> Ruling strength of world-bearing powers.
>   It is I.

With this, my dear sisters and brothers, we have in a sense completed the first part of the First Class of the School.

We have allowed the communications that we could receive from the spiritual worlds—for this school has been established by the spiritual world itself—we have let these pictures and inspirations, which can come to us from the spiritual world, pass before our souls. They present our soul with the path for understanding the true human "I," which lives amidst the Seraphim, Cherubim and Thrones.

My dear sisters and brothers! You have heard in the general anthroposophic lectures that these inner teachings of the heart first resounded in the suprasensory Michael School. Then, in mighty pictures and in the imaginative *cultus* at the beginning of the nineteenth century, these heart teachings were placed before those souls destined to be in the company of Michael, who were taught the revelations of the suprasensory School during the fifteenth, sixteenth, and seventeenth centuries. The School was led in the spiritual world by Michael and his companions in the way described. And now, before us, we have this anthroposophic School founded by Michael himself. We find ourselves living in this School. These are the words of Michael, words that should characterize the path that leads into the spiritual world and to the human "I." These are Michael's words. In a certain sense, these Michael words of the esoteric Michael School constitute its first section.

If in September—as will be announced—we find our way together again in these Class Lessons, then it will be the will of the Michael power to describe the revelations of the imaginative cultus of the beginning of the nineteenth century. That will be the second section. What has now been presented to our souls in the form of mantric verses will stand before us then in pictures that will be, as far as possible, the suprasensory pictures of the imaginative "cultus" of the beginning of the nineteenth century brought down to Earth. The third stage of the school will lead us directly into the interpretations of the mantras given in the suprasensory Michael School during the fifteenth, sixteenth, and seventeenth centuries.

We should feel how we ourselves go through all this in the spiritual world itself. But then we should also look back again and again to the sense-perceptible, physical world of Earth and, with true humility, take part in all that prevails in the earthly world of the senses.

Therefore, in conclusion, let our souls once more listen to the sounds—if we are receptive, if we have the inner sense for it—that come from every stone, plant and animal, from every drifting cloud and bubbling spring, from every rustling wind, from mountains and forests, from everywhere and everything happening on and around the Earth...if only we have the sense to hear it.

We were within the realm of the Seraphim, Cherubim and Thrones. Even the Guardian's voice sounded from afar. Now in humility we go back, past the Guardian of the Threshold, returning to the realm of sense-illusion. Once again we let these words resound in us:

> O Man, Know Thy Self!
> Thus sounds the Cosmic Word.
> You hear it with strength of soul,
> You feel it with might of spirit.
>
> Who speaks so powerfully through the world?
> Who speaks so tenderly within your heart?
>
> Does it work through the far-spread rays of space
> Into your senses' experience of life?
> Does it sound through the weaving waves of time
> Into the evolving stream of your life?

Is it you, yourself, who,
By sensing space,
By experiencing time,
Begets this word,
Feeling yourself estranged in the psychic void of space,
Because you lose the force of thought
In the annihilating stream of time?

(...)

The words that conclude Lesson Nineteen

With this, my dear sisters and brothers, in a sense we have completed the First Class of this School. We have allowed the communications that we can receive from the spiritual worlds to pass before our souls, for this is a school established by the spiritual world itself. We have dwelled on these pictures and inspirations that can come to us from the spiritual world. They present to our soul the path that leads us to take hold of the true human "I" among the Seraphim, Cherubim, and Thrones.

1.)

Zum Schluss der XIX. Stunde:—

„Damit meine lieben Schw. u. Brüder, ist in gewissem Sinne der erste Abschnitt dieser ersten Classe der Schule absolviert.
Wir haben diejenigen Mitteilungen, die wir bekommen können aus den geistigen Welten, denn diese Schule ist eine Schule eingesetzt von der geistigen Welt selber, wir haben diejenigen Bilder u. Inspirationen, die da kommen können aus der geistigen Welt, an uns vorüberziehen lassen. Sie stellen vor unseren Seelen dar, welches der Weg ist hin bis zu der Ergreifung des wahren Menschen-Ich in der Umgebung der Cherubim, Seraphim u. Throne.
meine lieben Schw. u. Brüder, es war

Handwritten note of Ludwig Polzer-Hoditz from a book in which he had written all the mantras (Archive Perseus Verlag).

Passages Omitted from the Text

First Lesson

(…) Page 3: The words of omitted text:

With this lesson, I want to restore the esoteric institution of the School of Spiritual Science to the task from which it has been under threat of estrangement in recent years.[1]

It will not be the task today in this initial, introductory lesson, to further elaborate on this thought. Even so, I want to indicate the importance of this moment and point out the earnest character of our movement that is increasingly endangered and undermined every day. This earnestness must come to expression especially within our school. It is by no means superfluous to say this, because it has not been evident that this earnestness has actually been taken seriously.

A kind of preparatory introduction will be given today, dear friends. I would like to emphasize above all that in this school the spiritual life must be received along with its true significance. In all of its depths, you must bear in mind that with this school an institution has been founded in which from the spirit of our time, a spiritual life can be revealed. The spiritual life can be deepened in every sphere, but there must be a center from which this deepening can come about, and for those who want to belong to the School, the center must be seen as the Goetheanum in Dornach.

Therefore, I would like to begin this school with those members of the School for whom it was possible to issue membership cards. You must be aware that within the School, every word is spoken with full responsibility toward the spirit that reveals itself in our age and time. It is the same spirit that has revealed itself to humankind for hundreds and thousands of years. And yet, it reveals itself in a particular way in each epoch. This spirit wants to give human beings what they can find in no other way except through the spirit.

We must be clear from the beginning that it is not out of hostility toward what comes to people from the sense world that we should turn our attention to the revelations of the spirit in a School of Spiritual Science. We must recognize that the world of the senses has great and necessary revelations to give us along with practical aids and indications for life. We must not allow anything to cause us to belittle what comes to us from the world of the senses.

But here, everything depends on our receiving the revelations of the spirit with all earnestness. I must say at the very outset that much in the way of prejudice, self-will and headstrongness that is still deeply rooted—even among members of the School—will have to go. We will need to explore how we can find a way to the sources of our selfishness and headstrongness that prevent us from rightly perceiving what the School should be. For many of us do not yet think seriously enough about the School. This must gradually be accomplished. Over time, it is only possible for those individuals to be in the School who can take it seriously in all its details.

On the one hand, this is made necessary by the subject itself and, on the other hand, by the difficult path we will have to tread in the face of all the hindrances and undermining forces coming from all directions every day, and that are increasingly making themselves felt. Members of the School are by no means sufficiently aware of this. All this, my dear friends, will need to be properly considered.

Foremost among what will engage us in the School, will naturally be the receiving of what can be given from the spirit. Then members of the School will also be required to follow the arduous path of facing the hindrances and undermining forces that are there.

I have discussed these things in our weekly newssheet *What Is Happening in the Anthroposophical Society*.[2] In it, I made clear the distinction between the General Anthroposophical Society and this school. It is necessary that this difference be clearly felt by the members of the School; members will also have to live in the sense of this difference until the School will eventually only have as its members those who are really prepared to make themselves true representatives of the anthroposophic cause in all details of life. I speak these words to emphasize how serious it actually is.

Second Lesson

(...) Page 22: The words of omitted text:

Dear friends, to feel the full weight of the words I am now speaking, it will be good for our striving after knowledge if all friends who are present—and especially all those who have been in the Anthroposophical Society for some time—will ask themselves the following question: How often have I resolved to do something as part of my anthroposophic life and after a while have completely forgotten about it? Perhaps I would have carried it out if I had thought about it, but then I forgot about doing it. It vanishes like a dream vanishes from my life.

It is not without meaning or significance to pose such a question to us. And it could be very important if a large number of our friends would what to put something before their souls that is current.

The Christmas Conference was intended to pour real esoteric life into the stream of the anthroposophic worldview, which is carried by the Anthroposophical Society. Many might ask: How often since then have I forgotten what I certainly felt as something beautiful during the Christmas Foundation Meeting? How often have I lived in thought and feeling as though the Anthroposophical Society continued as if it remained the same as it was before Christmas? Perhaps there are still some among us who are saying to themselves that in my case this is not true. Then it could be most necessary that they asked themselves again: Am I not deceiving myself, thinking it is not so in my case? Have I, in all things that concern anthroposophic activity, truly borne in mind that a new phase in the Anthroposophical Society was to begin at Christmas? To ask ourselves these questions is a real question of knowledge and it is of great importance. Then the necessary earnestness will move in souls.

It is good that this belongs to the lifeblood of the Anthroposophical Society and therefore with the very lifeblood of every member who has asked to be received into the Class. It is important for there to be an outcome from such a decisive moment in our lives. And so, it would be good that each individual who wants to belong to the Class would say to themselves: Could there be something I can do differently now that the Anthroposophical Society is newly founded, different from how I did things before? Could I introduce something new in my life as an anthroposophist? Could I change the way I worked until now by introducing something new, something that was not there before?

This would be of enormous significance if taken seriously by each individual who belongs to the Class. For in that way it would be made possible, dear friends, for this Class to work on without being burdened by heavy weights. Everyone who merely continues in the old way burdens the progress of this Class. It usually goes on unnoticed, yet it is true.

(...) Page 32: The words of omitted text:
The next lesson will take place next Friday.

Fourth Lesson

(...) Page 67: The words of omitted text:
My dear friends, it is necessary to add something else. The School must live in great earnestness and the things I spoke about on Wednesday, about the conditions of the School, must be taken seriously.[3] I have been obliged to withdraw the membership card from a person who—by omitting to do what was necessary—could have brought about a great misfortune. I mention this here to show that the purposes indicated during the Christmas Conference must indeed be adhered to with all seriousness. I ask that in the future you do not take it as a mere manner of speaking when I emphasize that this esoteric school is desired in all seriousness by the spiritual

world. When someone does not wish to be a representative of the Anthroposophic Movement in the right way, this School must reserve the right to withdraw that person's membership card.

I must point this out in all sincerity and thus do not neglect to mention that already one person's membership card was withdrawn, at least for certain time, until this person definitely shows that the opposite is the case. We can only grow into the School in the right way when we stop the many flippant views about the Anthroposophic Movement, views that have created so much trouble in the Anthroposophic Movement. We must grow with complete sincerity into this esoteric life. I have to say again that what was meant with the Christmas Conference has not yet been absorbed by every soul. The leadership of the School will be alert and will indeed follow through with firmness when the School is not taken seriously. Let us bear this in mind as part of today's lesson.

Fifth Lesson

(…) Page 86: The words of omitted text:

We shall continue next Friday. Tomorrow, and the day after tomorrow, there will be the general anthroposophic lecture at eight o'clock. On Sunday there will be a Eurythmy performance at 5 o'clock.

Sixth Lesson

(…) Page 107: The words of omitted text:

I had to keep you here longer today because of my travel to lecture abroad. Consequently, the next two Friday lessons cannot take place. The next lesson will be given on Good Friday.[4] Tomorrow's lecture will be for the Anthroposophical Society. On Sunday, there will also be a Eurythmy performance at five o'clock. The first part will be given by younger eurythmists, children and young ladies, and then a performance will be given by men, the gentleman of our guard. That will be on Sunday at five o'clock. On Sunday at eight o'clock, the second lecture will be given of the two scheduled for eight o'clock on Saturday and Sunday.

Seventh Lesson

(...) Page 108: The words of omitted text:

Quite a few new members of this School have come here today, and I must therefore, once again, say a few words about the principles of the School.[5] The first thing to be said about the School is that it forms the esoteric impulse of the Anthroposophic Movement, of the Anthroposophic Movement that received its renewal through the Christmas Conference here at the Goetheanum.[6] There used to be other esoteric circles,[7] all of which will gradually have to be absorbed into this School, for it is a fact that through the Christmas Conference a new spirit has entered into the Anthroposophic Movement insofar as it flows through the Anthroposophical Society.

Repeatedly, also outside of Dornach, I have spoken[8] of the difference between the Anthroposophic Movement as it existed before Christmas and the Anthroposophic Movement that we now have since Christmas. Initially, the Anthroposophical Society was in a way an administrative society for the teachings of Anthroposophy, since the content of Anthroposophy was, we might say, cultivated within the Anthroposophical Society. Since Christmas, it has not only been a matter of cultivating Anthroposophy through the Anthroposophical Society, but also of doing it. This means that every action and every thought that passes through the Anthroposophical Society must be in itself Anthroposophy.

As a result, my dear friends, the renewal that has taken place must be received with a sufficient depth of understanding. Above all, it must be received with profound seriousness. For there will be a distinction between the Anthroposophical Society in general and this esoteric School within the Anthroposophical Society. In keeping with the spirit of openness that was established at the Christmas Conference, the Anthroposophical Society will require no more of its members than that they stand honestly by what Anthroposophy is; we might say that members are, in a way, listeners of Anthroposophy; that they make of this Anthroposophy whatever they can with their hearts and souls.

The situation is different in the case of the School. Those who become members of the School declare by doing so that they desire to become true representatives of the Anthroposophic Movement. In this esoteric School, which will eventually be extended to three classes, there will have to be the freedom that exists for every member within the Anthroposophical Society. But at the same time, there will also have to be complete freedom for the Executive Council at the Goetheanum, which is responsible for the School. This means that the content of the School must only be given to those whom the School recognizes to be proper members.

Therefore, whatever a member of the School presents must be such that Anthroposophy is revealed to the world. If there are members, who in the opinion of the Executive Council are unable to be true representatives of the Anthroposophic Movement, then the Executive Council must be free to withdraw membership from such people. The relationship must be mutual.

Increasingly, a very strict spirit will have to enter into the regulation of the School. We cannot make progress with the Anthroposophic Movement if we are unable to feel ourselves as a school that wants to build a rock to be the foundation for Anthroposophy. There is going to be much difficulty in connection with Anthroposophy, and the members of this School must know that they will have to deal with these difficulties. They are not only anthroposophists; they are also members of an esoteric school.

It must be the obligation, an innermost obligation, to regard the establishment of the Executive Council—as it is at presently constituted—in an esoteric manner. The members must become increasingly aware of this; they are not yet fully aware of this and something will have to be done so that they do become aware of this. For the very fact that and Executive Council is created esoterically says a great deal.

Furthermore, all those who consider themselves to be rightful members of the School must regard the School as having been founded not by human beings but by the will of the spiritual powers who rule the world today. They must understand that it has been established from the spiritual world and that it wants to work in accordance with the spiritual world; it feels responsible to this spiritual world only; it feels in the strictest sense responsible to the spiritual world. Therefore, anything coming up that reveals a lack of seriousness with regard to the School must lead to the cancellation of membership if a member does not take the matter seriously.

In past years, negligence to a marked degree has found its way into the Anthroposophical Society. One of the tasks of the members of this School will be to ensure that this negligence ceases. Above all, we must make ourselves responsible so we can stand by every word we speak as being the truth. Untrue statements, even when they come from what we call good intentions, are things that work destructively within an esoteric movement. We must have no illusions regarding this fact and be absolutely clear about it. Intentions are not what matter; they can be taken lightly. Objective truth is what matters. It is one of the first duties of pupils of esoteric teaching to feel obliged not only to say what they believe is true, but to also check that what they say is objectively true. Only if by means of objective truth we serve the divine spiritual powers, whose forces move through the School, shall we be able to make it through all the difficulties that will be meeting Anthroposophy.

We must not forget what certain influential people have said. My dear friends, I am speaking here within the circle of the School and what is said here remains within the circle of the School. We must not forget that certain people are saying something like the following:[9] Persons in positions of influence are saying: that those who represent the principles of the Roman Church will do their utmost in the near future to make the individual states of the former German Empire independent so that—and I'm only reporting this—from these independent states, with the exclusion of Prussia, the Holy Roman Empire of the German nation can once more be established, which having been established from such a prominent quarter, will of course spread its influence over neighboring regions. These persons say that they will have to do this in order to destroy in root and branch the most dangerous and frightful movements. They add that if they fail to reestablish the Holy Roman Empire of the German nation—and they say it will be successful—but if they fail, then they will find other means to destroy in root and branch those most contrary and dangerous movements. The movements they are referring to are the Anthroposophic Movement and the Movement for Religious Renewal.

My quotations are almost verbatim. You will see that the words I speak from time to time are founded on a firm foundation when I tell you that our difficulties will not decrease but will increase by the week. I speak today especially to the hearts of those who stand by their membership of the School in all seriousness. Only by being members of the School in complete earnestness, which must be an active sincerity, will we be able to build the firm rock that we need to find our way through the difficulties facing us in the future.

From what I have said you can deduce that Anthroposophy—and religious renewal that is simply another branch of Anthroposophy—is taken more seriously by our opponents than it is by many of those who live within the membership. The fact that the Holy Roman Empire of the German nation, which came to an end in 1806, is to be reestablished in order to clear away such movements, shows how seriously it is taken. It does not matter how many members belong to a movement founded in the spirit. What matters is how much strength from the spiritual world lives in that movement. The opponents see that there is a great strength in it and, to combat it, they choose means that are not slight, but sharp and powerful.

Eighth Lesson

(...) Page 120: The words of omitted text:

Because a significant number of anthroposophic friends, who have not been present here before, have come to attend the class today, I am obliged to say a few introductory words about the institution of the School. We must, in all seriousness, adhere to the new impulse that entered into the Anthroposophic Movement with the Christmas Conference at the Goetheanum. This new impulse must in particular be taken up in the consciousness of the members of our School of Spiritual Science. I have mentioned this several times, but then I know that many anthroposophic friends here today have thus far not heard me speak about it, and for that reason I have to emphasize it again.

Until the Christmas Conference, the need to separate the Anthroposophic Movement from the Anthroposophical Society was always stated explicitly.

The Anthroposophic Movement represents the spiritual wisdom and spiritual life impulse that flows into human civilization and can and must be obtained in our time directly from the spiritual world. This Anthroposophic Movement doesn't exist because it pleases human beings; it exists because spiritual powers that lead and guide the world and bring about human history consider it right to do so. These spiritual powers let the spiritual light that can come through Anthroposophy in a manner suitable for today, flow into human civilization.

For this purpose, the Anthroposophical Society was founded, so that as an administrative society, it could administer the anthroposophic body of knowledge and life wisdom. Several times it had to be emphasized that Anthroposophy is something that hovers above the Society and that the Anthroposophical Society is its exoteric administrator.

This has changed since the Christmas Conference at the Goetheanum. The opposite is the case since the Christmas Conference. It is only because the opposite is the case that together with the Executive Council—which was formed at the Christmas Conference and with whom the necessary work can be carried out—I was prepared to take on the presidency of the newly founded Anthroposophical Society. What happened because of this can be described in one sentence. That sentence is: Everything that happens now through the Anthroposophical Society must itself be Anthroposophy. Since Christmas, Anthroposophy must be done in the Anthroposophical Society. Every single action must have a direct esoteric character. The establishment of the Dornach Executive Council at the Christmas Conference was thus an esoteric action, an action that must be thought of as having come directly from the spiritual world. Only if this truly lives in the consciousness of our anthroposophic friends can the Anthroposophical Society that was founded at that moment, thrive. Thus the

Passages Omitted from the Text

Anthroposophic Movement and the Anthroposophical Society have now become identical.

It was stressed at the Christmas Conference that the Executive Council at Dornach is an initiative council. Obviously, administration is also necessary, but administration is not what it considers as its first task. Its task is to cause Anthroposophy to flow through the Anthroposophical Society and to do everything that will lead to this goal.

This makes clear the position of the Dornach Executive Council in the Anthroposophical Society. It must be clear from now on that every relationship within the Anthroposophical Society is not built on some bureaucratic measure, but it is built throughout on human substance. Therefore, at the Christmas Conference, the statutes that were presented did not contain paragraphs that members must confess to or agree with; the statutes simply describe the intention of the Executive Council.[10] This is how the Anthroposophical Society is constituted today. It is founded on human relationship.

Though it may be a detail, I have to stress once again that every member receives a membership card that I myself have signed so that some personal relationship, however abstract, is immediately established. It has been suggested that I should have a rubber stamp made with my signature. I will not do this, although it is not exactly easy to get through the signing of twelve-thousand membership cards. Even so, I will not follow this suggestion because even if it is abstract, personal relationship arises with every individual member if my eyes rest for a moment on the name of the person who is to receive the membership card. This is the beginning of direct and tangible work within our society, and obviously all of the other relationships will be all the more truly human.

I must stress another subject and make it clear to the consciousness of the membership; I emphasize it because it has already been transgressed against. Members must be conscious of the fact that if they use the name "General Anthroposophical Society" they must first obtain the agreement of the Executive Council at the Goetheanum. Similarly, if something is issued from the Goetheanum and Dornach and is to be further used in an esoteric sense, then this can only be done if an understanding is first reached with the Executive Council at the Goetheanum. Therefore, we will, not recognize anything appearing in the name of the General Anthroposophical Society by way of formulations and teachings given from the Goetheanum unless an understanding has been reached first with the Executive Council at the Goetheanum. No abstract relationships; only concrete relationships will be possible in the future. The Goetheanum must take on concretely anything issued from the Goetheanum. Thus active members of the Anthroposophical Society wishing to use the heading "General Anthroposophical Society" for lectures given at one place or another, or formulations and the like that have been given here, must write to the recording secretary of the Anthroposophical Society at the Goetheanum, Frau Dr. Wegman, in order to obtain the agreement of the Executive Council at the Goetheanum. It is necessary that the Executive Council at the Goetheanum be properly regarded in the future as the center of the Anthroposophic Movement.

Now we must move on to the relationship of the School to the Anthroposophical Society. This too must also live in the consciousness of the membership. People become members of the Anthroposophical Society if in their hearts they have the desire to know and to live with the anthroposophic wisdom and life impulses as it wants to spread throughout the world. No other obligations are taken on except those that arise in heart and soul from Anthroposophy itself. Having belonged to the General Anthroposophical Society for a certain period of time—a minimum of two years has been decided on at present—members are then free to apply for membership in the School of Spiritual Science.

Becoming a member of the School of Spiritual Science is a matter of taking on a truly serious commitment to the Society, to the cause of Anthroposophy. This means that the member desires to be a true representative of Anthroposophy in the world. This is necessary today. The leadership of the School of Spiritual Science can under no other conditions decide to work together with its members.

Do not say, my dear friends, that this is a curtailment of your freedom. Freedom implies that all those who are involved are free. And so, just as members of the School can and must be free, so must the leadership of the School be free to decide with whom it does or does not want to work. If for some reason the leadership of the School is obliged to reach the opinion that a member cannot be a true representative of Anthroposophy in the world, it must then be possible for the leadership of the School either to refuse an application for membership or to withdraw membership if it has already been granted. In the future, this must be adhered to in the strictest sense so that there can indeed be a free collaboration between the leadership of the School and the membership.

As has already been stated in the member supplement to the *Goetheanum News*[11] we are step-by-step trying to make it possible for those unable to participate at the Goetheanum to take part in some way in the continuing work of the School. We can only take the fifth step after we take the fourth, the seventh step cannot follow directly on the first, and ever since the Christmas Conference there has been so much to do here. But everything will be done to the best of our ability. We shall be able to establish circular letters that will enable members living elsewhere to participate in what goes on in the School. So far we have only been able to make a beginning with a circular letter sent out by Frau Dr. Wegman to enable medical doctors to participate in the work of the School.[12] Gradually other possibilities will emerge and I beg you to be patient in this respect.

Remaining to be mentioned is a fact that must be understood as having been expressly established by the spiritual world, not by the impulses of human beings. A decision reached by the spiritual world has been brought down by the available means. Thus, the School must be regarded as an institution of the spiritual world for the present age just as has always been the case in the Mysteries. So, today, we may say that the School must develop in our time to become a true Mystery School. Accordingly, it will be the soul of the Anthroposophic Movement.

This points to the serious manner that membership in the School must be taken. It goes without saying that everything achieved through esoteric work up to this point flows into the work of the School. For the School is the esoteric foundation and source of all esoteric work within the Anthroposophic Movement. Those persons, for whatever reason, who want to establish something esoteric in the world, have to do so without connection to the Executive Council at the Goetheanum. They must be in full agreement with the Executive Council at the Goetheanum or they will be unable to use anything that flows from the Goetheanum in their teaching or impulses. Those wishing to proceed with esoteric work under any conditions other than those just mentioned cannot be a member of this school. They will have to continue with their esoteric work outside of the School and without the recognition of the School. They will have to realize that nothing originating in the School can be included in their work. The connection with this school must be seen as being entirely concrete. It must be clear to every member of the School of Spiritual Science at the Goetheanum in Dornach that the School must consider a member to be a true representative of Anthroposophy in the world and, that a member is an exoteric representative of Anthroposophy in a manner appropriate to the membership of the School.

At the time when I was not yet part of the leadership, not yet president of the Anthroposophical Society, an attempt was made to model the Goetheanum on other schools of higher learning. But this is not possible under present conditions. Here, esoteric aspects will be found that cannot be found at other schools of learning. And here, this is not an institution that can compete with other schools of higher learning. The starting point here will be the point at which every honestly striving individual comes upon questions in any field of life that cannot be answered outside of the esoteric realm.

Something real took place at the Christmas Conference and what took place there must be taken seriously. The impulses that are to issue from the Goetheanum must fulfill their tasks. Taking our departure from the earnest necessity to fulfill these tasks, members of the School must cut short all the nonsense that keeps on making them shy away from admitting freely and honestly: I am a representative of that Anthroposophy coming from the Goetheanum. Some members shy away from doing this. They keep on maintaining that it is better to remain silent about Anthroposophy and to prepare people slowly. They think it a better policy to proceed in silence and gradually bring people into contact with us. But this does not usually lead people to us, and those who wish to proceed in this way would do better to relinquish their membership in the School at once. I can assure you that membership in the School will be taken with extreme seriousness in the future. This will be accepted with heartfelt accord by those members of the School who are really behind the cause of Anthroposophy in all of their work and striving. But those who persist in maintaining that you cannot immediately confront people with Anthroposophy, but should first maneuver your way into people's confidence, such members might as well make the decision to carry on with their opinions outside of the School.

All of these things are preconditions that had to be mentioned today because so many anthroposophic friends are here who have so far not participated in the work of the School. We have had to listen to this introduction and wait so long for the lesson to begin today because so many friends are here for the first time. Thus, in a sense, today's lesson is a kind of preparation. I shall give a second lesson at a time to be announced to which only those present today will be admitted. Please ask those wishing to come still later to be patient. We shall not get anywhere if new people are present every time a lesson is given. With today's lesson, we have reached the limit of those who, for the moment, can be members. Of course, others can become members, but only those present today will be able to come to the next lesson, which will simply be a continuation of today's lesson.

Tenth Lesson

(...) Page 159: The words of omitted text:

I want to conclude by saying that without first obtaining permission, you may not pass on either the content of what is said here or the mantras. There must be a proper sequence of events. Only after permission has been obtained may information be passed on to either individuals or to groups. In particular, my dear friends, it is strictly inappropriate to send any of the mantras or their interpretations by mail. It is not permissible to send these things by mail and I beg you to abide earnestly and strictly by this requirement.

Eleventh Lesson

(...) Page 160: The words of omitted text:

You are all undoubtedly very deeply affected this morning by the news that Miss Maryon has departed from the physical plane, even though this event was long expected and followed a long period of really severe suffering that lasted more than a year. Tomorrow, when all the members of the Anthroposophical Society are present, I will share what I have to say about Miss Maryon's departure from the physical plane. For today, let me just mention that the First Class has lost a truly devoted pupil, for Miss Maryon was foremost among those who, with fervor and devotion, was attached to what the School had to bring. Despite her severe illness, she not only participated in the esoteric work being developed here, but also practiced the exercises given here; she let them work on her and she lived with them with exceptional care.

In her case, this was all founded on the fact that she was actually already an esoteric pupil when she came to us. She belonged to an esoteric school that was working in quite a different direction when she made the transition to the Anthroposophical Society, and she rapidly made a complete transition to Anthroposophy from that esoteric school. For her, the esoteric element was essential; she lived intensely within it during the year she was with us on the physical plane and she will now continue to do so, having departed from the physical plane, but most certainly not from Anthroposophy.

For today, this is all I have to say and, indeed, anymore would be inappropriate because she has only just left the physical plane. Tomorrow, when members and friends have gathered here, it will be my task to say what there is to be said.[13]

(...) Page 173: The words of omitted text:

Many of the friends who, above all, want to take part in these esoteric lessons of the School, are unable to attend regularly on Fridays. These Friday lessons will in the future take place on Sunday mornings, from eleven to twelve o'clock. The next lesson will therefore take place on Sunday in a week, from eleven to twelve o'clock so that friends who live nearby and are busy on Friday and Saturday, when most of the others could attend, will also be able to come regularly. For many of you attending on Fridays has been a great sacrifice and that is why the lessons have been moved to Sunday morning from eleven to twelve o'clock.[14]

Thirteenth Lesson

(...) Page 205: The words of omitted text:

From now on, the lesson will take place on Saturday at the same time.

Fourteenth Lesson

(...) Page 220: The words of omitted text:

I can announce that the next class lesson will take place Saturday, June 21, because I have an task in Silesia to a course of lectures on agriculture.[15] Therefore, the next lesson will be on June 21 at 8:30 p.m.

Fifteenth Lesson

(...) Page 235: The words of omitted text:

The next class lesson will take place a week from today, next Saturday at 8:30 p.m. Tomorrow there will be painting for the children in the building office.

Sixteenth Lesson

(...) Page 236: The words of omitted text:

Before these words speak to our souls—since again today many newly admitted members of the esoteric school are here—I must indicate once more, briefly, what is the meaning of this School. Today, I will briefly mention the importance of seeing that in this School communications to human souls come directly from the spiritual world. All that lives in the School and is here presented to human souls is to be seen as communication from the spiritual world itself. From this you will recognize that membership in the School must be regarded as a very serious matter.

The kind of seriousness with which this School must be imbued has become possible only since the Christmas Conference through the entire constitution of the Anthroposophical Society. Since the Christmas Conference, the Anthroposophical Society as such has become an entirely public matter, a public institution through which flows an esoteric stream of life. An esoteric stream that human hearts are welcoming today far more than they ever welcomed the more exoteric character that prevailed before. No more is required from members of the Anthroposophical Society than they feel themselves to be listeners of anthroposophic wisdom; beyond that, no more is demanded than would be expected from every decent human being in life.

Even more, belonging to this School requires even more that a member of this School acknowledge the requirements, the serious requirements of this School. The basic requirement is that everyone who wants to belong to the School shall take a stand in life and be a true representative of the anthroposophic cause in the world, in all directions and in every detail.

To be a representative of the anthroposophic cause in the world must naturally entail—with regard to anything one does or wants to do in

Passages Omitted from the Text

connection with the anthroposophic cause, however remote—that one will first get in touch with the leadership of the School, which means the esoteric council at the Goetheanum. The point is that through the School a real stream should flow into the anthroposophic movement, which today is represented by the Anthroposophical Society.

Therefore, it is necessary that membership in the School shall be understood to mean that one who belongs to the School receives Anthroposophy into one's full humanity, into one's entire being, while at the same time feeling oneself to be part of the stream of life and work that wants to go out from the Goetheanum. That we make such demands, my dear friends, cannot be looked upon as an infringement of individual freedom since membership in the School rests on a mutual relationship. The leadership of the School must be free to give what it has to give to those it feels justified in giving it. Moreover, since there is no obligation to be a member of the School, since it is a matter of personal freedom, the leaders of the School must also be free to lay down their requirements without anyone being able to say that freedom of will has thereby been impaired. It is a free agreement between the leadership of the School and those who want to be a member.

However, because the strict character of the School must be taken very seriously, it cannot be otherwise than that the leadership of the School has the right to cancel membership if they consider it necessary based on events that may have occurred. Moreover, my dear friends, as evidence that the leadership strictly observes this proves that, in the relatively short period of time that the School has existed, sixteen members have been expelled from the School for more or less time. I must emphasize once again: this measure—for we are entering deeply into the esoteric life—will, without question, have to be strictly applied in the future, no matter what the personal aspect may be for those it affects.

(...) Page 238: The words of omitted text:

Those who do not yet have these mantras will be able to receive them from other members of the School. But in doing so a certain procedure

The First Class of the Michael School

must be observed: not the one who receives the mantras but the one who gives them must first ask permission to give them.

Seventeenth Lesson

(...) Page 262: The words of omitted text:

My dear friends, I must remind you of something that was said when the Class was first established, which was emphasized even before that time, during the Christmas Conference. People must not keep assuming that something that has been arranged in a certain way out of deep reasons can be altered from the outside or arranged differently from what was originally established. For that reason, I have to announce something that those who are already in the Class should most definitely endeavor to make clear to others who intend to seek membership. What I have to announce is this: in future, without exception, no application to join the Class will be taken into account unless it is made directly to the recording secretary of the Executive Council, Dr. Wegman, or to me. Applications for membership in the class will only be considered if they are directed to one of these two addresses; what has been established right from the beginning must remain in force. Members have once again begun to arrange things as they please, without adhering to what has been established. I also wish to take this opportunity of drawing your attention to something else, my dear friends, since it is now extremely important that the Anthroposophical Society should be led with the competence that has been established.

Repeatedly, letters I have received have contained the sentence: if I do not receive a reply, I shall take this to be an affirmation. Those who have written in this way already know what I have to say. I now request all of those who have written in this way, and all of those who still intend to do so, to take into account that every letter containing the sentence: that no reply is taken to mean the affirmative, may be assumed to contain its own refusal. Letters containing this sentence will in future not be answered at all because it is impossible to make progress when such assumptions are made. Letters written in this manner will automatically be taken to contain their own refusal.

Eighteenth Lesson

(...) Page 276: The words of omitted text:

The next class lesson will take place not today in a week but today in two weeks at 8:30.[16]

Nineteenth Lesson

(...) Page 289: The words of omitted text:

My dear sisters and brothers, it has to be said that the rules to which attention has repeatedly been drawn with respect to the esoteric School, are unfortunately being observed in a different way by many who have applied for membership and then became members.

Yesterday, I was obliged to remind you emphatically about a number of matters.[17] It is difficult to believe that members have been using their blue membership cards to keep their seats reserved. It has also happened in three cases that people have left notebooks containing the mantric verses of the School lying about—two notebooks and one folder to be precise. The folder, which contained the verses in typewritten form, was found lying in the street. The texts in one of the notebooks were copied in the manner described yesterday, and the other notebook was found in the Glass House. It was necessary because of this for me to exclude three members of the School immediately before the beginning of the lesson we have just heard.

This brings us to a total of nineteen exclusions from the School. One might have expected that a greater degree of seriousness would emerge from souls who have already heard here about the significance of the School. Yet one person loses the mantras in the street, another leaves them lying about, and a third leaves them in the Glass House, making it necessary to exclude three quite prominent members from the School. I must assure you, my dear sisters and brothers, that the rules I told you about at the beginning and that I have since repeatedly mentioned, must be applied with the utmost strictness. A serious esoteric School such as this can only be maintained if members really do adhere to what has been asked of them in the name of the spiritual powers who lead it.

This is how things are with truly esoteric matters. The attributes that were hitherto frequently prevalent in the Anthroposophical Society can on no account be allowed to prevail further. Something that is by its very nature filled with seriousness must simply be taken absolutely seriously.

Mantras of the Michael School in English and German

FIRST TABLET

O Man, Know Thy Self!
Thus sounds the Cosmic Word.
You hear it with strength of soul,
You feel it with might of spirit.

Who speaks so powerfully through
 the world?
Who speaks so tenderly within
 your heart?

Does it work through the far-spread
 rays of space
Into your senses' experience of life?
Does it sound through the weaving
 waves of time
Into the evolving stream of your life?

Is it you, yourself, who
By sensing space,
By experiencing time,
Begets this word,
Feeling yourself estranged in the psychic
 void of space,
Because you lose the force of thought
In the annihilating stream of time?

SECOND TABLET

Know first the earnest Guardian,
Who stands before the gate of spirit land,
Denying entry to your senses' power
And to the strength of your intellect,
Because in the weaving of your senses
And in the forming of your thoughts
First you must find—
From the nothingness of space,
From time's delusive powers—
The strength to conquer
The truth of your own being.

THIRD TABLET

I came into this sense world
Bearing thought's heritage
 within me,
Led by a divine power.
Death stands at journey's end.
I want to feel the Being of Christ.
He awakens spiritual birth in
 matter's death.
In spirit, thus, I find the world
And know myself amid the
 world's evolving.

ERSTE TAFEL

O Mensch, erkenne dich selbst!
So tönt das Weltenwort.
Du hörst es seelenkräftig,
Du fühlst es geistgewaltig.

Wer spricht so weltenmächtig?
Wer spricht so herzinniglich?

Wirkt es durch des Raumes Weitenstrahlung
In deines Sinnes Seinserleben?
Tönt es durch der Zeiten Wellenweben
In deines Lebens Werdestrom?

Bist du es selbst, der sich
Im Raumesfühlen, im Zeiterleben
Das Wort erschafft, dich fremd
Erfühlend in Raumes Seelenleere,
Weil du des Denkens Kraft
Verlierst im Zeitvernichtungsstrome.

ZWEITE TAFEL

Erkenne erst den ernsten Hüter,
Der vor des Geisterlandes Pforten steht,
Den Einlass deiner Sinnenkraft
Und deines Verstandes Macht verwehrend,
Weil du im Sinnesweben
Und im Gedankenbilden
Aus Raumeswesenlosigkeit,
Aus Zeiten Truggewalten
Des eignen Wesens Wahrheit
Dir kraftvoll erst erobern musst.

DRITTE TAFEL

Ich trat in diese Sinnes-Welt,
Des Denkens Erbe mit mir führend,
Eines Gottes Kraft hat mich hereingeführt.
Der Tod, er steht an des Weges Ende.
Ich will des Christus Wesen fühlen.
Es weckt in Stoffes-Sterben Geist-Geburt.
Im Geiste find' ich so die Welt
Und erkenne mich im Weltenwerden.

FIRST LESSON

Where on Earth foundations,
    color upon color,
Life, creative life, manifests itself;
Where from earthly substance,
    form on form,
The lifeless world is fashioned;
Where sentient beings, powerful in will,
Warm themselves with joy
    in their existence;
Where you, yourself, O Man, acquire
Your body from earth, air and light:

There you enter with your own true being
Deep into night-enveloped cold
    and darkness;
From the dumb expanse you ask in vain
Who you are and were and will become.
For your own being the light of day
    fades into
Soul's night and spirit-darkness;
With anxious seeking you turn your soul
To the light that takes its strength
    from darkness.

And from the darkness there lights up
To you—
Revealing your own likeness,
Yet also shaping you into an image,
Solemn spirit words powerfully working
    in the cosmic ether,
Words that your heart can hear—

The spirit messenger, who alone
Can shed light upon your path.
Before him lies the far-spread world
    of the senses;
Behind him yawns the depths of the abyss.

And before his darkened realm of spirit,
Close to the yawning chasm of existence,
His creative word sounds
    with all primeval power:
Behold, I am the only gate to knowledge.

From the far reaches of the beings of space,
Who experience their being in light;
From the beat of the course of time,
Which finds its expression in creation;
From the depths of the heart's experience,
Where the world fathoms itself in your Self:

There resounds in the speaking of the soul,
There shines forth from the thoughts
    of the spirit,
Working from divine, healing powers,
Weaving in cosmic, formative forces,
The Eternal Word of existence:
<u>O Man, Know Thy Self!</u>

316

Behold the foremost beast;
    its crooked back,
Its bony head, its parched form,
Dull blunt blue appears its skin.
Your fear of creative spirit being
Begat this monstrous foe within your will;
Only courage on the path of knowledge
    will overcome it.

Yet, beware of the abyss!
For its beasts would soon devour you
If in heedless haste you passed me by.
Your cosmic age has set them within you
As the enemies of knowledge.

Behold the second beast;
    it bares its teeth
In its distorted countenance,
    and tells lies with scorn.
Yellow, streaked with gray, its
    loathsome shape.
Your hatred of the spirit's revelations
Begat this weakling in your feeling;
Your fire for knowledge must tame it.

Behold the third beast with cloven snout;
Glassy is its eye, its posture slouching.
Dirty red its form appears.
Your doubt in the power of spirit light
Begat this spectral
    form within your thinking;
Your creative work in knowledge must
    make it yield.

Only when you have overcome these three
Will your soul develop wings
To soar across the deep abyss
That severs you from the field of knowledge
Where the dearest longings of your heart,
Aspiring to wholeness, wish to consecrate themselves.

ERSTE STUNDE

Wo auf Erdengründen, Farb' an Farbe,
Sich das Leben schaffend offenbart;
Wo aus Erdenstoffen, Form an Form,
Sich das Lebenslose ausgestaltet;
Wo erfühlende Wesen, willenskräftig,
Sich am eignen Dasein freudig wärmen;
Wo du selbst, o Mensch, das Leibessein
Dir aus Erd' und Luft und Licht erwirbst:

Da betrittst du deines Eigenwesens
Tiefe, nachtbedeckte, kalte Finsternis;
Du erfragest im Dunkel der Weiten
Nimmer, wer du bist und warst und werdest.
Für dein Eigensein finstert der Tag
Sich zur Seelennacht, zum Geistesdunkel;
Und du wendest seelensorgend dich
An das Licht, das aus Finsternissen kraftet.

Und aus Finsternissen hellet sich
– Dich im Ebenbilde offenbarend,
Doch zum Gleichnis auch dich bildend,
Ernstes Geisteswort im Weltenäther,
Deinem Herzen hörbar, kraftvoll wirkend –

Dir der Geistesbote, der allein
Dir den Weg erleuchten kann;
Vor ihm breiten sich die Sinnesfelder,
Hinter ihm, da gähnen Abgrundtiefen.

Und vor seinen finstern Geistesfeldern,
Dicht am gähnenden Abgrund des Seins,
Da ertönt sein urgewaltig Schöpferwort:
Sieh, ich bin der Erkenntnis einzig Tor.

Aus den Weiten der Raumeswesen,
Die im Lichte das Sein erleben,
Aus dem Schritte des Zeitenganges,
Der im Schaffen das Wirken findet,
Aus den Tiefen des Herzempfindens,
Wo im Selbst sich die Welt ergründet:

Da ertönt im Seelensprechen,
Da erleuchtet aus Geistgedanken
Das aus göttlichen Heileskräften
In den Weltgestaltungsmächten
Wellend wirkende Daseinswort:
O, du Mensch, erkenne dich selbst.

Doch du musst den Abgrund achten;
Sonst verschlingen seine Tiere
Dich, wenn du an mir vorübereilt'st;
Sie hat deine Weltenzeit in dir
Als Erkenntnisfeinde hingestellt.

Schau das erste Tier, den Rücken krumm,
Knochenhaft das Haupt, von dürrem Leib,
Ganz von stumpfem Blau ist seine Haut;
Deine Furcht vor Geistes-Schöpfer-Sein
Schuf das Urgetüm in deinem Willen;
Dein Erkenntnismut nur überwindet es.

Schau das zweite Tier, es zeigt die Zähne
Im verzerrten Angesicht, es lügt in Spotten,
Gelb mit grauem Einschlag ist sein Leib;
Dein Hass auf Geistes-Offenbarung
Schuf den Schwächling dir im Fühlen;
Dein Erkenntnisfeuer muss ihn zähmen.

Schau das dritte Tier, mit gespalt'nem Maul,
Glasig ist sein Auge, schlaff die Haltung,
Schmutzigrot erscheint dir die Gestalt;
Dein Zweifel an Geistes-Licht-Gewalt
Schuf dir dies Gespenst in deinem Denken;
Dem Erkenntnisschaffen muss es weichen.

Erst wenn die Drei von dir besiegt,
Werden Flügel deiner Seele wachsen,
Um den Abgrund zu übersetzen,
Der dich trennet vom Erkenntnisfelde,
Dem sich deine Herzenssehnsucht
Heilerstrebend weihen möchte.

SECOND LESSON

The third beast with its glassy eye,
Is the |evil| counter-image
Of thinking, that in you denies itself,
And chooses its own death,
Forsaking spirit powers who,
Before its earthly life, sustained
Its life in fields of spirit.

The second beast with mocking face
Is the |evil| counter- force
Of feeling that hollows out your very soul
And makes for emptiness of life;
Whereas enlightening spirit-fullness
Was given you before you were on Earth
From the might of spirit-sun.

The first beast's ghostly skeleton
Is the |evil| creative might
Of will that estranges your own body
From all the forces of your soul
And offers it to adverse powers
Who want to rob the world's being
In future times from Divine Being.

ZWEITE STUNDE

Des dritten Tieres glasig Auge,
Es ist das |böse| Gegenbild
Des Denkens, das in dir sich selbst
Verleugnet und den Tod sich wählet,
Absagend Geistgewalten, die es
Vor seinem Erdenleben geistig
In Geistesfeldern lebend hielten.

Des zweiten Tieres Spottgesicht,
Es ist die |böse| Gegenkraft
Des Fühlens, das die eigne Seele
Aushöhlet und Lebensleerheit
In ihr erschafft statt Geistgehalt,
Der vor dem Erdensein erleuchtend
Aus Geistessonnenmacht ihr ward.

Des ersten Tieres Knochengeist,
Er ist die |böse| Schöpfermacht
Des Wollens, die den eignen Leib
Entfremdet deiner Seelenkraft
Und ihn den Gegenmächten weiht,
Die Weltensein dem Göttersein
In Zukunftzeiten rauben wollen.

THIRD LESSON

See how thinking weaves in you;
Experience, then, world-illusion.
Selfhood hides itself from you;
Dive down into the semblance.
Ether's essence wafts in you;
Selfhood's being should revere
Guiding beings of your spirit.

Perceive how feeling streams in you;
How semblance mixes there with being.
Your Self to semblance feels inclined;
Immerse yourself in seeming being.
And world soul forces dwell in you;
Your Selfhood, it should deeply ponder
Powers of life within your soul.

Let work the impulse of will in you;
It rises up from worlds of illusion
Creative in its very essence.
To this devote all your life,
For filled it is with cosmic spiritual might.
Your very being should now grasp
World creative might in your spiritual "I."

DRITTE STUNDE

— ◡
Sieh in dir Gedankenweben:
◡ —
Weltenschein erlebest du,
— ◡
Selbstheitsein verbirgt sich dir;
◡ —
Tauche unter in den Schein:
— ◡
Ätherwesen weht in dir;
— ◡
Selbstheitsein, es soll verehren
◡ —
Deines Geistes Führerwesen.

◡ —
Vernimm in dir Gefühle-Strömen:
◡ —
Es mengen Schein und Sein sich dir,
◡ —
Die Selbstheit neigt dem Scheine sich;
◡ —
So tauche unter in scheinendes Sein:
◡ —
Und Welten-Seelenkräfte sind in dir;
◡ —
Die Selbstheit, sie soll bedenken
◡ —
Der eignen Seele Lebensmächte.

— ◡
Lass walten in dir den Willens-Stoß:
— ◡
Der steigt aus allem Scheineswesen
— ◡
Mit Eigensein erschaffend auf;
— ◡
Ihm wende zu all dein Leben:
— ◡
Der ist erfüllt von Welten-Geistesmacht;
— ◡
Dein Eigensein, es soll ergreifen
— ◡
Weltschöpfermacht im Geistes-Ich.

FOURTH LESSON

Feel how from the depths of Earth
Forces press into your being,
Into members of your body.
You will lose yourself in them
If you give your will over
Powerlessly to their surging.
Dim and dark they make your "I."

Feel how from the worldwide spaces
Godly powers send their spirit-radiance
Lighting up your inmost soul.
Find yourself in them with love.
Wisdom weaving they then create
You as a Self within their spheres,
Strong for spirit works of Good.

Feel how in the heights of heaven
Selfhood selflessly can live,
If in spirit-fullness it will follow
Powers of thought and striving to
   the heights,
And will bravely then receive the Word
That rings forth from heights above
   with Grace
Into Man's true being.

VIERTE STUNDE

Fühle wie die Erdentiefen
Ihre Kräfte deinem Wesen
In die Leibesglieder drängen.
Du verlierest dich in ihnen,
Wenn du deinen Willen machtlos
Ihrem Streben anvertrauest;
Sie verfinstern dir das Ich.

Fühle wie aus Weltenweiten
Göttermächte ihre Geisteshelle
Dir ins Seelenwesen leuchten lassen.
Finde dich in ihnen liebend,
Und sie schaffen weisheitwebend
Dich als Selbst in ihren Kreisen
Stark für gutes Geistesschaffen.

Fühle wie in Himmelshöhen
Selbstsein selbstlos leben kann,
Wenn es geisterfüllt Gedankenmächten
In dem Höhenstreben folgen will
Und in Tapferkeit das Wort vernimmt,
Das von oben gnadevoll ertönet
In des Menschen wahre Wesenheit.

FIFTH LESSON

Light battles with darkness
In that realm where your thinking
Would like to penetrate spirit-being.
You find, toward light aspiring,
That spirit takes your Self away.
You can, if lured by powers dark,
Lose your Self in matter.

Warmth battles with cold
In that realm where your feelings
Would like to live in spirit-weaving.
You find, in loving warmth,
Your Self scattered in spirit-bliss;
You can, if coldness hardens you,
Crush your Self in suffering.

Life battles with death
In that realm where your own will
Would like to reign as creative spirit.
You find, when grasping life,
Your Self will vanish in spirits' might.
You can, if subdued by death's
    own power,
Encramp your Self in nothingness.

FÜNFTE STUNDE

Es kämpft das Licht mit finstren Mächten
In jenem Reiche, wo dein Denken
In Geistesdasein dringen möchte.
Du findest, lichtwärts strebend,
Dein Selbst vom Geiste dir genommen;
Du kannst, wenn Finstres dich verlockt,
Im Stoff das Selbst verlieren.

Es kämpft das Warme mit dem Kalten
In jenem Reiche, wo dein Fühlen
Im Geistesweben leben möchte.
Du findest, Wärme liebend,
Dein Selbst in Geisteslust verwehend;
Du kannst, wenn Kälte dich verhärtet,
Im Leid das Selbst verstäuben.

Es kämpft das Leben mit dem Tode
In jenem Reiche, wo dein Wollen
Im Geistesschaffen walten möchte.
Du findest, Leben fassend,
Dein Selbst in Geistesmacht verschwinden;
Du kannst, wenn Todesmacht dich bändigt,
Im Nichts das Selbst verkrampfen.

SIXTH LESSON

To earthly nature you descend
When unfolding your force of will.
When as thinker you tread the Earth,
Then power of thought will show
   to you
Yourself in your animal nature.
Fear of Self
Must change to courage in your soul.

Of light-shine's power you retain
Mere thoughts within your inner self.
When light-shine thinks itself in you
An untrue spirit-being will arise
In you as Selfhood's vain delusion.
But mindfulness of earthly needs
Maintains you as a human being.

With watery nature do you live
Merely through feeling's
   dreamy weaving.
Send wakening through your
   watery being.
Your soul will then emerge
In plant-like dull existence;
Paralysis of Self
Must lead to wakefulness.

Of world-formation you retain
Mere feelings in your inner self.
When cosmic form then feels
   itself in you
Your faint experience of the spirit
Will choke you in your
   Selfhood's being.
But love of values of the Earth
Will save your human soul.

In fleeting air you dream your thoughts
Merely in forms of memory-pictures.
Take hold of the airy being with
   your will.
Your soul will threaten you
   with pain,
Rigidified and cold as stone.
But Selfhood's death from cold
Must yield to spirit's fire.

Of cosmic life you do retain
Mere willing in your inner self.
When cosmic life takes full hold
Consuming spirit bliss will kill
Your experience of Self.
But earthly will, devoted to the spirit,
Lets the divine in us hold sway.

SECHSTE STUNDE

Du steigst ins Erden-Wesenhafte
Mit deines Willens Kraftentfaltung;
Betritt als Denker du das Erdensein,
Es wird Gedankenmacht dir dich
Als deine eigne Tierheit zeigen;
Die Furcht vor deinem Selbst
Muss dir in Seelen-Mut sich wandeln.

Du lebest mit dem Wasserwesen
Nur durch des Fühlens Traumesweben;
Durchdring erwachend Wassersein,
Es wird die Seele sich in dir
Als dumpfes Pflanzendasein geben;
Und Lahmheit deines Selbst
Muss dich zum Wachen führen.

Du sinnest in dem Lüftewehen
Nur in Gedächtnis-Bilderformen;
Ergreife wollend Lüftewesen,
Es wird die eigne Seele dich
Als kalterstarrter Stein bedroh'n;
Doch deiner Selbstheit Kälte-Tod,
Er muss dem Geistesfeuer weichen.

Du hältst von Lichtes-Scheines-Macht
Gedanken nur im Innern fest;
Wenn Lichtesschein in dir sich selber denkt,
So wird unwahres Geisteswesen
In dir als Selbstheitwahn ersteh'n;
Besinnung auf die Erdennöte
Wird dich im Menschensein erhalten.

Du hältst vom Weltgestalten
Gefühle nur im Innern fest;
Wenn Weltenform in dir sich selber fühlt,
So wird ohnmächtig Geist-Erleben
In dir das Selbstheitsein ersticken;
Doch Liebe zu den Erdenwerten
Wird dir die Menschenseele retten.

Du hältst vom Weltenleben
Das Wollen nur im Innern fest;
Wenn Weltenleben dich voll erfasst,
So wird vernichtend Geistes-Lust
In dir das Selbst-Erleben töten;
Doch Erdenwollen geist-ergeben,
Es lässt den Gott im Menschen walten.

SEVENTH LESSON

Behold the Three,
They are as One,
When you bear in Earth existence
The stamp of being human.

△ Experience the cosmic form of your head.
⋈ Feel the cosmic beat of your heart.
▽ Think the cosmic strength of your limbs.

These are the Three
The Three that live as One
In Earth existence.

Spirit of the head,
You can <u>will</u> it;
And will <u>becomes</u> for you
Heaven's weaving of manifold forms in the senses.
    You weave in worlds of <u>wisdom</u>.

Soul of the heart,
You can <u>feel</u> it;
And feeling <u>becomes</u> for you
The seed for awakening cosmic life in
    You live in worlds of <u>appearance</u>.

Strength in the limbs,
You can <u>think</u> it;
And thinking <u>becomes</u> for you
Purposeful human striving of the will.
    You strive in realms of <u>virtue</u>.

thinking
willing

Enter:
The door is open!
You will become
A true human being.

SIEBENTE STUNDE

O schau die Drei,
Sie sind die Eins,
Wenn du die Menschenprägung
Im Erdendasein trägst.

◁ Erlebe des Kopfes Weltgestalt.

⊠ Empfinde des Herzens Weltenschlag.

▷ Erdenke der Glieder Weltenkraft.

Sie sind die Drei,
Die Drei, die als das Eins
Im Erdendasein leben.

Des Kopfes Geist,
Du kannst ihn wollen;
Und Wollen wird dir
Der Sinne vielgestaltig Himmelsweben;
   Du webest in der Weisheit.

Des Herzens Seele,
Du kannst sie fühlen;
Und Fühlen wird dir
Des Denkens keimerweckend Weltenleben;
   Du lebest in dem Scheine.

Der Glieder Kraft,
Du kannst sie denken;
Und Denken wird dir
Des Wollens zielerfassend Menschenstreben;
   Du strebest in der Tugend.

     Tritt ein
Das Tor ist geöffnet
     Du wirst
Ein wahrer Mensch werden.

EIGHTH LESSON

See behind thinking's sensory light,
How in the darkened spirit-cell
Will ascends from the body's depths.
Let lifeless thinking flow through
    the strength of your soul
Into the cosmic void.
And will now rises up
As cosmic thought-creating.

See in the soul the weaving of feeling,
How in the dimness of dreams
Life streams in from worlds afar.
Let, through the peace of your heart,
Human feeling waft away in sleep.
And cosmic life becomes
    spiritually active
As the power of man's true being.

See above the bodily working of will,
How thinking descends from the
    forces of the head
Into slumbering fields of action.
Let our will be transformed,
Through the soul's perception, into light.
And thinking now appears
As will's magic essence.

ACHTE STUNDE

Sieh hinter des Denkens Sinneslicht,
Wie in der finstren Geisteszelle
Wollen sich hebt aus Leibestiefen;
Lasse fließen durch deiner Seele Stärke
Totes Denken in das Weltennichts;
Und das Wollen, es erstehet
Als Weltgedankenschaffen.

Sieh in des Fühlens Seelenwehen,
Wie in dem Träumedämmern
Leben aus Weltenfernen strömt;
Lass in Schlaf durch die Herzensruhe
Menschenfühlen still verwehen;
Und das Weltenleben geistert
Als Menschenwesensmacht.

Sieh über des Wollens Leibeswirken,
Wie in schlafende Wirkensfelder
Denken sich senkt aus Haupteskräften;
Lass durch die Seelenschau zu Licht
Menschenwollen sich verwandlen;
Und das Denken, es erscheinet
Als Willenszauberwesen.

NINTH LESSON

Life {

O Man, touch and sense through your body's whole being
How earthly forces support your existence.   Earth

O Man, live and experience in the whole sphere of your touch
How water-beings mold your existence.   Water

O Man, feel and perceive in the whole weaving of your life
How powers of air nurture your existence.   Air

O Man, think and perceive throughout your flow of feelings
How fire spirits help your existence.   Fire
}

Love {

O Man, behold yourself in the kingdom of the elements.

O Man, let hold sway in the depths of your soul
The cosmic powers that guide the planets.

O Man, come into being through the cosmic circling.
}

Piety {

O Man, preserve in your spirit's creativity
The heavenly revelation of the stars immobile.

O Man, create yourself through heaven's wisdom.
}

Bring into your thinking
Feeling and will
Which irradiate the light-filled soul
As pure reflection.
And you are a spirit
Among pure spirits.

Bring into your feelings
Thinking and will
Which weave throughout the soul
With warmth as noble love.
And you are a soul
In the realm of the spirits.

Bring into your powers of will
Thinking and feeling
Which actively live in your soul
As spirit-impulse.
And you see yourself
As a body from spiritual heights.

NEUNTE STUNDE

Leben {
O Mensch, ertaste in deines Leibes ganzem Sein,   Erde
Wie Erdenkräfte dir im Dasein Stütze sind.

O Mensch, erlebe in deines Tastens ganzem Kreis,   Wasser
Wie Wasserwesen dir im Dasein Bildner sind.

O Mensch, erfühle in deines Lebens ganzem Weben,   Luft
Wie Luftgewalten dir im Dasein Pfleger sind.

O Mensch, erdenke in deines Fühlens ganzem Strömen,   Feuer
Wie Feuermächte dir im Dasein Helfer sind.
}

O Mensch, erschaue dich in der Elemente Reich.

Liebe {
O Mensch, so lasse walten in deiner Seele Tiefen
Der Wandelsterne weltenweisende Mächte.

O Mensch, erwese dich durch den Weltenkreis.
}

Frommsein {
O Mensch, erhalte dir in deines Geistes Schaffen
Der Ruhesterne himmelkündende Worte.
}

O Mensch, erschaffe dich durch die Himmelsweisheit.

Trag' in Fühlenskräfte   Trag' in Willensmächte
Die als edle Liebe   Die als Geistestriebe
Durch die Seele wärmend weben   Um die Seele wirkend leben
Denken und Wollen   Denken und Fühlen
Und du bist Seele   Und du schaust dich selbst
Im Reich der Geister.   Als Leib aus Geisteshöhen.

Trag' in Denk-Erleben
Das als reines Sinnen
In der Seele lichtvoll glänzt
Fühlen und Wollen
Und du bist Geist
Unter reinen Geistern.

TENTH LESSON

1. I live in the dark realm of Earth,
2. I weave in the shining light of the stars,
3. I read in the deeds of the spirits,
4. I hear in the speech of the gods,
5. Earth's darkness fills me with longing,
6. The shining stars comfort me,
7. The deeds of the spirits are teaching me,
8. The speech of the gods works creatively in me,
9. Earth's darkness extinguishes me.
10. The starlight's shining awakens me.
11. The deeds of the spirits call to me.
12. The speech of the gods begets me.

ZEHNTE STUNDE

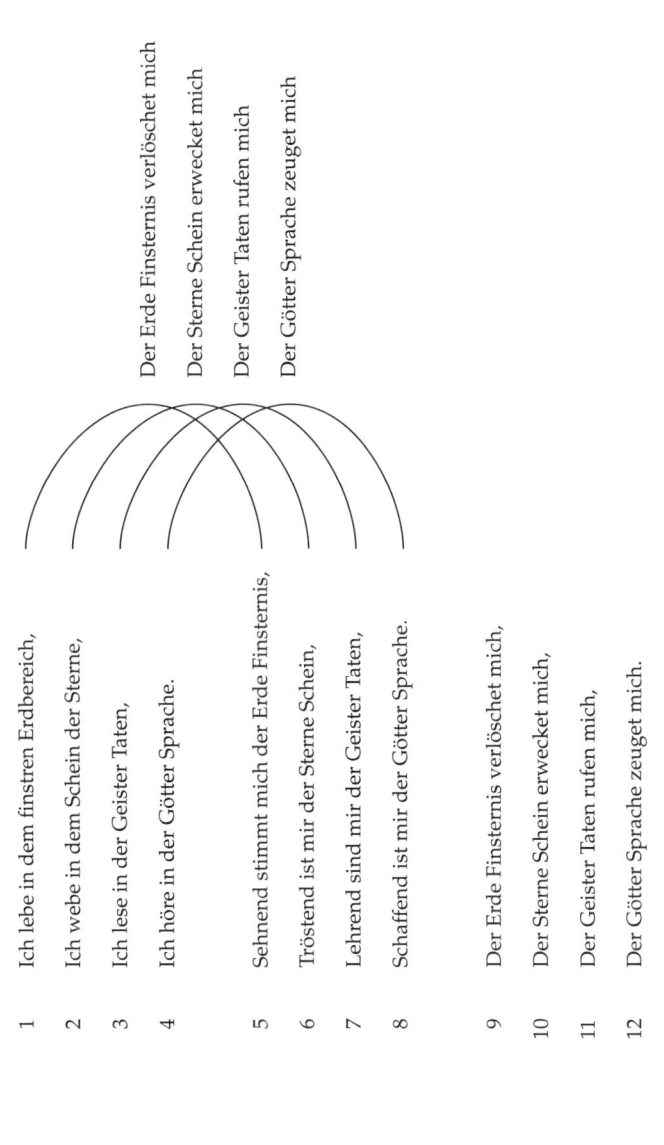

1 Ich lebe in dem finstren Erdbereich,
2 Ich webe in dem Schein der Sterne,
3 Ich lese in der Geister Taten,
4 Ich höre in der Götter Sprache.

5 Sehnend stimmt mich der Erde Finsternis,
6 Tröstend ist mir der Sterne Schein,
7 Lehrend sind mir der Geister Taten,
8 Schaffend ist mir der Götter Sprache.

9 Der Erde Finsternis verlöschet mich,
10 Der Sterne Schein erwecket mich,
11 Der Geister Taten rufen mich,
12 Der Götter Sprache zeuget mich.

ELEVENTH LESSON

Cosmic starry spaces,
Homeland of the gods!
    From the head held on high
    Human spirit-radiance speaks
        "I am"
Thus do you (the gods) live within the earthly body
    As human being.

Circling cosmic sun,
Paths of spirit action!
    Human soul's weaving sounds
    In the center of the heart
        "I live"
Thus do you (the gods) tread the earthly path
    As human creative force.

World foundation powers,
Radiant love of the Creator!
    Create in the body's limbs
    Streams of human action
        "I will"
Thus do you (the gods) strive in earthly activity
    As human sense-world deeds.

ELFTE STUNDE

Welten-Sternen-Stätten,
Götter-Heimat-Orte!
   Spricht in Haupteshöhe
Menschen-Geistes-Strahlung
      Das «Ich bin»:
So lebet Ihr im Erdenleibe
Als Menschen-Wesenheit.

Welten-Sonnen-Kreise,
Geister-Wirkens-Wege!
   Tönt in Herzensmitte
Menschen-Seelen-Weben
      Das «Ich lebe»:
So schreitet Ihr im Erdenwandel
Als Menschen-Schöpferkraft.

Welten-Grundes-Mächte,
Schöpfer-Liebes-Glänzen!
   Schafft in Leibesgliedern
Menschen-Wirkens-Strömung
      Das «Ich will»:
So strebet Ihr im Erdenwerke
Als Menschen-Sinnes-Taten.

TWELFTH LESSON

I. Listen to the realm of thinking:

1) The Guardian: He speaks who wants to show you
Your paths in spirit light
From Earth life to Earth life:
Behold your senses' luminous nature.

Angeloi

2) The Guardian: He speaks who wants to bear you
In realms of being, set free from matter,
To other souls on wings of soul:
Behold the forces working in your thinking.

Archangeloi

3) The Guardian: He speaks who wants to give you
A firm ground for existence
Among the spirits in the creative realm
Far from Earth:
Behold your memory's image-forming.

Archai

II. Listen to the realm of feeling:

1) The Guardian: He speaks who as a thought
Calls you to cosmic existence
From the sun rays of the spirit:
Feel the stirring of life in your breath.

Exusiai

2) The Guardian: He speaks who gives you
Cosmic existence in spirit realms
From the life forces of the stars:
Feel the surging weaving in your blood.

Dynamis

3) The Guardian: He speaks who wants to create for you
Spirit sense from earthly will
In the light of lofty realms divine:
Feel the powerful resistance of the Earth.

Kyriotetes

ZWÖLFTE STUNDE

I. Vernimm des Denkens Feld:

Hüter

1.) Es spricht, der dir die Wege
Von Erdensein zu Erdensein
Im Geisteslichte weisen will:
Blick' auf deiner Sinne Leuchtewesen.

Angeloi

Hüter

2.) Es spricht, der dich zu Seelen
Im stoffbefreiten Seinsgebiete
Auf Seelenschwingen tragen will:
Blick' auf deines Denkens Kräftewirken.

Archangeloi

Hüter

3.) Es spricht, der unter Geistern
Im erdenfernen Schöpferfelde
Den Daseinsgrund dir geben will:
Blick' auf der Erinnerung Bildgestalten.

Archai

II. Vernimm des Fühlens Feld:

1.) Es spricht, der als Gedanke   Hüter
Aus Geistes-Sonnenstrahlen
Dich zum Weltendasein ruft:
Fühl' in deines Atems Lebensregung.

Exusiai

2.) Es spricht, der Weltendasein   Hüter
Aus Sternen-Lebenskräften
Dir in Geistesreichen schenket:
Fühl' in deines Blutes Wellenweben.

Dynamis

3.) Es spricht, der dir den Geistes-Sinn
In lichten Götter-Höhenreichen   Hüter
Aus Erdenwollen schaffen will:
Fühl' der Erde mächtig Widerstreben.

Kyriotetes

341

THIRTEENTH LESSON

III. Behold the realm of will.

The Guardian: 1) He speaks who guides the dull cosmic forces
From their dark subterranean depths
Into your limbs to quicken you:
Thrones: Behold the fiery nature of your instincts.

The Guardian: 2) He speaks who lets the clear rays of spirit
Filled with grace from God's fields of action
Circulate through your blood:
Cherubim: See how conscience guides your soul.

The Guardian: 3) He speaks who brings the fruit of former lives
Through deaths and births with balanced karma
To breath of life in present time on Earth:
Seraphim: Behold your destiny's spiritual trials.

DREIZEHNTE STUNDE

III. Vernimm des Willens Feld:

Hüter   1.) Es spricht, der die Weltenkräfte, die dumpfen
              Aus den Erden-Untergründen, den finstren
              In deiner Glieder Regsamkeiten lenket:
Throne   Blick' auf deiner Triebe Feuer-Wesen.

Hüter   2.) Es spricht, der die Geistesstrahlen, die hellen
              Aus Gottes-Wirkensfeldern, gnadevoll
              In deinem Blute kreisen lässt:
Cherubine   Blick' auf des Gewissens Seelen-Führung.

Hüter   3.) Es spricht, der das Menschensein, das vollbrachte
              Durch Tode und Geburten, sinngerecht
              Zum Atmen bringt in gegenwärt'ger Zeit:
Seraphine   Blick' auf deines Schicksales Geistes-Prüfung.

FOURTEENTH LESSON

I) The Guardian: Where is the solidity of the Earth that sustained you?
   The heart answers, inspired by:

   Christ: I forsake its solid ground as long as the spirit supports me.
   Lucifer: I feel rapturous joy that I no longer need its support.
   Ahriman: I will hammer it even firmer with the power of the spirit.

II) The Guardian: Where is water's formative force that pervaded you?
   The heart answers, inspired by:

   Christ: My life extinguishes it as long as the spirit forms me.
   Lucifer: My life melts it away that I may be free of it.
   Ahriman: My life solidifies it that I may transport it to the realm of spirit.

III) The Guardian: Where is the quickening power of the air that awakened you?
   The heart answers, inspired by:

   Christ: My soul breathes heaven's air as long as the spirit surrounds me.
   Lucifer: My soul, wrapped in spirit bliss, couldn't care less.
   Ahriman: My soul sucks it up that I may learn how the gods create.

IV) The Guardian: Where is the purifying fire that set your "I" aflame?
   The heart answers, inspired by:

   Christ: My "I" burns in the fire of God as long as the spirit ignites me.
   Lucifer: My "I" has the force of flame through the spirit's solar power.
   Ahriman: My "I" has fire of its own that burns alone through self-development.

VIERZEHNTE STUNDE

I) Hüter: Wo ist der Erde Festigkeit, die dich stützte?

    Christus: Ich verlasse ihren Grund, so lang der Geist mich trägt.
    Lucifer: Ich fühle wonnig, dass ich fortan der Stütze nicht bedarf.
    Ahriman: Ich will durch Geistes Kraft fester noch sie hämmern.

II) Hüter: Wo ist des Wassers Bildekraft, die dich durchdrang?

    Christus: Mein Leben verlöscht sie, so lang der Geist mich formt.
    Lucifer: Mein Leben zerschmilzt sie, dass ich erlöst von ihr werde.
    Ahriman: Mein Leben befestigt sie, dass ich sie ins Geistgebiet versetze.

III) Hüter: Wo ist der Lüfte Reizgewalt, die dich erweckte?

    Christus: Meine Seele atmet Himmelsluft, so lang der Geist um mich besteht.
    Lucifer: Meine Seele achtet ihrer nicht in Geistes Seligkeit.
    Ahriman: Meine Seele saugt sie auf, dass ich göttlich schaffen lerne.

IV) Hüter: Wo ist des Feuers Reinigung, die dir das Ich erflammte?

    Christus: Mein Ich lodert im Gottesfeuer, so lang der Geist mich zündet.
    Lucifer: Mein Ich hat Flammenmacht durch Geistes Sonnenkraft.
    Ahriman: Mein Ich hat Eigenfeuer, das rein durch Selbstentfaltung flammt.

FIFTEENTH LESSON

The Guardian:	What becomes of the solidity of the Earth that sustained you?
	From the third hierarchy comes the response:
Angeloi:	Sense how we are sensing in your thinking.
Archangeloi:	Experience how we have experience in your feeling.
Archai:	Perceive how we perceive in your willing.
The Guardian:	What becomes of water's formative force that pervaded you?
	From the second hierarchy comes the response:
Exusiai:	Recognize the spirit's cosmic creating in the human body's creating.
Dynamis:	Feel the spirit's cosmic life in the human body's life.
Kryotetes:	Will the spirit's cosmic process in the human body's being.
The Guardian:	What becomes of the quickening power of air that awakened you?
	From the first hierarchy comes the response:
Thrones:	With knowing grasp your inner being within your divine cosmic being.
Cherubim:	Enkindle warmth of inner life within your divine cosmic life.
Seraphim:	Awaken your inner light within your divine cosmic light.

3rd Hierarchy · 2nd Hierarchy · 1st Hierarchy

FÜNFZEHNTE STUNDE

Der Hüter: Was wird aus der Erde Festigkeit, die dich stützte?

Angeloi: Empfinde, wie wir in deinem Denken empfinden.
Archangeloi: Erlebe, wie wir in deinem Fühlen erleben.
Archai: Schaue, wie wir in deinem Wollen schauen.

[3. Hierarchie]

Der Hüter: Was wird aus des Wassers Bildekraft, die dich durchdrang?

Exusiai: Erkenne Geistes-Welten-Schaffen im Menschen-Körper-Schaffen.
Dynamis: Erfühle Geistes-Welten-Leben im Menschen-Körper-Leben.
Kyriotetes: Wolle Geistes-Welt-Geschehen im Menschen-Körper-Sein.

[2. Hierarchie]

Der Hüter: Was wird aus der Lüfte Reizgewalt, die dich erweckte?

Throne: Ergreife wissend Innen-Sein in deinem Gottes-Welten-Sein.
Cherubine: Erwarme am Innen-Leben in deinem Gottes-Welten-Leben.
Seraphine: Erweck' in dir Innen-Licht in deinem Gottes-Welten-Licht.

[1. Hierarchie]

SIXTEENTH LESSON

The Guardian speaks:
    Where is the purifying fire that set your "I" aflame?

Angeloi, Exusiai, Thrones:
    Awaken for yourself in the expanse of cosmic ether the flaming script of life.

Archangeloi, Dynamis, Cherubim:
    Create for yourself in cyclic waves of time your soul's atonement forces.

Archai, Kyriotetes, Seraphim:
    Ask for yourself from eternal deeds of being the spirit's redemptive powers.

The Guardian:
    Has your Spirit understood?

The "I":
    The cosmic spirit in me
    Has held its breath
    And may its presence
    Illuminate my "I."

The Guardian:
    Has your soul comprehended?

The "I":
    The cosmic souls within me
    Lived in the council of stars
    And may their harmonies,
    Resounding, fashion my "I."

The Guardian:
    Has your Body experienced?

The "I":
    The cosmic forces in me
    Judge the deeds of men
    And may their verdicts
    Guide the "I" in me.

SECHZEHNTE STUNDE

Der Hüter spricht:

    Was wird aus des Feuers Reinigung, die dir das Ich entflammte?

Angeloi, Exusiai, Throne:

    Erwecke dir in Weltenätherweiten die Lebensflammenschrift.

Archangeloi, Dynamis, Cherubine:

    Erschaffe dir in Zeitenwellenkreisen die Seelensühnekräfte.

Archai, Kyriotetes, Seraphine:

    Erbitte dir in ew'gen Wesentaten die Geisterlösermächte.

Der Hüter:

    Hat verstanden dein Geist?

Ich: Der Weltengeist in mir
    Er hielt den Atem an
    Und seine Gegenwart
    Mög' erleuchten mein Ich.

Der Hüter:

    Hat begriffen deine Seele?

Ich: Die Weltenseelen in mir
    Sie lebten im Sternenrat
    Und ihre Harmonien
    Mögen klingend schaffen mein Ich.

Der Hüter:

    Hat erlebt dein Leib?

Ich: Die Weltenkräfte in mir
    Sie richten Menschentaten
    Und ihre Wahrspruchworte
    Mögen lenken mir das Ich.

SEVENTEENTH LESSON

The Guardian:
See the ether-colored rainbow,
Powerful orb of light.
Let light's creative force
Pass through your eyes
And your "I" penetrate its circle.
Then behold from yonder
    vantage point
Colors flowing in the cosmic chalice.

Angeloi, Archangeloi, Archai:
Feel how our thoughts
Have color-breathing life
In the chalice's flowing light.
We carry sense-illusion
To realms of spirit-being.
Imbued by the world we turn
Ourselves to serve the higher spirits.

Exusiai, Dynamis, Kyriotetes:
What we received from you,
From the dead world of sense-illusion,
    is enlivened;
We waken it to existence.
We bestow it upon the rays of light
Which reveal the nothingness
    of matter,
Weaving love into spiritual existence.

Thrones, Cherubim, Seraphim:
Within your worlds of will
Feel our cosmic working.
Spirit shines in matter
When we create thinking.
Spirit creates in matter
When we live in willing.
The world is the I-willed Spirit-Word.

350

SIEBZEHNTE STUNDE

Der Hüter:

    Sieh' des Äther-Farbenbogens
    Lichtgewalt'ges Rund,
    Lass' durch deiner Augen
    Lichterschaffene Kraft
    Dein Ich den Kreis durchdringen,
    Und dann schau von jenseit'ger Warte
    Farbenflutend die Weltenschale.

Angeloi, Archangeloi, Archai:

    Empfind' unsrer Gedanken
    Farbenatmend Leben
    In der Schale Lichtesfluten;
    Wir tragen Sinnenschein
    In Geistes-Wesensreiche
    Und wenden weltdurchdrungen
    Uns höhern Geistern dienend zu.

Exusiai, Dynamis, Kyriotetes:

    Euer Empfangenes
    Aus totem Sinnenschein Belebtes:
    Wir wecken es im Sein;
    Wir schenken es den Strahlen,
    Die des Stoffes Nichtigkeit
    In des Geistes Wesenheit
    Liebewebend offenbaren.

Throne, Cherubine, Seraphine:

    In deinen Willenswelten
    Fühl' unser Weltenwirken;
    Geist erglänzt im Stoffe,
    Wenn wir denkend schaffen;
    Geist erschafft im Stoffe,
    Wenn wir wollend leben;
    Welt ist Ich-wollend Geistes-Wort.

EIGHTEENTH LESSON

I. <u>Angeloi:</u>
   Human beings are thinking!
   We need the light from the heights
   That we may illuminate their thinking.

   <u>Dynamis:</u>
   Receive the light from the heights
   That you can illuminate thinking
   When human beings are thinking.

II. <u>Archangeloi:</u>
   Human beings are feeling!
   We need the warmth of soul
   That we may live in feeling.

   <u>Kyriotetes and Exusiai:</u>
   Receive the warmth of soul
   That you can live in feeling
   When human beings are feeling.

III. <u>Archai:</u>
   Human beings are willing!
   We need the forces of the depths
   That we can work in willing.

   <u>Kyriotetes, Dynamis, and Exusiai:</u>
   Receive the forces of the depths
   That you can work in willing
   When human beings are willing.

ACHTZEHNTE STUNDE

I) Angeloi:
Es denken die Menschenwesen!
Wir brauchen das Licht der Höhen,
Dass wir im Denken leuchten können.

Dynamis:
Empfanget das Licht der Höhen,
Dass ihr im Denken leuchten könnt,
Wenn Menschenwesen denken.

II) Archangeloi:
Es fühlen die Menschenwesen!
Wir brauchen die Seelenwärme,
Dass wir im Fühlen leben können.

Kyriotetes und Exusiai:
Empfanget die Seelenwärme,
Dass ihr im Fühlen leben könnt,
Wenn Menschenwesen fühlen.

III) Archai:
Es wollen die Menschenwesen!
Wir brauchen die Tiefenkraft,
Dass wir im Wollen wirken können.

Kyriotetes, Dynamis und Exusiai:
Empfanget die Tiefenkraft,
Dass ihr im Wollen wirken könnt,
Wenn Menschenwesen wollen.

NINETEENTH LESSON

The human "I" knows itself to be in the realm of the Spirit Word borne by Seraphim, Cherubim, and Thrones.

The Guardian speaks from afar:
Who speaks in the Spirit-Word
With a voice
That burns in the cosmic fire?

From the realm of the First Hierarchy:
The flames of the stars are speaking.
Seraphic powers of fire flame forth;
They also burn in my heart.
In primal being's fount of love
The human heart finds the
Creative language of spiritual fire:

It is I.

The Guardian speaks from afar:
What thinks in the Spirit-Word
With thoughts that are
Fashioning cosmic souls?

From the realm of the First Hierarchy:
The radiance of the stars is thinking.
Cherubic formative forces shine forth;
They also shine within my head.
In primal being's fount of light
The human head finds
Thinking that works formatively in the soul.

It is I.

The Guardian speaks from afar:
What wields strength in the Spirit-Word
With forces
That live in the cosmic body?

From the realm of the First Hierarchy:
The star-world-body wields strength.
The Thrones' sustaining powers body forth;
They also embody my limbs.
In primal being's fount of life
The human limbs find
Ruling strength of world-bearing powers.

It is I.

NEUNZEHNTE STUNDE

Der Hüter spricht aus der Ferne: Der Hüter spricht aus der Ferne: Der Hüter spricht aus der Ferne:

(Das Menschen-Ich weiß sich im Bereich des seraphisch-cherubinisch-Throne-getragenen Geistes-Wortes)

Wer spricht im Geistes-Wort
Mit der Stimme,
Die im Weltenfeuer lodert?

Was denkt im Geistes-Wort
Mit Gedanken,
Die aus Weltenseelen bilden?

Was kraftet im Geistes-Wort
Mit Kräften,
Die im Weltenleibe leben?

Aus dem Reich der ersten Hierarchie:
Es sprechen Sternen-Flammen,
Es flammen seraph'sche Feuer-Mächte;
Sie flammen auch in meinem Herzen.
In des Urseins Liebe-Quell
Findet Menschen-Herz
Schaffendes Geistes-Flammen-Sprechen:

Es ist Ich.

Aus dem Reich der ersten Hierarchie:
Es denken der Sterne Leuchter,
Es leuchten cherubin'sche Bilde-Kräfte;
Sie leuchten auch in meinem Haupte.
In des Urseins Lichtes-Quell
Findet Menschen-Haupt
Denkendes Seelen-Bilde-Wirken:

Es ist Ich.

Aus dem Reich der ersten Hierarchie:
Es kraftet der Sternen-Welten-Leib,
Es leiben der Throne Trag-Gewalten;
Sie leiben auch in meinen Gliedern.
In des Urseins Lebens-Quell
Finden Menschen-Glieder
Kraftendes Welten-Träger-Walten:

Es ist Ich.

The Meditative Path of the Michael School Today

by Thomas Meyer

"The Goetheanum is present wherever people
work in the sense of Rudolf Steiner."
Ludwig Polzer-Hoditz

Rudolf Steiner and the Time Spirit Michael

According to Rudolf Steiner's spiritual research, Michael is the leading time spirit of a period beginning in the fall of 1879 and lasting for another 220 years or so, until around the year 2230.

This spiritual individuality is an Archangel functioning as an Archai and is distinct from the spirit of the age guiding the entire Fifth Post-Atlantean cultural age, which began in 1413. Rudolf Steiner named this cultural period the "Anglo-Saxon Germanic Age," which exists spiritually under the influence of the constellation of the fishes (Pisces). It will last for a total of 2,160 years. In the year 3573, the time spirit inspiring the Anglo-Saxon Germanic cultural age will be replaced by another time spirit who will inspire the *Slavic*, or Sixth Post-Atlantean, cultural age. The time spirit of the Anglo-Saxon Germanic cultural age has a complex path of development. This spirit of the age grew from the Nordic–Germanic folk element, was educated by a former Greco–Roman time spirit, and must come to an understanding with the earlier time spirit of the Egyptian cultural epoch, who today stands at the level of a Spirit of Form. An overview of Rudolf Steiner's view of cosmic evolution follows on the next page.

We must discern between the two time spirits of our Fifth Post-Atlantean cultural age, one coming from the Nordic folk tradition and guiding the age, and the time spirit Michael, who reigns for a cycle of approximately 350 years. We must also discern between these two time spirits and the guiding time spirit of the entire sevenfold Post-Atlantean epoch. This spirit was originally the folk spirit and later the time spirit of the Old Indian age. This being will guide the development of humanity until the end of the Seventh Post-Atlantean cultural age.

The First Class of the Michael School

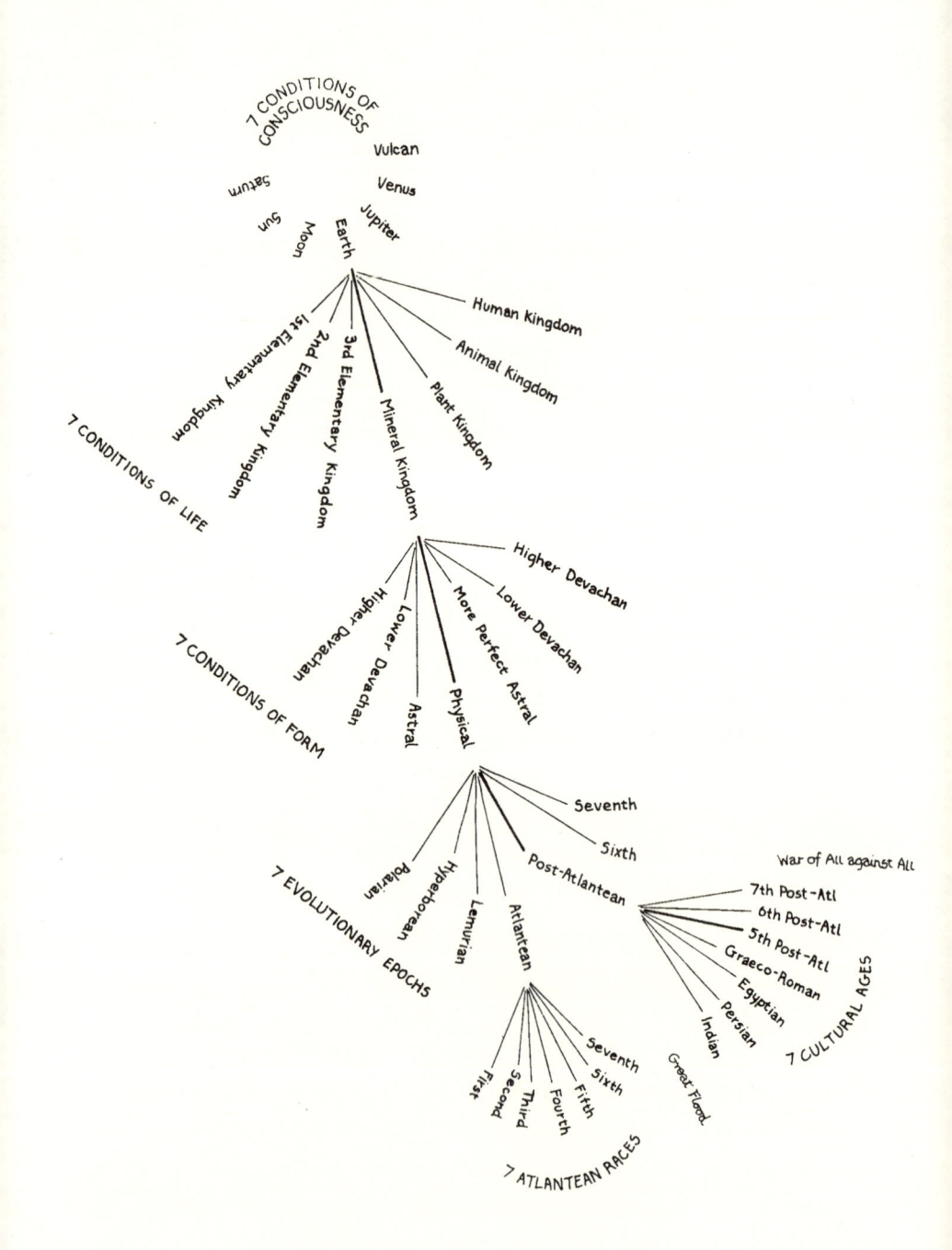

Rudolf Steiner's view of cosmic evolution

360

Steiner points to the leading spirit of the Fifth Post-Atlantean cultural age and the spirit leading the entirety of the seven Post-Atlantean cultural ages in the lecture cycle on folk souls, which he gave in June 1910 for a Theosophical audience in Oslo, Norway.[1]

Of these three time spirits, who are naturally interrelated on a time-spirit level, the third is considered in the following paragraphs, which focus on the workings of the time spirit Michael, who in 1879 assumed his responsibilities as time spirit.

The Michael Age is characterized by certain *spiritual* qualities that arise during his rule, including the attempt to make these qualities productive in a cosmopolitan way for the whole of humanity. In the *previous* Michael Age, the newest quality for spiritual development was *Aristotelianism*, which spread in a cosmopolitan way through the campaigns of Alexander the Great, and even later when Aristotelianism was partially modified by Arabism. In the time of the Scholastics[2]—above all by Thomas Aquinas and Albertus Magnus—Aristotelianism was modified again for humanity in a Christian manner, meaning it had to be brought into accordance with the impulse of Christianity.

According to Rudolf Steiner, the decisive factor for our Michael age, which began in 1879, is to grasp cosmic spiritual facts and beings with *healthy common sense*. In the past this activity was reserved for religious faith. Throughout the life and work of Rudolf Steiner, an ideal repeatedly expressed by the Michaelic guiding phrase "spiritualization of the intellect."

In 1902, Steiner confirmed words from Willhelm Hubbe-Schleiden, an associate of the Theosophical stream and later the person who publicly proclaimed the Order of the Eastern Star, created around Krishnamurti. On August 16, 1902,[3] two months before becoming General Secretary of the German Section of the Theosophical Society, Rudolf Steiner wrote, "I want...to do everything to bring the theosophy of today into the direction your words indicate: '*Today, the way into the spiritual realm leads through the realm of the intellect.*'"

Long before this statement was made, Rudolf Steiner's thinking was moving in the same direction. The whole of his *Philosophy of Freedom* supports it. In it, the spiritual being of thought is the center point that "must be grasped before anything else can be grasped." This work was created in 1893, at a time when Steiner himself reached beyond the zenith of his intellectual soul development.

During this period, Steiner deeply experienced the powerful beginnings of Michael's work, which was active behind the scenes of outer events. For the first time, Rudolf Steiner related this to his audience through the Michael lectures of 1924 in Torquay, England. They took place during the summer school organized by D. N. Dunlop. On August 12,[4] Steiner told his audience, "I lived with all the forces of the intellectual soul through what was taking place in this world behind the veil, in the sphere of Michael's activity, and it was there that the great challenge arose once and for all to deal earnestly with the reality of the spiritual world, to bring these momentous questions to the light of day."

On August 2, a few days before Steiner made those essential remarks concerning his esoteric development, and specifically those he made about his relationship to the being of Michael, he held the final lesson of the Michael School in Dornach, which he had founded—or, rather, brought down to earth. With the conclusion of this final lesson, Steiner completed the first phase of this School.[5] Again, three weeks prior to this on July 19, 1924,[6] in Arnhem, he characterized these "great demands" by Michael as follows:

> Let us now consider what it is that Michael...has to administer in the spiritual cosmos. It is Michael's task to administer a power that is essentially spiritual, reaching its zenith in the human faculty of intellectual understanding. Michael is not the spirit who, if I may put it so, cultivates intellectuality per se; the spirituality he bestows strives to bring enlightenment to humankind in the form of ideas and in the form of thoughts—but ideas and thoughts that grasp the spiritual. His will is that the human being shall be a free being who understands in concepts and ideas what comes as revelation from the spiritual worlds.

A distinct characterization of Michael as the "Administrator of the Cosmic Intelligence" can be found in the first part of *Anthroposophical Leading Thoughts*.[7] Rudolf Steiner completed his literary work with these thoughts and a series of autobiographical recollections. The part concerning Michael was published by Marie Steiner in 1930, some five years after Steiner's death, as *The Michael Mystery*. Later on, these thoughts were gathered and edited in the collected works as *Anthroposophical Leading Thoughts*.[8] The picture that emerges from Rudolf Steiner's bequest of Michael considerations goes far beyond Michael's work as the time spirit. It shows Michael as "the spiritual being...who, from the beginning, directed his gaze toward humankind." He is active in the cosmic intelligence, and it is "Michael's will to keep the intelligence, which is developing within humanity, permanently in connection with the divine-spiritual beings."[9]

Steiner passed through his first moon node in the autumn of 1879. Those who know the characteristics of moon nodes in human life have to assume that the young Steiner already experienced the *commencement* of the Michael time in his *astral body,* which typically develops between fourteen and twenty-one years of age.

Exactly twenty-eight years after the dawn of the Michael age, a crucial encounter occurred with a personality closely related to carrying and realizing the Michael impulse with the founding of the Michael School here on earth. This encounter was with Ita Wegman during Pentecost 1907 at the Theosophical Congress in Munich, Germany. This was also when the consensual separation took place between Annie Besant (representing the Eastern path of esoteric development) and Rudolf Steiner (representing the Western path of esoteric development).

All members of the German Section of the Theosophical Society had to decide freely which path they wanted to take. This choice also had to be made by the thirty-one-year-old Ita Wegman, who had by that time been a student of Rudolf Steiner for five years. The following occurred when she declared that she had decided to follow the path of Rudolf Steiner: "His eyes lit up. He took my hand, *gave me the Michael sign,* and told me important things that I am not at liberty to repeat. Ancient karma that we both shared was renewed."[10]

Four-times-seven years after the dawn of the Michael age, Rudolf Steiner gave—for the first time, as far as we know—the sign of Michael to a human being. This sign had been sought in European occult traditions without reward, not even for Agrippa of Nettesheim. It seems to have been spiritually conceived by Rudolf Steiner. In any case, it was the first time it was recorded by him.

It is the same sign that other students of Steiner would see and experience only when he returned from England in September 1924. A separate contemplation is dedicated to this sign.[11]

The Suprasensory Michael School

Some of the previously mentioned Michael revelations from 1924 belong to the pinnacle of Rudolf Steiner's spiritual activity on earth.

These revelations were (as were the karma revelations from the same year) the fruit of an enormous *risk*. In November 1923, the Anthroposophical Society found itself in a desperate state. Steiner taught within the Anthroposophical Society at that time without being a member. The risk in question is connected with Steiner's decision to assume chairmanship of the new General Anthroposophical Society, founded over Christmastime 1923. The risk arose because the spiritual powers that had, until that point, supported and inspired his research, could withdraw their help because they could not possibly start dealing with *earthly* affairs. Steiner took the risk to guide the newly founded Society toward the future and away from the old Society, which had become stagnant and rampant with quarreling. The spiritual world responded to this sacrificial deed of love with an even greater level of participation and the demand that Steiner continue his research. Yes, these demanding forces even banished the power of the anti-Michaelic demons, which until then had prevented the spiritual researcher from speaking whenever he wanted to mention Michaelic secrets. All that

Steiner had to say regarding the Michael School belongs to these now-freely spoken Michaelic revelations in the summer of 1924.

Between July 20 and September 14 in Arnhem, Dornach, Torquay, and London, Rudolf Steiner spoke consciously in a variety of ways about the "School of Michael," the "Michael School," a "cosmic" and "spiritual" school. Once he even spoke of a suprasensory "institution of wisdom."[12] When was this suprasensory school founded? Who were its "students"—or perhaps better to say its "participants"? And what was taught there? We may enter this question concisely against the background of Steiner's own words.

The suprasensory Michael School was started by Michael around the fourteenth century, before he became a time spirit in 1879. Essentially, the school continued through the nineteenth century. It was the time on *earth* after the Scholastics and after the annihilation of the Templar Order. The Age of Discovery had begun, and it was the time when Francis Bacon and Amos Comenius laid the groundwork for the onset of the natural sciences and the materialistic approach to education. This was supposed to be modified in Goethe's time by the impulse of Goetheanism, although it was not really taken up.

On August 27, 1924, in London,[13] Rudolf Steiner revealed:

> All those discarnate souls who belonged to Michael took part in this great School in the suprasensory world during the fourteenth, fifteenth, and sixteenth centuries. All the beings of the hierarchy of Angels, Archangels and Archai who belonged to the Michael stream and many elemental beings took part in it.

In essence, two groups of human souls gathered around Michael: those who were shaped by a more Platonic spirituality and those who were shaped by a more Aristotelian spirituality. The former worked mainly before the beginning of the Michael School in or around the School of Chartres; the latter mainly in or around the order of the Dominicans. At the turn of the twelfth to the thirteenth century, both groups made a spiritual agreement in the suprasensory world to work together on earth again at the end of the twentieth century. The specific presentations of these interrelationships should be read directly from the lectures of Steiner.[14]

What was taught in the Michael School? In London on August 27, 1924,[15] Rudolf Steiner explained:

> In this suprasensory school, a wonderful review was given of the wisdom of the ancient mysteries. Detailed knowledge in regard to the ancient mysteries was imparted to the souls partaking in this School. They looked back to the Sun Mysteries, to the mysteries of the other planets. But a vista of the future was given, too—a vista of what should begin in the new Age of Michael.

One of the zodiac verses by Steiner says, "May what is coming rest on what has been." This law of spiritual development is also valid for the work of Michael. In his school, the great and, in a true sense, generous review of the *old* mysteries was the spiritual starting point for the foundation of the *new* mysteries for the present time and for the future.

The Interview that Failed

The spiritual encounter in the ninth century between the individualities incarnated previously as Harun al-Raschid and his ingenious advisor on the one side and Aristotle and Alexander on the other, belongs to a decisive event that preceded the Michael School. After death, Harun al-Raschid and his clever advisor became conscious of how much of their work in Bagdad was based on the thoughts Aristotle had brought into the world and that Alexander the Great had disseminated throughout. They developed a sort of longing to meet the real individualities of these two friends. In Torquay on August 12, 1924, Rudolf Steiner said that they were seeking a spiritual "interview" with them. The individualities of Aristotle and Alexander had incarnated shortly before in the time of the Grail, when they sought to harmonize the Aristotelianism in their souls with the Mystery of Golgotha in Greco–Roman times. Harun al Raschid and his advisor held on to the pre-Christian Aristotelianism. They were unable to connect with a transformed Aristotelianism, or what was in the process of being metamorphosed. In this respect, the interview had a negative outcome, and the consequences made world history. Francis Bacon, the reincarnated Harun al Raschid, rebelled against the philosophy of Aristotle. He opposed *Organon*—Aristotle's logical writings—with his famous *Novum Organon*, in which everything is based on sensory perception as the only reality. Amos Comenius, the reincarnated advisor, became the founder of pedagogy with a materialistic tendency, the father of "visual learning," which views thinking as bound solely to the sense world. The earthly and spiritually one-sided work of Bacon and Comenius was so strong that the results worked back into the spiritual world once again, straight into the sphere where the great teachings of Michael took place.

> When Amos Comenius and Bacon had once again passed through the gate of death, a remarkable thing came to pass in the spiritual world. After Bacon had passed through the gate of death, it so happened that because of the particular mode of thinking he had adopted in his incarnation as Bacon, a whole world of 'idols,' demonic idols, went forth from his etheric body, spreading into the spiritual world...that was inhabited by the individualities who were pupils of Michael. The idols spread into this world.[16]

Rudolf Steiner further explains that it was the task of the individuality of Aristotle, and particularly his pupil Alexander, to paralyze the destruction of these anti-Aristotelian idols in the sphere of the Michael School. He showed that the idols that could not be paralyzed became, during the time of the French Revolution, the "occult inspirations of materialism in the nineteenth century." This can give us an impression of the spiritual force connected with the work of Bacon and Comenius.[17] It also gives an impression of the connection of Alexander and Aristotle with Michael's battle against demons.

Against the background of Steiner's descriptions from 1924, a new light is shed on the intimate scene between Rudolf Steiner and Ita Wegman at Pentecost in Munich in 1907. This very old karma that was "renewed" was part of the prenatal connection in which both individualities as Michael knights in the suprasensory Michael School did battle against the demonic powers, including "the idols of Bacon."

With this in mind, our gaze is directed toward the reality of the subearthly ahrimanic counter-school, which Steiner describes in the summer of 1924, mainly in Arnhem.

The Michael Devotional Ritual at the Conclusion of the School[18]

As the eighteenth turned into the nineteenth century, the ages-long training came to a certain conclusion. This happened during a suprasensory devotional ritual in which the Platonists and the Aristotelians characterized previously participated and that Rudolf Steiner describes as follows: "It was like a great cosmic, spiritual festival, lasting for many decades as a spiritual happening in the world immediately bordering on the physical."[19] Both groups of souls longed for a new Christianity, and the new Christianity was celebrated at this spiritual gathering before it came to earth. Soon afterward, toward the end of the nineteenth century, the Aristotelian-oriented souls descended to earth to find what was suprasensorially prepared in the Michael School and its devotional ceremony in Anthroposophy, which had been founded by Rudolf Steiner.

The more Platonically oriented souls would descend into incarnation toward the end of the twentieth century to connect with the incarnated Aristotelian souls and work together to "prevent civilization from complete decadence."

The new Christianity was suprasensorially prepared in this devotional ritual and was in no way a simple outer reformation of the existing Christianity. It was Michaelic Christianity, capable of answering "the great demands" and "the great questions of life." You can see this woven into the esoteric literature of a poet who was inspired by the Michaelic devotional ritual. In Goethe's "Fairy Tale of the Green Snake and the Beautiful Lily," a new age is announced in which the human being must cross the threshold in full consciousness. At the crossing of the threshold, the old instinctive collaboration of the soul forces of thinking, feeling, and willing is dissolved; this is represented in the "mixed king." The time of the mixed king is over, even when protested by Retardus in Rudolf Steiner's mystery drama, *The Portal of Initiation*. This new Christianity is nothing other than the path of knowledge into the suprasensory world, demonstrated in the suprasensory school with its devotional ceremony. On this path the human being develops faculties to work in the *sensory* world with new ideas. This is even more necessary today than it was ninety years ago to "prevent civilization from complete decadence."

The Earthly Michael School and the Role of Ita Wegman

The most important outcome of the Christmas Conference was the establishment of the School of Spiritual Science in Dornach. It would be filled with the ages-long teachings of the Michael School and its Devotions,[20] now on *earth* for *ears to hear* and for those with *healthy common sense* to perceive. After the preceding explanations, it will be of no surprise that Rudolf Steiner needed the cooperation of *Ita Wegman*. The karma of both individualities originated from the time of Alexander and, previously, from an even earlier Michael epoch in the time of Gilgamesh. After the Goetheanum fire of Christmas 1923, this karma also began to reveal itself in Ita Wegman's soul, meaning that she became increasingly aware of her experiences as a pupil of Michael in past incarnations and in the suprasensory Michael School. The Michael sign she received in 1907 may have assisted her in this. Now, in 1924, she received the following verse in addition to other meditations to support her spiritual memory: "Remain in Time and Eternity / A Student in the light of Michael / In the Love of the Gods / In the Heights of the Cosmos."[21]

With reference to the School of Spiritual Science, Rudolf Steiner called Ita Wegman his "assistant." And after the autumn of 1924, every member of the School that wanted to join the First Class had to make a pledge to Rudolf Steiner and Ita Wegman that was confirmed by a handshake.

In the introduction to the First Class lesson in Dornach on February 15, 1924, Rudolf Steiner explained that, as such, this School is in essence not an earthly institution, but one that has been established from the spiritual world. He said: "I would like to emphasize here above all that...with this School an institution has been founded from that spirit that can give the revelations of spiritual life to *our time.*"²²

Dictation from the Spiritual World

The identity of the spirit of our time has already been described. Even more clearly, in a later passage from the fourteenth lesson in May 1924, it is said:

> You must also bear in mind, my dear friends, that it is a reality in the fullest sense that this esoteric school has been established not by human will, but by the spiritual world.... Everything given in this esoteric school in the Goetheanum *emerges in speech through my lips* but is *dictated by the spiritual world*.... This must be so in every duly constituted esoteric school, in the present and in the immediate future, as it was the case in the holy mysteries of ancient times. Moreover, *this* esoteric school is the real School of Michael, and the institution of those spiritual beings who receive the direct inspiration of Michael's cosmic will.²³

The suprasensory Michael School was brought into the sensory world by this means through Rudolf Steiner's deed. During the *suprasensory* Michael School, a vast overview of the old mysteries was taught and, during the devotional ritual, a preview of Anthroposophy was given as the new content of the Christian mystery. Now, on February 15, 1924, the suprasensory Michael School became *sense-perceptible,* and *a nineteen-step meditative path toward true self- and world-knowledge was given.* In other words, after February 1924, the suprasensory Michael teachings were continued *on earth* by Rudolf Steiner. There was a pause after the devotional ceremony during which Michael prepared for his function start in 1879 as our time spirit. Then Rudolf Steiner continued the Michael teaching *on earth.* Steiner is *the carrier* of continuity between the suprasensory phase of the Michael School ending in the devotional ritual and the second phase of the teaching in the nineteen Class lessons.

According to the intentions of Michael, all the lessons of the Michael School on earth appeal to a healthy common sense. At the beginning of the tenth lesson, Steiner emphasizes, "We should appreciate the fact that common sense in the act of understanding spiritual knowledge is the initial stage of esoteric striving." Common sense should be utilized not only to understand Steiner's comments, but also to understand the mantric verses. Then in the transition to meditation, a healthy understanding will yield to an immersion experience of the spiritual mantric substance. Additional attention must be paid to the rhythm, sound, and composition of the words, which Steiner explains precisely in the third lesson.[24]

―⁂―

The real teacher in both phases of the Michael School is *Michael*. There is nonetheless an essential modification. In the second phase, initiated by Steiner, Michael teaches in collaboration with "spiritual beings who are directly inspired by the cosmic will of Michael." Who are these beings?

The Guardian of the Threshold

In the end, beings from all nine hierarchies who remain connected with Michael are doing "the teaching" on the meditative path of the second phase of the Michael School. The Guardian of the Threshold is a being who needs special consideration here because his collaboration was not necessary in the *suprasensory* phase of the Michael School. This tangible spiritual being is of an Archangelic level[25] and had, if any, a very different function to fulfill in the first phase of the purely suprasensory Michael School. There was no need for a wakeful, protecting Guardian of the Threshold, because the first phase of the School took place completely on the *other side* of the threshold in the spiritual world. Rudolf Steiner tells us that the Guardian has an essential and central function in the suprasensory *earthly* phase of the Michael School. He can be met as an admonishing, protecting, and counseling guide on the nineteen stages of the meditative path. Through him we gain access to all of the beings of the hierarchies and what *they* have to teach us on the meditative path.

On September 11, 1924, Steiner indicates that the Guardian of the Threshold is "appointed by Michael." Consequently, it becomes clear that in the earthly phase of the Michael School this seemingly nameless being is, in some respects, the most important helper of Michael. Regardless of the different form of the content, it is easy to miss the fact that the appointment of the Guardian in the earthly phase represents the literal and essential difference between the two phases of the Michael School.

Temporary Conclusion of the Earthly Michael School

At the end of the nineteen Class lessons on April 2, 1924, Steiner announced that the "first part" of the First Class (not the First Class itself) is concluded. Indeed, the human being's true self that was sought from the first lesson appears in the last lesson as a being that is spoken, thought, and carried by a choir of beings from the hierarchies. True self-knowledge is born through spiritual world-knowledge. At this milestone, the nineteenth level has reached a certain conclusion. However, Steiner expects there will be a continuation of the First Class teachings through a second and even a third part. Both parts should serve the meditating soul's spiritual memory of the suprasensory devotions and the earlier suprasensory Michael School.

It is clear from all that has been presented that the gates of the suprasensory Michael School on earth were closed temporarily after the nineteenth lesson. This fact was not changed by the seven recapitulation lessons given in Dornach between September 6 and 20, 1924. These recapitulation lessons did not bring new mantric teachings, though for many the numerous integral clarifications by Steiner provided welcome additions. It is certainly remarkable that after his return from England—where Rudolf Steiner spoke in 1913 for the first time to members of the Anthroposophical Society about Michael—he also made the sign of Michael there for the first time and depicted it on the blackboard. The sign and seal of the Rose Cross were added at this time to show evidence of the connection between the Rosicrucian stream and the Michael stream. In short, a certain *devotional* element was added, as a herald of the content of the second part that was supposed to lead into the suprasensory reality of the devotional ritual.

Because Dornach was the *birthplace* of the suprasensory earthly phase of the Michael School, it is not only understandable but should also be self-evident that *during this phase* Steiner considers the Goetheanum to be the center of the new Michael School. He wants the members of the First Class to do the same.

It will become clear from this fact why Steiner applied such strong rules and discipline for acceptance as a Class member and for attendance at the Class lessons.[26] The nineteen provisional "exclusions" of unnamed and "prominent" personalities testify to this discipline during the course of the nineteen lessons. These exclusions were not of an arbitrary, personal nature but integral to the serious character of the Michael teachings given in the School. To maintain their original effectiveness, the content had to be protected from the world in quiet meditation and with conscientious care. Among Class members, both were apparently missing and as a result the mantras had already lost their effectiveness during Steiner's lifetime, and undoubtedly so after Steiner's death. In the seventh and last recapitulation lesson in Dornach on September 20, 1924, Steiner forewarns, "They [the mantras] lose their effectiveness when they come into unauthorized hands." The texts are available today on the internet and in bookstores and are freely accessible to anyone who wants to read them.

Why and how we can work today in a meaningful way—under totally different circumstances—with the contents of the suprasensory earthly Michael School will be made clear next.

The Role of Ludwig Polzer-Hoditz

Ludwig Polzer-Hoditz (1869–1945) was one of Rudolf Steiner's earliest esoteric students. He heard his first lecture by Rudolf Steiner on the four stages of self-knowledge on November 23, 1908. He was admitted to the esoteric school in February 1912 and to its devotional component in January 1914, where certain rituals of the Freemasons were taken from their spiritual source and explained. For the remainder of his life, Ludwig Polzer-Hoditz remained connected with the mantras given in this school, and an ever more trusting relationship developed with Rudolf Steiner. Polzer-Hoditz belonged to the small circle of people whom Steiner, also in correspondence, addressed as "Friend."

In 1917, on the stage of world politics, through Polzer-Hoditz's mediation an attempt was made to offer a memorandum on the threefold social order to the Austrian emperor, whose chief of cabinet was Polzer-Hoditz's brother Arthur. Steiner's very last letter, written on March 25, 1925, began with "My dear friend Count Polzer!" The letter was sent to Prague and received by Polzer-Hoditz exactly at the time of Steiner's death. All this and more can be read in the biography of Polzer-Hoditz.[27]

Ludwig Polzer-Hoditz was present at the burning of the Goetheanum in Dornach. After the war, around September 30, 1923, and at Polzer-Hoditz's request, he participated in Steiner's esoteric lessons in Vienna. In 1923/24, he also participated at the Christmas Conference in Dornach, the new founding of the Anthroposophical Society.

He was admitted to the School of Spiritual Science, which was inaugurated on February 15, 1924. Although it is uncertain how many "esoteric lessons" he experienced, it is certain that he visited Steiner's studio on September 24, 1924, with a request for permission to read the Class lessons in Vienna. And, it is equally certain that Polzer-Hoditz was already holding the First Class lessons in Vienna at Michaelmas 1924.

"Independent and Responsible Only to the Spiritual World"

He had another conversation with Steiner in Dornach on November 11, 1924. "He answered my question lovingly and emphatically about how I should give the Class lessons in Vienna and Prague: 'Do it as you want!'" Soon after this conversation, Polzer-Hoditz borrowed, according to his own words, stenographic notes from Lily Kolisko and the transcribed text of the first fourteen lessons and wrote them down. He wrote down the last five lessons in Dornach from "original text loaned to him for a couple of days by Ita Wegman." That text could have been the stenographic notes and transcribed text of Helene Finckh. He received the text of the recapitulation lessons from Marie Steiner.

In 1931, seven years after he began holding Class lessons on Michaelmas 1924, Ludwig Polzer-Hoditz concludes, "He continued the Class work given to him by Dr. Steiner in Vienna and Prague without interruption and at regular intervals of four to five weeks."[28]

The permission given to him was also given to Ita Wegman and to Lilly Kolisko, who was to give the Class lessons to the teachers in Stuttgart. Later, permission was given to other students of Steiner so they could give the lessons in other countries. Wegman and Kolisko read the Class intermittently compared to Polzer-Hoditz's regular and more frequent intervals. On March 20, 1931, Polzer-Hoditz felt compelled to make a statement because "ever and again incorrect representations were distributed" regarding his Class work. "Initially, I did not read the text of the lessons, but represented them independently without denying the character of the Class Lessons"[29]

From 1926 onward he "read the text verbatim, because the Class members had expressed the wish that he do so," though he emphasizes that, to make them clear, it is "impractical to explain the mantras to a small circle." To maintain continuity with the esoteric lessons he had experienced before the war, Polzer-Hoditz at times began to read the later lessons with elements from the earlier esoteric lessons. In Paradubitz in Bohemia, he had a rose cross erected and three candles lit to take into account the additional devotional element that Steiner had initiated in the recapitulation lessons after his return from England.

Ludwig Polzer-Hoditz concluded in 1931 that, soon after Steiner's death on March 30, 1925, it was clear "that no other member of the Executive Council had any idea of what Dr. Steiner had discussed with me regarding the Class work." "He [Rudolf Steiner] did not feel at all a need to inform any of the members of the Executive Council about what he discussed with me about the work." The statement of March 1931 ends with the sentence, "Based on all these circumstances and these concurring facts, especially the seven years of uninterrupted work, I feel empowered, independent, and responsible only to the spiritual world."

Ludwig Polzer-Hoditz's Concern for the Continuity of the Class Work

After carrying out the Class work regularly for seven years, Ludwig Polzer-Hoditz was not spared misunderstandings and worse during the next seven years. The height of the crisis occurred in 1935, when Polzer-Hoditz decided to work against the expulsion of two members of the Executive Council (Ita Wegman and Elizabeth Vreede), as well as other prominent leading members (among whom were Eugen Kolisko and D. N. Dunlop). He did this based on his nightly experiences, which guided him. The speech that Polzer-Hoditz gave in Dornach during the General Meeting of Easter 1935 is a monument of vision and courage in a time of the increasingly dark spiritual confusion that seized large and leading parts of the Anthroposophical Society.[30]

In his speech, Polzer-Hoditz shows profound insight into the original conditions of the School of Spiritual Science and the revelations of the Time Spirit in the Class Lessons. These conditions were bound to the developing relationship between Rudolf Steiner and Ita Wegman previously mentioned. Just as Marie von Sivers (Steiner) was his coworker in all esoteric events *before* the war, Ita Wegman was his coworker after the Christmas Conference.

According to Polzer-Hoditz, the initiative for the esoteric Michael School originated with Ita Wegman. "With the acceptance of this initiative," he says, "the necessary esoteric union of destiny was created between Rudolf Steiner and Ita Wegman, which is a necessary condition for the mysteries of our time." He fully acknowledges Marie Steiner's previously mentioned collaboration and says, "Before the war, Mrs. Steiner was collaborating with Rudolf Steiner on all esoteric events. One thing was as important as the other, like *everything* in Rudolf Steiner's life." In addition, Polzer-Hoditz points to the increasing devotional character of the Class in September 1924, and says:

> It was because of the increasing devotional character of the Michael-Mystery that he spoke to Dr. Wegman about the handshake and pledge that needed to be given at admission. This signified the meaning of their joint destiny for the Michael-Mystery.... This

joint destiny for the founding of a Mystery calls for coworkers in the truest sense, as documented by Rudolf Steiner through deeds involving Mrs. Steiner and Dr. Wegman.

At this time, Polzer-Hoditz turned against "the talk of old and new esotericism":

> Rudolf Steiner never had anything to do with an esotericism that divides new and old. Quite the opposite; from the beginning and also from before the war, Rudolf Steiner dedicated his forces to the necessary reappearance of the mysteries as they need to be in the present and in the future. With Anthroposophy, he gave humanity a spiritually conscious content and wisdom having the precise character essential for the present by being equally valid for both masculine and feminine spirits. Connected with this is the need to represent this duality in the devotional representation of Anthroposophy, and therefore the collaboration was also because of the feminine spirit. We are present in a Class lesson, an event that can connect us with the mystery stream of all ages; it is not an academic lecture. If we abandon this consciousness and don't bring it continuously to life [he admonished], we abandon what Rudolf Steiner brought to earth as a heavenly institution.

It was clear to Polzer-Hoditz that Rudolf Steiner did not want "a spiritual and esoteric centralization to occur after his death." He experienced with increasing concern how after Steiner's death the mentality of centralization was running rampant, in complete contradiction to Steiner's intentions. He pleaded for a decentralized admittance of members by local group leaders; he pleaded for matters concerning the Class to be built on *trust* and handled with trust, the same trust that Rudolf Steiner had given him in complete freedom. Anthroposophy was entrusted to Rudolf Steiner, and this trust—"after his death and without his leadership—had to be brought to *Anthroposophy itself, to the people who carry it, and to those who are going to carry it.*" How little of this *new* trust was present can be demonstrated by recounting an event mentioned by Polzer-Hoditz in one of his talks.

The First Class of the Michael School

Ever since that moment on January 1, 1927, when Dr. Boos forcefully disturbed the Class lessons and almost pushed Dr. Wegman away from the podium, I knew that if this situation cannot be made good on a Class level by the entire Executive Council in a unanimous way, the General Anthroposophical Society will decline, will flatten into intellectualism. And, in spite of increased attendance at conferences, it will continue lose its original character.

Eight years after this experience of "the case of Boos" in the Class, the Executive Council in Dornach was broken up and the Society was split in two. Polzer-Hoditz's speech could not prevent the decision to exclude; the speech went unheeded and seemingly had little effect.

Undeterred, he continued his Class work in Vienna and Bohemia, "independently and responsible only to the spiritual world," as he had written in March 1931. But this independence was not appreciated by the Executive Council, which remained at the Goetheanum. The following took place after the disastrous general meeting of Easter 1935.

> Soon after the meeting, the Executive Council in Dornach demanded in writing that I return the Class lesson texts and stop Class readings. I answered briefly that I could not grant the current three-person Executive Council an esoteric character and that it had no right to take from me an authority it had not given me, an authority given directly to me by Dr. Steiner. I agreed with Dr. Wegman that I would inform her about any requests for admission to the Class.[31]

The clear desire from Dornach for a pretentious leadership, heading toward spiritual centralization, was supported by the Austrian General Anthroposophical Society.

Ludwig Polzer-Hoditz felt obliged to resign from the Austrian Society in July 1935. In a letter to Herald Koch reviewing this time, Charles Kovac wrote, "When it came to the unfortunate split in the Executive Council, it also had an effect in Vienna, where the First Class was read by Polzer-Hoditz and by someone else (I forgot his name). I stayed with Polzer-Hoditz and continued to attend his lectures." This was reported by

Charles Kovacs, who was born in Vienna in 1907 and became a teacher in Edinburgh. We also owe to Kovacs a solid characterization of *how* Polzer-Hoditz gave the lessons and *the effect* they had.

> In his Class lessons, Polzer-Hoditz inserted part of the Freemason's rituals: the three hammer blows and the invocation of the Spirits of the past, present, and future. However, the strongest experience was—and I never experienced this with any other Class reader—the direct experience of one's own ether body and through it the etheric environment.

Continuing Class Work Outside of the Anthroposophic Institutions

Although Ludwig Polzer-Hoditz quietly continued his efforts in freedom, disturbances and intrigues against his Class work within the Anthroposophical Society did not cease.

Slogans and half-truths whipped up antipathetic sentiment against Polzer-Hoditz's Class lessons. "Those who want to receive the Class as Dr. Steiner gave them should go to the Society; those who attend the free groups cannot participate in the Class lessons of the Society. Count Polzer-Hoditz does not give the Class as Dr. Steiner did." Because of these slogans and half-truths directed against his participation in the Class, Polzer-Hoditz had to make another clarifying statement in December 1935, directed solely toward members of the Michael School.[32] Polzer-Hoditz objected to the arguments by saying that Steiner himself did not always give the Class lessons in the same way. He stressed:

> Never was a mantric word spoken by me in the Class that did not come from Rudolf Steiner. The fact that Class holding has to be created in the greatest possible living way and not fixed dogmatically will be clear to all esotericists who do not want the Michael Mystery to go the way of the Roman Catholic Church, which led to dogmatic arguments in its councils.

This explanation by Polzer-Hoditz did not end the intrigues against his Class work. Consequently, on May 30, 1936, he decided to resign from the General Anthroposophical Society. He hoped that by taking this step the agitations around his Class work would stop—at least within the General Anthroposophical Society—which it apparently did.

May 30 belongs to the death days meticulously written down in Polzer-Hoditz's notebook. It was the death day of D. N. Dunlop, who died on that day in London a few weeks after the general meeting at Easter 1935. It is impossible that Polzer-Hoditz's resignation on May 30 was by pure chance. Dunlop had come to know and appreciate Polzer-Hoditz and had been able to absorb his speech at the 1935 general meeting through a translation made for him by George Adams. Dunlop was also deeply connected with the Class work. A leather-bound booklet exists with the first eight Class lessons translated into English and handwritten by Eleanor Merry for "DND" (as friends called him), because he could speak only a little German. The leather cover was engraved with a Michael sign by the hand of Eleanor Merry, who also added it as a title page. This sign by her hand is reproduced on the cover of this book.

In a certain sense, Polzer-Hoditz felt relieved after taking his step *to protect* the Class work for which Dr. Steiner gave him responsibility. He had tried to arbitrate the Dornach conflict in a peaceful and reasonable manner; he could not allow the Class work to become a bone of contention in the General Anthroposophical Society. Therefore, for the work to be continued it had to be severed completely from the birthplace of the School of Spiritual Science. Furthermore, Polzer-Hoditz regularly gave the Class in Vienna, Prague, Belgrade, Budapest, and several places in Bohemia. He admitted new members and passed the information on to Ita Wegman. After her expulsion from the Executive Council, he continued to regard her—next to Rudolf Steiner—as the noteworthy midwife of the second phase of the Michael School.

The hidden spiritual battle between true Michaelic impulses and the hotheaded, pseudo-Michaelic efforts found in Hitlerism can be illustrated by an example—namely, the *Anschluss*, the annexation of Austria by Hitler on March 11, 1938. This was a clash between quiet esoteric work and raging politics. In unpublished memoirs, Polzer-Hoditz writes, "I gave a Class lesson in Vienna during that time when the upheaval took place. It was very sudden. When I walked over the ditch to give the Class lessons people still called out 'Austria,' and on the way back they called 'Sieg Heil' and swastikas appeared everywhere."

I disclosed in Polzer-Hoditz's biography that his work was not limited to giving Class lessons. He took initiatives continually to bring new impulses to influential representatives of Central-European political life. I want to refer here only to the beginning of March 1938, when he delivered a memorandum to Milan Hodza, the secretary of the prime minister of the Czechoslovak Republic, after Polzer-Hoditz's last Class lesson in Prague for a while. He wrote, "This was the last of such efforts." With a certain resignation and with deep insight into the necessity of such efforts, he adds: "Why should I be heard, when the great teacher was not heard, and yet I know that through Anthroposophy all efforts on this path are not in vain and will continue to work. Failure is never a decisive factor for the truth of a spiritual impulse."

This attitude was also at the core of Polzer-Hoditz's Class work. He could continue his work in a only limited way during the years following Hitler's annexation of Austria.

Concern about Individual Continuity

A new and growing concern arose. To whom should he give the texts and mantras and also the deeper understanding of the Michael School? It will be clear from what has already been said that it was in no way a question of institutional succession, but only of individual human succession. In 1938, during this time of serious concern about succession, he encountered Menny Lerchenfeld once again; she was twenty-eight and the daughter of Otto Count Lerchenfeld. He communicated with her in various conversations and letters about how *she* represented for him a bridge with the youth. "There has to be continuity with young people, which has been missing so far," he wrote to her. He spoke to her about the Christmas Conference and the Michael School. He prepared a box for her that contained the esoteric writings, sealed and put it in a safe place, and then set it aside for the time after the end of his life. Menny Lerchenfeld even wrote on one occasion about the moment when "even I can pass it over to other hands." It was to be different. The young friend did not feel up to the task of providing continuity for the Michael School by becoming an individual carrier. Beginning in 1940, Polzer-Hoditz and his wife Bertha were in Buchenbach, near Freiburg, where his wife had to be for health reasons. Here he entered a new circle of destiny to which the poet Paul Michaelis belonged. The box destined for Menny Lerchenfeld is missing. Michaelis took over part of his esoteric heritage, burnt some of it, and possibly also Polzer-Hoditz's hand written copies of the Class texts. Polzer-Hoditz's little booklet survives, in which he had written several Class mantras, including verses for meditation, death dates, quotes from lectures and verses from earlier esoteric lessons,.

When, on October 13, 1945, Polzer-Hoditz crossed the threshold in Vienna, his efforts toward *individual* succession based on trust were unfulfilled.

The End of the School of Spiritual Science and Efforts to Centralize the Class Work

After World War II, the leadership of the General Anthroposophical Society tried to reconnect the unpublished contents of the Michael School with its birthplace in Dornach. In other words, this leadership attempted to establish an *institutional* succession. On what grounds was this done? Could one speak in truth of an existing School of Spiritual Science? This was a school that contained unfinished First Class content at the time of Steiner's illness in 1924. Can you speak this as a true School of Spiritual Science when the content of the First Class is not complete and people are not empowered to carry it forward? Furthermore, strife had erupted there about how to handle the Michaelic spiritual content, which obliged Polzer-Hoditz at the end of his life to make his work completely independent of the School and the Society.

The above-mentioned Charles Kovac made a revealing remark about the "School of Spiritual Science" in this respect. In the previously mentioned letter from 1995, he wrote: "As I see it now, there was so much agitated animosity among us younger anthroposophists that, in this mood of turbulence, all esoteric progress was blown away by the storms. We did not know—and many today still do not know—that this was the beginning of the end of the School of Spiritual Science. Manfred Schmidt-Brabant will still not admit to it." This last mentioned personality was the chairman of the General Anthroposophical Society during these crucial years at the end of the century. This personality realigned matters surrounding the Class into an institutional succession in that he even promoted the formation of a Second Class wished for by many members. In 1993, this idea was hyped in the conference program for members of the School of Spiritual Science. At this time, a first publication of the Class text had become unavoidable because of the expired publication rights and because pirated copies were already circulating. The publication in 1992, as well as the manuscript print of 1977, were certainly welcome. They signified a natural and a certain letting go of the idea of an institutional succession, and of the absolute connectivity between the content of the Michael School and the General Anthroposophical Society. Would both again be renewed by an absurd attempt to speak about the "Second Class"?

Relevant Facts for this Edition

Rudolf Steiner brought the *second* phase of the Michael School down to earth and gave Ludwig Polzer-Hoditz the serious task to work with its contents. Ludwig Polzer-Hoditz was the first human being who in freedom decided to sever this work from the School of Spiritual Science in Dornach, its birthplace. Everyone dealing truthfully with the content of the Michael School needs to remember this fact. With this in mind, it is vital to *make one editorial change* in this publication: to move Rudolf Steiner's introductions and inserts about the Christmas Conference and the School of Spiritual Science in Dornach as a necessary esoteric center of the Anthroposophical Society, to a section *at the end* of all nineteen Class lessons.

These introductions and inserts were fully justified at the time and in the birthplace of the earthly Michael School. Succeeding developments do not allow these introductions and inserts to possess the same absolute and everlasting value as the Class Lessons themselves. The corresponding paragraphs are an example of how Steiner's words when spoken by others can, with best intentions and subjective integrity, become an objective untruth. We are unaware of how long Polzer-Hoditz included these explications and inserts in the Class Lessons he gave.

An institution whose officers carry out expulsions and dismissals, such as we had to present here, cannot claim—then or now—to be an esoteric *center* for the anthroposophic Michaelic movement.

The mantras of the Michael School are, in the truest sense, sustenance for people today, not only for the life between birth and death, but even more so for the time spent in the spiritual world after death. There, all souls who have crossed the threshold will experience beings and processes they can only cope with when *on earth* they have already experienced something about these beings and processes.

Rudolf Steiner spoke in the eighteenth lesson about the circumstance when "human beings remain dull and unwilling in regard to... what can be learnt through initiation science." The souls of the deceased have to live through the agony of not understanding, which can be compensated for only in the next incarnation. "They go through the gate of death. They hear what they should have heard already while on earth. They do not understand it. Like unintelligible clanging, like mere sound, mere cosmic noise, so do the words of power sound to them when the gods are speaking to one another." And, "For in the spirit land, it is equivalent to death if having gone through the gate of death we do not understand what resounds there." These words alone, when taken seriously, should be enough to eradicate all egoistic personal and group reservations for a proper distribution of the contents of the Michael School without outside requirements. The contents of the Michael School should be made available to all people seeking them because, as sustenance for life on earth and after death, they are not solely the property of a group of people who are close to the School's place of birth and the associated institutions located there.

The Purpose of Working with the Content of the Michael School

It would naturally follow from this account that a completion of the First Class with the second and third "parts" points toward a future necessity. Through *whom* this continuation can in reality be undertaken is an open question. Polzer-Hoditz once expressed the following in a letter to Menny Lerchenfeld: "Four-times-twelve will be called by him as leaders, and all true anthroposophists will be able to work freely under them." Those who are *called by Steiner* may be the first who are worthy to participate in the *completion* of the First Class. Surely there will be introduced and observed comparable rules like those present during the realization of the "first part" of the Class, so the new mantras can be as effective as initially the old ones were.

Nonetheless, why would we have any interest at all in working with these "old" mantras of the School that have lost their original power? Many people may well ask this question. The answer is as unattractive as it is necessary: It is so there will be people who can form a *bridge* and carry a real continuity between the first part of the First Class of the suprasensory Michael School and the future revelations of the content of the second and third parts of the First Class. How can the First Class be *completed* while there are so few people on earth who are conversant with the Michaelic course of instruction from 1924?

Ludwig Polzer-Hoditz was a participant in the marvelous birthing event of the first part. He attended to this young Michaelic child, first within and later outside of the institution in which it saw its first light on earth. Today, it can be found on the street, in bookstores, "online," and scarcely alive. It needs the care of people who know about its origin, love its being, and have a heartfelt interest to see it prosper.

This publication is intended for these people.

Who Is the Guardian of the Threshold?

The Guardian of the Threshold plays a central role throughout the several lessons of the first section of the Michael School. The Guardian is introduced in the first lesson as the "spirit messenger." He is a constant companion on the meditative path through the nineteen lessons. He is the mediator of all the cautions and teachings given to the spiritual seeker. He is also the intermediary for all of the teachings that come from the sphere of the nine hierarchies and touch the spiritual ear of the meditant. All that he speaks, he speaks at "Michael's command." This points to a spiritual collaboration with the individuality of the archangel Michael and, sooner or later, may kindle a question about the Guardian's individuality and being.

This spiritual being isn't the "lesser Guardian," who is also described as the "double" in Rudolf Steiner's book *How to Attain How to Know Higher Worlds?* Even less relevant in this context is the ahrimanic double, who shortly after birth enters the human being and shortly before death leaves the same, as Steiner indicates in 1917.[33]

According to our understanding, Rudolf Steiner gave the most concise insights into the being of the Guardian in the lecture cycle *Initiation, Eternity and the Passing Moment*,[34] after the first performance of the third Mystery Drama, *The Guardian of the Threshold*, where the Guardian was presented for the first time. On August 27, 1912, he characterized the spiritual being of the *Guardian of the Threshold* as follows: "Here we stand at the boundary between the life of the senses and spiritual life, confronted... by a reality that only works suprasensorially, but as concretely and alive as a human being. This is the Guardian of the Threshold.... When we learn to know him, we know he belongs to the category of beings who, to a certain extent, have taken part in life since primeval times on earth, but who have not gone through what one experiences as a being of soul.... There we meet a being about whom we may say: I have a being before me who experiences and lives through a great deal in the world, although he does not concern himself with all the love and grief and pain that can be experienced on earth, nor with the failings and immorality found there. He neither knows nor wishes to know anything of what has taken place up to now in the depths of human nature. Christian tradition expresses this in the words: When confronted by the mystery of man's becoming, such beings veiled their faces.[35] A whole world is expressed in this contrast between such beings and human beings."

The Human Path of Incarnation at the Conclusion of Lemuria

Rudolf Steiner does not point in the larger sense with these words to the first beginnings of humanity, but to the stage of humanity caused by the "fall" when the human being was expelled from paradise at the end of the Lemurian epoch. This event designates the beginning of the human being's path of development on earth as an upright being influenced first by Lucifer and then later by Ahriman. The time when this development occurred was in the last *age of the fishes* (Pisces) in the seventh and final Lemurian age.

A legend from Sri Lanka, a region on at the edge of Lemuria, points to this connection. On top of Adam's Peak, the island's holiest mountain, there is an imprint on a rock. It is supposed to be the imprint of the foot of Adam who, after his expulsion from paradise, placed his foot on the earth for the first time.

Before this development—the actual incarnation of humanity—and before all succeeding incarnations, the beings mentioned by Rudolf Steiner in his Munich lecture were veiling their faces. One of those beings is the Guardian of the Threshold. Steiner says in relation to the spiritual encounter with the Guardian Being: "A feeling arises: passing through various earth cultures you have of necessity acquired imperfections, but you must return again to the original state. You must retrace your path on earth. This being can show you the way because he does not possess the mistakes you have made. Now you stand before a being as a real admonition, majestic and grandiose as a stimulus toward all you are not. This being demonstrates this most vividly to you and it is possible to feel your own being completely filled with the knowledge of what you are and are not. There one stands before this living admonition."

Steiner also revealed the hierarchical rank to which this being belongs: "This being belongs to the rank of Archangels." Thus, this being belongs to the same order of beings as Michael.

Finally, "The meeting actually takes place and has the effect of suddenly revealing to us what we have become as earthly human beings in sensory existence. This is direct self-knowledge in the truest and broadest sense of the word. You see yourself as you are. You also see yourself as you ought to become."

The Guardian of the Unborn in the Human Being

On the meditative path through the nineteen First Class lessons, the spiritual seeker encounters no other Guardian than the being characterized here. The basic function of the Guardian is twofold. First, he is to prepare the traveler on the path for the actual crossing of the threshold and, second, to awaken in the soul what has remained pure and uncorrupted by the fall into the sense world. The Guardian of the Threshold is also the one who guards what is as yet unborn in the human being. That which is unborn in us doesn't descend into earthly life. It is the true spiritual I Being of which our earthly I is essentially a distorted picture. To achieve consciousness of this true I, Rudolf Steiner gave the following meditation[36]:

> I gaze into the Darkness.
> In it there arises Light —
> Living Light!
> Who is this Light in the Darkness?
> It is I myself in my reality.
> This reality of the "I"
> Does not enter into my earthly life.
> I am but an image of it.
> But I shall find it again
> When with good will for the Spirit
> I shall have passed through the Gate of Death.

The Guardian wants to remind us of this I. And to this I, this being who is deeply hidden in the image of self and who has never left Paradise, the meditative path should lead. The Guardian only gazes upon what remained pure and innocent in the human being during our higher spiritual infancy, in spite of the fall from paradise into the world of egoism and murder.

The Guardian wants to call on our inner Cain nature so that "The original state of Cain before murdering his brother can be restored," as Rudolf Steiner indicated in one of many versions of the Temple Legend.[37]

Phanuel

Is it possible to achieve an even more concrete picture of the Guardian/Archangel? Was this being known in the older mystery schools? A lecture in Berlin from 1908[38] can lead us further here. Rudolf Steiner points out on April 20, 1908, that in olden times people knew names of other Archangels in addition to the well-known Archangels Uriel, Gabriel, and Michael: "You need only read in the *Book of Enoch* to find the names of other Archangels. So, for instance, there is Phanuel, an important Archangel who not only has the task of guiding a people or nation, but another task as well. We are aware that initiation consists of the human being striving upward to an ever-higher consciousness and that, even now in the course of earthly evolution, is ascending to even higher levels of consciousness.

The people in the mystery centers knew well that guiding, leading forces were also necessary. Because of this, they brought those who were to be initiated under the protection of the Archangel who was called Phanuel. He was the protector who was called upon by the candidate for initiation."

When you follow Steiner's lead, you can find a place in the apocryphal *Book of Enoch* that is pertinent to our discussion. After characterizing Michael, Raphael and Gabriel, it says: "Phanuel is the fourth, the one who presides over repentance and the hope of those who will inherit eternal life."[39]

The initiates are the ones who will inherit "eternal life." What is translated here as "repentance" and "hope" relates to the two basic functions of the Guardian. He first shows us what our souls have become since our fall into the sense world; this fall can lead us to *repentance*, meaning to knowledge of being fallen and leading us to the resolve to freely regain "eternal life." And, second, by showing us our innermost paradisiacal nature that is deeply hidden from our normal consciousness—our true I Being which does not descend in to earthly life—he awakens in us the highest *hope* of development when we earnestly tread the path of initiation; all this despite our fall into matter. As it was in the past, so it is in the present. We can perceive in Phanuel a tangible archangel individuality who was "assigned by Michael" to relate to us the cautions, teachings and mantras of the suprasensory Michael School on earth.

During the profound cycle given in The Hague in 1913[40] in an unpublished question and answer session, a participant asked the following question. "Does a person in the course of incarnations meet the Guardian once or several times?" Rudolf Steiner answered "Only once. *Whoever meets him once, knows him forever.*"[41]

That we can have spiritual experiences without passing the Guardian is a fact we all know from personal experience. All this becomes clear from the study of Spiritual Science. Also, the *Mystery Dramas* of Rudolf Steiner show this to us. The Guardian shows up only after the important protagonists (Capesius, Johannes, Thomasius, and Maria) *after* they had their review experience of a past life. Although such experiences may be achieved more quickly and easily before meeting the Guardian, the *assessment* of these experiences always contain some uncertainty. They can easily divert one into luciferic or ahrimanic ways, which idea is portrayed in the last scene of Rudolf Steiner's Mystery Drama *The Trial of the Soul*. It is characteristic of the Michaelic spiritual path that the Guardian of the Threshold is present to continually give warnings, advice and guidance. We should courageously come closer and closer to this Guardian, to heed his admonitions. "Assigned by Michael," he speaks to us: Michael was the countenance of Yahweh, and today he is the countenance of Christ.

Thus, three beings—Phanuel, Michael, and Christ—have first been considered to provide a background for this special and unique nineteenfold meditative path of the Michael School. The path would not exist without their collaborative working and, it is in this that it differs from earlier and contemporary spiritual paths. A spiritual path without Phanuel cannot lead to Michael and Christ, only to Lucifer and Ahriman. Whoever seriously and with perseverance enters the meditative path of the Michael School will "always" know this forever.

The Structure and Levels of the Nineteen Lessons

While considering the entire path of the nineteen lessons, a clear separation can be perceived in the *warnings given by the Guardian of the Threshold*. The first part of the path covers the first through the seventh level and the second part covers the eighth through the nineteenth level. A culmination of the earlier lessons occurs with the seventh lesson, which is also a turning point on the path. From the first lesson the meditant's attention is focused on thinking, feeling and willing, on what these forces became under the influence of anti-spiritual forces of the time and what they need to become to cross the abyss.[42]

All the lessons up to the seventh serve to deepen the dual view of the threefold soul in its current state and the state it is able to attain in the future. Within the first seven lessons, one can discern a part that is more diagnostic and a part that stimulates development: the fourth lesson or level forms the mid- or transition-point between these two, appealing to a deeper feeling element, which is itself in the middle of the three soul forces.

> Feel how from the depths of earth...
> Feel how from the worldwide spaces...
> Feel how in the heights of heaven...

Here, within the *feeling experience*, there must be developed a distinct consciousness of the depths, widths, and heights.

The soul forces continuing toward the threshold become increasingly separate from each other and are increasingly held together in a body-free state by the newborn I.

At the seventh level, the double-sidedness of the three soul forces is revealed to the "threshold-crosser," as Steiner once described the meditant. In addition to the collaboration by the three soul forces in the physical body during normal consciousness, there will be an experience of the differentiated threefoldness in a higher consciousness.

> Behold the Three,
> They are as One,
> When you bear in Earth existence
> The stamp of being human.
>
> Experience the cosmic form of your head.
> Feel the cosmic beat of your heart.
> Think the cosmic strength of your limbs.
> These are the Three
> The Three in Earth existence
> That live as One.

Then the relationship between the threefoldness of the body and the threefoldness of spirit (thinking), soul (feeling) and strength (willing) will be pointed out to the meditant. At the same time an important change occurs between this side and the other side of the threshold.

> The spirit of the head:
> You can will it...

While in sensory world experience thinking relates to the spirit of the head, in suprasensory experience thinking relates to the *will*. While in sense world consciousness will relates to the strength of one's limbs, in suprasensory experience will relates to *thinking*. Only feeling remains constant between thinking and willing in both worlds. You might say it is a constant middle point of a lemniscate through which a reverse turning occurs between thinking and feeling. For the first time in this level of the Class, physical gestures are added to give orientation and strength to the experience.

When this transformation has become fully conscious, the Guardian lets resound the words of monumental importance:

> Enter:
> The door is open!
> You will become
> A true human being.

Entrance to the Objective Spiritual World

Through this door the meditant is guided further outward—step-by-step—on the path into the objective *spiritual world*. The meditant learns ever more deeply to grasp the threefoldness of the soul with its corresponding reversals (willing / cosmic thought-creating and thinking / as will's magic essence) and the continuity of feeling from the spiritual point of view beyond the threshold.[43]

On the ninth level, the meditant needs to learn to experience his or her body, soul and spirit from a spiritual point of view. On all subsequent levels, the spiritual experience becomes freer from the body and soul; it is ever more turned outward toward world knowledge in an all-encompassing spiritual manner. The spiritual experience goes into "situation meditations" in the objective spiritual world and into collaboration by all nine hierarchies. In the final lesson, the self-knowledge that was demanded in the first lesson is *born* from a spiritual world-knowledge. The meditant grasps his or her "I" living as an entity originating in the world of the three highest hierarchies. Starting from an earthbound *egocentric* "I"-consciousness, the meditant begins to have a spiritual, *cosmic-centric* ego consciousness that arises from within, if this paradoxical expression can be permitted. At the same time, the meditant returns again in spirit to the head, heart and human limbs now connected with the cosmic-spiritual threefoldness of the soul, which can be experienced in the sphere of first hierarchy beings, where the meditant's true "I" also originates.

Said differently, the meditative nineteen leveled path manifests as a path of consciousness from the semblance-"I" to the true "I" of the human being. This path has a spiraling character, so to speak. On a higher level, the meditant arrives again at the beginning with the Self he or she was striving to know. At first it was a goal and then, on the nineteenth level, it can became an event.

After gaining the consciousness of a true self, born from the hierarchies, the meditant would have been guided to a *continuation* in the "second part" of the First Class, according to intentions expressed by Rudolf Steiner in the fall of 1924. This depiction—by a truly qualified person—is left up to a future *second* phase of the suprasensory Michael School on earth.

The Seven and the Twelve

The first part of the path of nineteen levels is in the sign of seven; the second is in the sign of twelve. Seven is the number of the soul, of the wandering stars and time. Twelve is the number of eternal spirit working into space from the twelve zodiac regions. The seven basic moods of the first seven lessons could be compared with the journey traversed by the soul through the seven *moods of the worldviews*. This journey passes through the spheres of the planets from the Moon sphere to the Saturn sphere.

Steiner calls the first worldview mood the mood of "occultism." In this soul mood "the world is Maya and one has to search for the inner side of things in another way than through sense perception and common knowledge." It is the mood in which we experience the sunlit sense world as spiritual darkness. These seven moods of knowledge are systematically presented in the lecture cycle *Human and Cosmic Thought*.[44] It will be easier to traverse the first seven stages of the Michaelic path when these moods are developed. Take, for example, the fourth level of the meditative path where the feeling *experience* is called for three times; here the meditant can find a relationship with the fourth mood of knowledge: "empiricism." The fifth level of meditation leads to an experience of a threefold *battle*; the fifth mood of knowledge is "voluntarism," which is in tune with all cosmic activity based on *will*. Or ultimately, the mood of "Gnosis," which stimulates a deep inward spiritual *basis* for reality. It is the best way to prepare for the meeting with the Guardian of the Threshold, who appears in the seventh lesson, the lesson of transition. The soul moves through all seven moods of knowledge, like the planets move through the cosmos of the zodiac, itself representing the twelve worldviews, which Steiner calls *worldview nuances* that indicate the spiritual.

Or you can think of the soul training in the Middle Ages by treading the path of the Seven Liberal Arts. These seven also relate to the spheres of the planets; only when students have gone through the seven planetary spheres are they mature enough to rise to the actual sphere of the spiritual cosmos.

These parallels are not pointed out here to emphasize a schematic equation, but to highlight the difference between the seven-ness and the twelve-ness in the structure of the meditative path of nineteen levels in the Michael School.

And it corresponds to the two sides of the human soul-spirit being, since the seven and twelve appear everywhere the human being seeks to unfold its *entire* being when developing and understanding itself.

The Form Language of the Michael Sign

Spiritual beings reveal themselves in forms. As the pentagram belongs to the human being, so also do forms belong to beings that live in the suprasensory world. Living into the language of these forms can lead to a first and also a deeper understanding of these beings. Such forms can be considered and used as a key for understanding these beings. This will be explained by the following two examples.

Rudolf Steiner has drawn two forms or signatures that can be read as the footprints of two spiritual beings who are of specific importance in the time of our development: the signature of the sun-demon Sorat and the signature of the Time Spirit Michael. The first sign or signature was already revealed and published in the history of recent occultism, for example by Agrippa of Nettesheim and then by Rudolf Steiner in his *Apocalypse* lecture cycle of 1908.[45, 46] It seems that Rudolf Steiner was the first to research and publish the Michael sign.

Rudolf Seiner made the Michael sign for the first time on August 27, 1924, in the second Class lesson given in London,[47] if it had not already been made during the first lesson given in London on August 25. It was drawn for the first time on the board for Class members in Dornach on September 6.[48]

The Sign of Sorat

Let us first try to grasp something in the form language of this sign. Overall, the form runs from *above* to *below*, and this expresses the *spiritual* world in relation to the *physical* world. Observing the two-pronged beginning reveals its dual origin. One could also say this duality is a split. A slightly curved diagonal movement goes downward from this split. The movement then undergoes an abrupt change of direction. It goes a short way in the altered direction, at which point the whole movement originating in the split suddenly stops. This last, short and almost straight piece, often represented as completely straight, can also be experienced as a hook. The thing has a hook[49]; there is a snag in it.

Rudolf Steiner gives clear and important indications about the entrance of the sun demon into history. In the timeline he connects it with the number 666 described in *The Apocalypse*, and with the doubling and multiples of that number. In the seventh century, Sorat revealed himself in the School of Gondishapur. In the fourteenth century, Sorat's work could be seen in the dissolving of the Templar Order and the torturing of many Templars At the turn of the millennium his work can be seen in the catastrophe of September 11 in the US and its effect on the whole of civilization. In Gondishapur, the

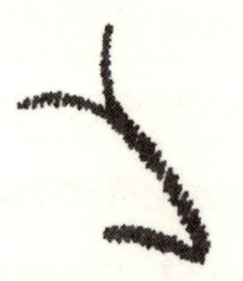

Figure 1: The Sign of Sorat from 1908

complete future evolution of the human being and the development of the higher spiritual members of Spirit Self, Life Spirit and Spirit Human were brought to a halt. The human being was developing the consciousness soul too early and was in danger of being bound to it.[51]

Through the eradication of the Templar Order—in contrast to the Roman Catholic Church—the *true* Christian spiritual development that lived in this order was to be cut off with one blow. The striving for truth for the whole of humanity was to be dulled or possibly completely destroyed through the events taking place at the millennium. The events were covered in very effective lies spread over the whole planet on a scale never before experienced.[52]

Common with all attacks by Sorat is that they work against spiritual impulses having their origin at a *higher* level than the sun demon: these impulses had to be redirected, stopped and cut off. Apparently it is an absolute dualism, the bending and abrupt ending of a spiritual impulse. Everywhere in public or private life, when events happen with this signature, one can speak of a direct influence of the sun demon. The contemplation of this sign can lead to a corresponding awakening in face of these spiritually destructive tendencies.

The Michael Sign

The Michael sign is completely different! The originating movement starts from spiritual heights and moves toward the depths of the earth in completely straight lines—lines that are different than the slightly curved lines found in the sign of Sorat. Yet, there is no split at the beginning, and the sign moves in one stroke while clearly changing directions. There is one stroke in four parts moving from above to below, with the last moving upward. At the same time the entire movement creates an *inner space*, an inner soul space between the second, third and fourth parts. From the beginning movement to the end we stand in an *inner soul space* in contrast to an objective outside space. One belongs to the spiritual world the other to the physical world.

The Michael Sign and "Acting Consciously"

We now apply what is here briefly mentioned to the human being insofar as he or she is striving in the Michaelic sense, meaning that as a being standing in the world, *acting consciously*, and corresponding to Rudolf Steiner's key formula given in his *Philosophy of Freedom*.

What is created while truly acting in freedom and from the spirit is the idea of the action (moral intuition). This idea should be realized on earth (movement from above downward, see Figure 2). *Before* its realization however, the idea is brought to an inner soul space where it is wrapped in sympathy and then "gives birth to the Love of the Deed" (end of the second and third part of the stroke) and then becomes individualized. Then it leaves the inner space again and becomes solidified into a picture with moral imagination, without which no concrete free deed is possible (end of the third, beginning of the fourth part of the stroke). A deed, individualized and substantiated in this way, imprints itself on the physical world.

Figure 2: The sign of Michael and "Conscious Action"

Such a deed can be an outer deed (for example the building of a house), an artistic deed or a scientific deed, at first invisible, but in some way directed to the development of the physical world. All deeds that are in this way a conclusion of this fourfold movement contribute to the overall *spiritualization* of the sense world. That is why the last part of the stroke rises upward.

Viewed in this way, the Michael sign is at the same time a sign of every truly free deed, meaning an ideal intuition carried out by love rather than duty. Viewed in this way, the sign reveals complete and simultaneous agreement with the essence of the *Philosophy of Freedom* and the being of Michael. Although the word Michael is not mentioned in this germinal work by Steiner, he appears in the human being acting from cognition.

With regard to human beings acting from cognition, the threefold spirit, soul, and body is expressed in this sign. The spirit relates to the spiritual outer space where the ideas are conceived; the soul relates to the inner space formed by the straight lines; the body relates to what in the last part of the stroke crystallizes through the body as a deed.

The inner space formed by the four straight lines has a completely different character than one formed by a circle or by curved lines. The first stands in total clarity between the spiritual and physical world and *connects to both*, the second encapsulates itself and loses the connection to the two objective outer spaces. Expressed in spiritually scientific words, the first carries the signature of Michael and the second the signature of Lucifer. It takes one look at contemporary times to confirm how much of encapsulated luciferic inner space there is at present compared with those that are the outcome of truly free Michaelic striving.

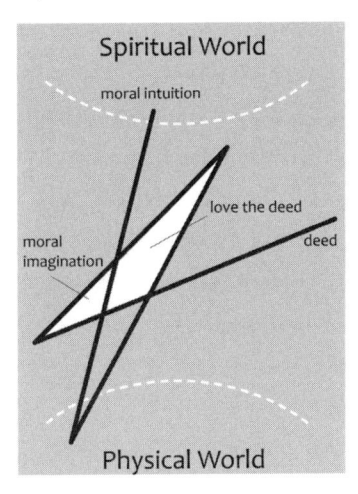

Figure 3: The Michael Sign in Action

The Rudimentary Caricature of the Michael Sign

Perhaps the signature of the Michael sign can become even clearer when one tries to abbreviate the four-part stroke. For example, if we omit the first part, the spiritual foundation of the action is left out; the action can only be born out the soul void of spirit. All action coming forth from subjective soul impulses (ambition, conceitedness, revenge) are missing the first part of the creative idea that needs to be the foundation for a Michaelic deed. When the second and third parts of the stroke are also omitted, the *soul foundation* is erased from the action as well. Then the action can only come about in an automatic and mechanical way without the soul's participation, at most from the cold necessity of duty. What then remains as the last part, when done as a gesture, is well known to all people who saw before them the picture of a right arm flung straight to the right as it was presented in the Third Reich. *One can see a ripped-off remnant of the Michael sign in this gesture.* It may nevertheless have awakened the subconscious memory of the complete *four-part stroke* as it was experienced more or less extensively before birth. Accordingly, it can be understood that it could have had a corrupting effect on millions of people. One can see in the Hitler greeting what was to inspire spirit denying, automatic and insane deeds, and the last remnant of a stunted—in the sense of Sorat—fourfold stroke.

These statements are not meant to be dogmatic or definitive and are offered as a suggestion to bring clarity and experience to the two signs. When possible, make the Michael sign through a real action in movement.[53] This then can slowly become an experience with reference to current events or in an individual life.

THOMAS MEYER was born in Basel in 1950. After studies in German and English literature and philosophy, he worked as a Waldorf school teacher. In 1990, he founded Perseus Verlag Basel (see www.perseus.ch), and in 1997 the monthly *Der Europäer,* now appearing in English as *The Present Age.* Among his many books, Meyer has published biographies of Ludwig Polzer-Hoditz and D. N. Dunlop (Temple Lodge, London), and edited the book *Light for the New Millennium,* about Rudolf Steiner's association with Helmuth von Moltke (Rudolf Steiner Press, London). Thomas Meyer lives with his family in Basel.

Notes

Introduction to the Third German Edition

1. Dr. Ita Wegman played an important role at Rudolf Steiner's side in forming the Christmas Conference and the School of Spiritual Science. See "The Earthly Michael School and the Role of Ita Wegman," page 375).

2. Letter from Marie Steiner on February 8, 1948 to engineer Werner Rosenthal in Stockholm.

3. The excised text, marked by an ellipsis, is reproduced in its entirety in "Passages Omitted from the Text" on pages 279ff of this book.

4. For more information, see "The Role of Ludwig Polzer-Hoditz" on pages 379ff in this book. See also Thomas Meyer, *Ludwig Polzer-Hoditz: A European*, Temple Lodge, 2014.

5. Rudolf Steiner, *Esoterische Unterweisungen für die erste Klasse der Freien Hochschule für Geisteswissenschaft am Goetheanum 1924* (Esoteric Instructions for the First Class of the Free College for Spiritual Science at the Goetheanum 1924), 4 vols, CW 270 (not translated into English).

6. The editorial proofs and comments by Jutta Schwarz that are related to the German language itself, are not relevant to the English-language translation and are not reproduced in this edition.

7. At the same time, Perseus Verlag in Basel had its twenty-first anniversary in February 2011.

Passages Omitted from the Text

1. *The Year of Destiny 1923 In The History of The Anthroposophical Society*, See CW 259; and, in *The Christmas Foundation Meeting of The General Anthroposophical Society 1923–1924*, CW 260.

2. Rudolf Steiner refers to writings now available in CW 260a: *The Constitution of the General Anthroposophical Society and The School of Spiritual Science.*

3. See the lecture of January 30, 1924, Rudolf Steiner, Dornach, CW 260a: *The Constitution of the General Anthroposophical Society and The School of Spiritual Science.*

4. Rudolf Steiner lectured from March 27 until April 11, 1924 in Prague and Stuttgart. The seventh class lesson was given a week before Good Friday, and on Good Friday, the eighth lesson was given.

5. Rudolf Steiner already spoke and wrote about this in Dornach; see CW 260a on *The Constitution of the General Anthroposophical Society and The School of Spiritual Science.*

6. See CW 260, *The Christmas Conference: For the Foundation of the General Anthroposophical Society, 1923/1924,* Anthroposophic Press, 1989.

7. Rudolf Steiner does not have in mind the early esoteric School (1904–1914), but individual circles that formed in 1920–1923.

8. All that Rudolf Steiner said about the significance of the Christmas Conference in different places can be found in CW 260a on The Constitution of the General Anthroposophical Society and The School of Spiritual Science.

9. From Rudolf Steiner's notebook, April 1924 (archive no. 571): "Dr. Eisele, leader of the Prussian press to Excellency Von Gillhausen. Anthroposophy, Christian Community—we will establish the Holy Roman Empire of the German nation—small states to counter the dominance of Prussia, because we will rule spiritual movements. If we do not succeed—and it will succeed—then we will in another way—we mean the Anthroposophic Movement and the Movement for Religious Renewal." The source of this quote has so far not be located—a Dr. Eisele was in Munich in 1921 and was the leader of the Bayern Press. Possibly Rudolf Steiner had mistakenly written down "Prussian" instead of "Bayern".

10. See CW 260, *The Christmas Conference: For the Foundation of the General Anthroposophical Society, 1923/1924.*

11. See CW 260, *The Christmas Conference: For the Foundation of the General Anthroposophical Society, 1923/1924,* p. ix.

12. The circular letter mentioned is printed in CW 316, *The Young Doctors Course.* No further circular letters were sent.

13. See *In Memoriam of Edith Maryon,* May 3, 1924, in CW 261, *Our Dead: Memorial, Funeral, and Cremation Addresses,* SteinerBooks, 2011.

14 This only occurred for the twelfth lesson. After that they were held on Saturday evenings.

15 See CW 327, *Agriculture Course: The Birth of the Biodynamic Method*, Rudolf Steiner Press, 2004.

16 This class lesson did not take place in two weeks as announced, but only after three weeks.

17 See CW 260a: *The Constitution of the General Anthroposophical Society and The School of Spiritual Science*. Words after the lecture of August 1, 1924.

The Meditation Path of the Michael School Today

1. Rudolf Steiner, *The Mission of the Folk-Souls*, Christiania (Oslo), Norway, June 1910, CW 121.

2. Scholasticism is a method of critical thought which dominated teaching by the academics, or "schoolmen," of medieval universities in Europe from about 1100–1700, and a program of employing that method in articulating and defending dogma in an increasingly pluralistic context. See more in the Wikipedia article on Scholasticism.

3. See CW 39, August 16, 1902.

4. Rudolf Steiner, *Karmic Relationships*, vol. 8 (Rudolf Steiner Press, 2015), lect. 1, Aug. 12, 1924, CW 240.

5. *The Nineteenth Lesson of the School for Spiritual Science* (see page 277).

6. Rudolf Steiner, *Karmic Relationships*, vol. 6 (Rudolf Steiner Press, 2002), lect. 8, Arnhem, July 19, 1924, CW 240.

7. *The Anthroposophical Leading Thoughts* was a newssheet published for members during Rudolf Steiner's lifetime.

8. Rudolf Steiner, *Anthroposophical Leading Thoughts*, CW 26, Rudolf Steiner Press, 1973.

9. Rudolf Steiner, *Anthroposophical Leading Thoughts*, letter of Oct. 19, 1924, CW 26.

10. Peter Selg, *Ich bleibe bei Ihnen, Rudolf Steiner und Ita Wegman* (I Remain with You: Rudolf Steiner and Ita Wegman), Stuttgart, 2000.

11. See the section "The Michael Sign" on Page 403 in this book.

12. Rudolf Steiner, *Karmic Relationships: Esoteric Studies*, vol. 8, lect. 3, August 21, 1924, CW 240.

13. Rudolf Steiner, *Karmic Relationships: Esoteric Studies*, vol. 8, lect. 6, Aug. 27,1924, CW 240.
14. Rudolf Steiner, *Karmic Relationships*, 8 vols. (Rudolf Steiner Press); see CWs 238 and 240.
15. Rudolf Steiner, *Karmic Relationships*, vol. 8, lect. 6, Aug. 27,1924, CW 240.
16. Ibid.
17. An indication by Steiner is in *The Riddle of Humanity* (Rudolf Steiner Press, 1990), lect. 15, Sept. 3, 1916, CW 170, points to activities by Bacon for materialism already in the Atlantean time.
18. The author uses the term *cultus* to indicate what Rudolf Steiner describes as "a great cosmic, spiritual festival, lasting for many decades as a spiritual happening in the world immediately bordering on the physical." This word has many meanings in the English-speaking world, and many of the meanings are not appropriate or adequate to describe the sense intended here. For this reason, the term *devotional event* is used in its place.
19. Rudolf Steiner, *Karmic Relationships*, vol. 6, lect. 7, July 18,1924, Arnhem, CW 240.
20. See *The Devotions as Conclusion of the Michael School* in "The Suprasensory Michael School."
21. Peter Selg, op. cit.
22. See the "Omitted Text of the First Class Lesson" in this book.
23. See the Fourteenth Lesson on page 206 of this volume.
24. Rudolf Steiner explains in a concise manner the difference between a thinking that understands and meditation in *A Way of Self-Knowledge and the Threshold of the Spiritual World*, part 2, "Trust in Thinking: The Nature of the Thinking Soul," CW 17.
25. See "The Human Path of Incarnation at the Conclusion of Lemuria" in this volume.
26. Consider the omitted text from Lesson One.
27. Thomas Meyer, *Ludwig Polzer Hoditz: A European*, Temple Lodge, 2014.
28. Polzer-Hoditz, in an announcement of Mar. 20,1931, from the archive of the Goetheanum—*History of the Class Work within the AAG after Steiner's Death*. See Johannes Kiersch, *A History of the School of Spiritual Science: The First Class*, Temple Lodge, 2006; and Peter Selg,

Rudolf Steiner and the School for Spiritual Science, SteinerBooks, 2012.

29. Polzer-Hoditz, in an announcement of Mar. 20, 1931, from the archive of the Goetheanum: *History of the Class Work within the AAG after Steiner's Death.*

30. The entire speech is in Thomas Meyer, *Ludwig Polzer Hoditz: A European,* Temple Lodge, 2014.

31. Polzer-Holzer wrote this quote in a typescript *In Memoriam* for Dr. Wegman after her death in March 1943.

32. This clarifying statement is included in its entirety in *Ludwig Polzer Hoditz: A European*, Temple Lodge, 2014. See "On the Matter of the Class," page 579.

33. Rudolf Steiner, *Geographic Medicine,* lect. 2, St. Gallen, Nov. 16, 1917, CW 178.

34. Rudolf Steiner, *Initiation, Eternity, and the Passing Moment* (Anthroposophic Press, 1980), 7 lectures, Munich, Aug. 25–31, 1917, CW 138.

35. Rudolf Steiner, *Initiation, Eternity and the Passing* Moment, lect. 1, Munich, Aug. 25, 1912. As of this writing, independent references to these "Christian traditions" have yet to be found.

36. Meditation given by Rudolf Steiner in London, Sept. 2, 1923, CW 228.

37. Rudolf Steiner, *From the History and Content of the Esoteric School: Letters, Documents, and Lectures, 1904–1914,* p. 197, CW 265.

38. Rudolf Steiner, *Good and Evil Spirits: And their Influence on Humanity,* Berlin, 1908, CW 102.

39. Enoch 40, quoted from Emil Kautzsch, *Die apokryphen und pseudepigraphen des Alten Testaments,* Tübingen, 1900.

40. Rudolf Steiner, *The Effects of Esoteric Development,* lect. 10, The Hague, March 29, 1913, CW 145.

41. In the Archive at Perseus Verlag, Basel.

42. This is nothing more than the "repentance" and "hope" connected with Phanuel.

43. Eighth Class Lesson or level.

44. Rudolf Steiner, *Human and Cosmic Thought,* Jan. 20–23, 1914, Berlin, CW 151. See also T. H. Meyer, *Representative Men: In the Light of Anthroposophy,* Great Barrington, MA: SteinerBooks, 2012, p. 105ff.

45. *The Apocalypse of St. John*, Rudolf Steiner, Nuremberg, June 17–30, 1908, CW 104. Steiner called Sorat one of the greatest ahrimanic demons (Sept. 12 1924, GA 346).

46. Rev. 13:11: "Then I saw a second beast coming out of the earth. It had two horns like a lamb, but it spoke like a dragon." Compare this with the artistic presentation by Charles Kovacs in his *The Apocalypse in Rudolf Steiner's Lecture Series*, (Floris Books, 2013), July 25, 2013.

47. *Esoterische Unterweisungen für die erste Klasse der Freien Hochschule für Geisteswissenschaft am Goetheanum 1924. I–IV* (Esoteric Instructions for the First Class of the Free College for Spiritual Science at the Goetheanum 1924, 4 vols.), vol. 3, CW 270.

48. *Esoterische Unterweisungen für die erste Klasse der Freien Hochschule für Geisteswissenschaft am Goetheanum 1924. I–IV*, vol. 4, CW 270.

49. This is a colloquialism in the German language, perhaps not without reference to such a spiritual sign.

50. Rudolf Steiner, *Inner Impulses of Evolution*; see lectures of Sept. 25 and Oct. 1, 1916, CW 171.

51. Rudolf Steiner, *Death as Metamorphosis of Life: Including "What Does the Angel Do in our Astral Body?" and "How Do I Find Christ?"* (SteinerBooks, 2008), Zurich, Oct. 16, 1918, CW 182.

52. Thomas Meyer, *Reality, Truth, and Evil: Facts, Questions, and Perspectives on September 11, 2001*. Temple Lodge, 2005.

53. The movement of the Michael sign starts with the right arm outstretched, then with an angle to make the first three parts, while the hand and the lower arm remain in line with the upper arm, ending in the last part again with the entire arm outstretched. It is noticeable that the movement downward in the Michael sign is steeper than the angle in the Sorat sign and that in *the last two movements enclose the space of the heart.*

About the Frontispiece

The spiritual-scientifically developed faculties of Rudolf Steiner include the capacity to let intuitively perceived spiritual beings speak through him as a fully conscious intermediary. According to Elisabeth Vreede, he once introduced an esoteric lesson with "My dear sisters and brothers! This esoteric lesson is such that it is not the responsibility of the one speaking." And then it was not Steiner speaking but the *Zarathustra-individuality inspiring through him*. In an enhanced form, he let *the time spirit Michael* and *the Guardian of the Threshold* in the nineteen lessons of the First Class speak through him, and through these two beings *the whole choir of the hierarchies*.

There is no known early or later portrait of Rudolf Steiner that makes this side of his occult activity immediately visible. This picture was taken upon the request of the painter Fritz Hass. He asked Rudolf Steiner if he could take a picture of him during a state of clairvoyance and was immediately allowed.

Although this picture was taken in 1907, it expresses Rudolf Steiner's intuitive inspirational activity more than any other during the nineteen Class lessons.

The editor

Rudolf Steiner's Blackboard Drawings

Picture 1: Fifth Lesson   *Picture 2: Sixth Lesson*

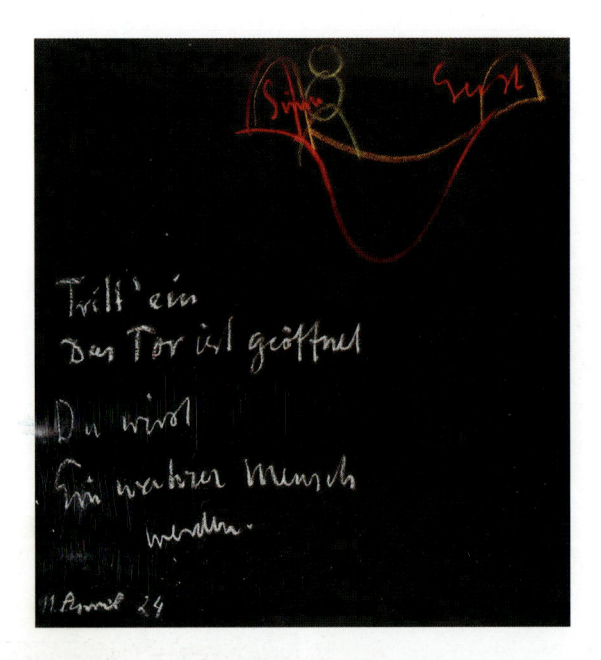

Picture 3: Seventh Lesson

Picture 4: Eighth Lesson

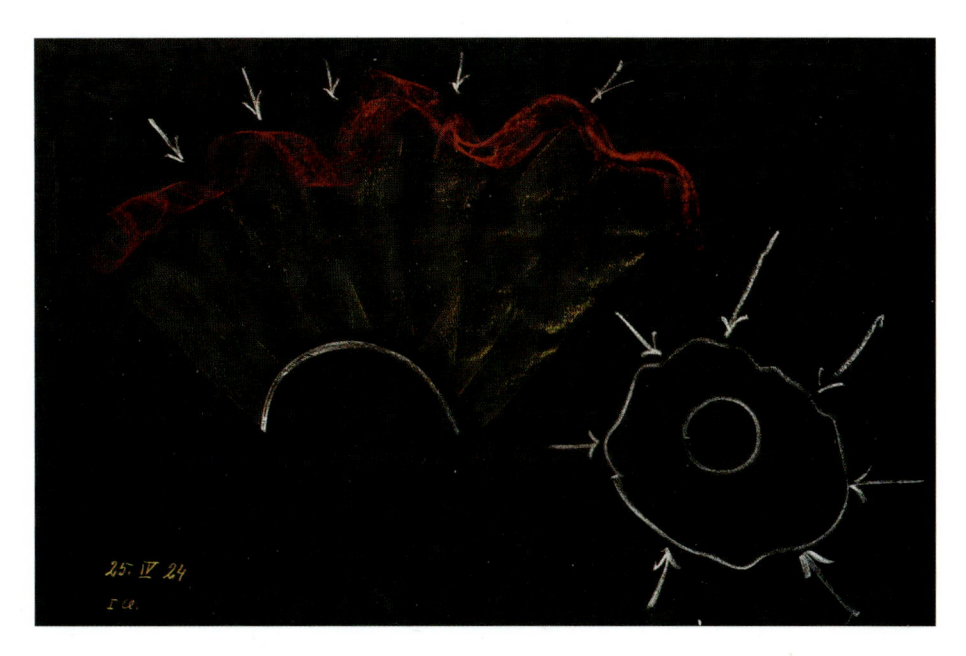

Picture 5: Tenth Lesson

Picture 6: Eleventh Lesson

Picture 7: Twelfth Lesson

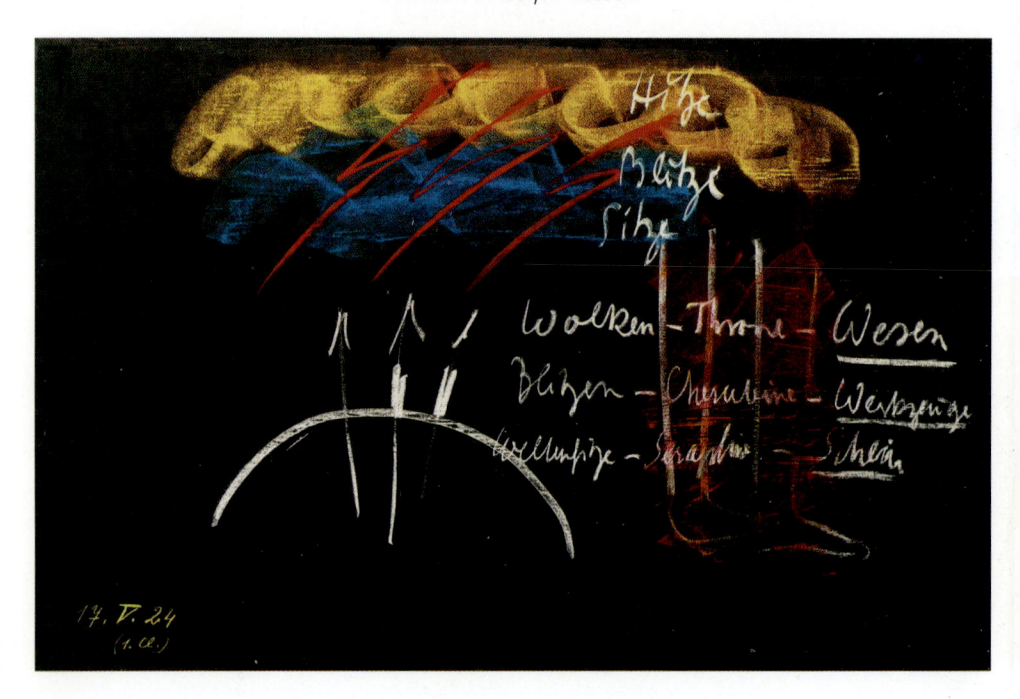

Picture 8: Thirteenth Lesson

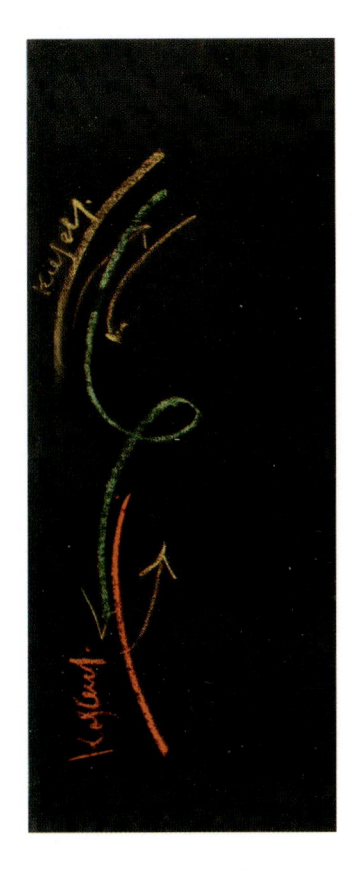

Picture 9: Fourteenth Lesson

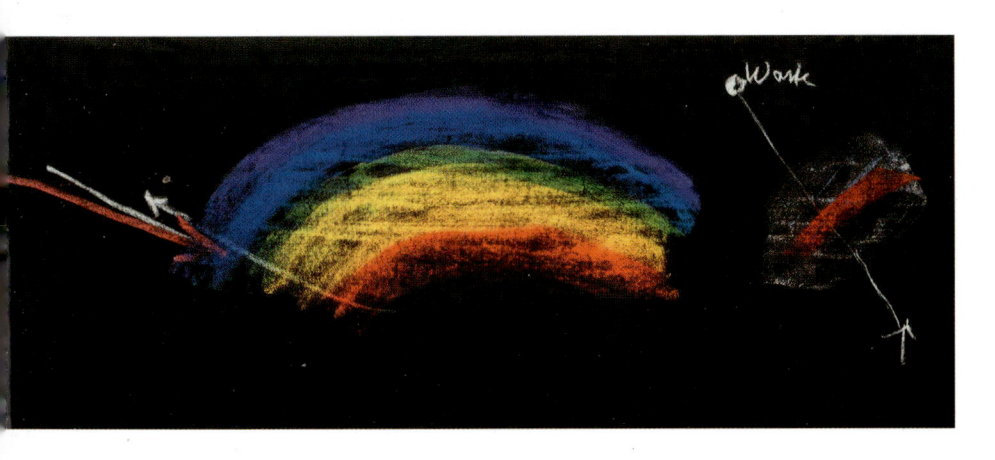

Picture 10: Seventeenth Lesson

Picture 11: Eighteenth Lesson